W9-BHO-553

PYRENEES PILGRIMAGE

WALKING ACROSS FRANCE

L. PEAT O'NEIL

To Betty and George,
Happy Hiking and Travels!
J. Peat O'Neil
August, 2021

Copyright © 2010 L. Peat O'Neil
All rghts reserved.

ISBN: 1-4392-6789-8
ISBN-13: 9781439267899

INSPIRATION

This will soon be looked upon as ignoble, nevertheless men of genius of every kind walk; wit may ride, but genius goes on foot. --Louis-Sébastien Mercier (1740-1814) Going on Foot, 1799

All thinkers are dreamers; reverie is thought in its fluid, undetermined state. There is no great mind that has not been possessed, charmed, frightened, or, at least, astonished, by the visions evoked by nature. --Victor Hugo (1802-1885) The Alps and Pyrénées, 1843

At present, in this vicinity, the best part of the land is not private property; the landscape is not owned, and the walker enjoys comparative freedom. But possibly the day will come when it will not be partitioned off into so-called pleasure grounds, in which a few will take a narrow and exclusive pleasure only - when fences shall be multiplied, and mantraps and other engines invented to confine men to the *road*. --Henry David Thoreau (1817-1862) Walking, 1851

To awaken quite alone in a strange town is one of the pleasant sensations in the world. You are surrounded by adventure. You have no idea of what is in store for you, but you will, if you are wise and know the art of travel, let yourself go on the stream of the unknown and accept whatever comes in the spirit in which the gods may offer it. --Freya Madeleine Stark (1893–1993) Baghdad Sketches, 1932

One travels in order to learn once more how to marvel at life in a child's way. --Ella K. Maillart (1903–1997) My Philosophy of Travel, 1950

Plans are deliberately indefinite, more to travel than arrive anywhere. --Robert Maynard Pirsig (1928-   ) Zen and the Art of Motorcycle Maintenance: An Inquiry Into Values, 1974

DEDICATION

To my wonderful, great mother, still strong at age 92, and all gardeners who nurture Gaia our home planet and heal sentient beings.

ACKNOWLEDGMENTS

Grateful thanks to Eli Flam and Christa Watters, editors of Potomac Review who published excerpts from this narrative in slightly different form. "Along the Pyrenees Trail" appeared in *Potomac Review* (Fall-Winter 2001-2002), 57-72. "Across the Pyrenees-II" appeared in *Potomac Review* (Spring-Summer 2002), 214-19.

Thanks to all the generous people who helped and encouraged me during my journey across France. In particular, I want to acknowledge those who looked after me while I recuperated from surgery on my wrist -- Serge Salles, Pierrette and Pierre-Henrí Lier and family; Eliane and Henrí Lier; Jean-Louis Lezat and family; Andrew and Linda Stockwell; Rosemary, Acadia and David Stanton; and the surgical and nursing staff at Lannemezan Hospital. My special thanks to the women of the Mounic family who comforted me immediately after the accident and drove me to the hospital.

For their research, editorial and design suggestions I thank Esther Andrews, Elizabeth Cale, Linda Green, Lisa McAllister, Sean Markey, Joan McKervey, Elvy O'Brien, Philippe-Joseph Salazar, Fran Sauve, Don Schlief, Rosemary Brown Stanton and Krystyna Wasserman.

TABLE OF CONTENTS

INTRODUCTION

The idea for this journey formed in a Bethesda bookstore. Scanning the shelves in the travel section, my hand paused on a guide to trekking the Pyrénées. I could do this, I thought. I've climbed higher mountains and traveled solo in remote regions. But could I do a long trek alone? The guidebook author was half my age, but nothing in the pages of Douglas Streatfield-James's book, *Trekking in the Pyrénées*, led me to believe the Pyrénées would be too difficult for a solo hiker.

It was a bleak day in March and I'd been walking on a suburban bike path -- the Georgetown Branch Trail -- casting about for a project to mark the beginning of my sixth decade. I had already considered and dismissed the idea of touring Sardinia on foot. After an itinerant visit there in 1980, I knew a woman alone in the hills of Sardinia would have problems. The pilgrimage to Santiago de Compostela in Spain drew my interest, but that was hardly a road less traveled. I briefly fantasized kayaking along southern Greenland or motorcycling around Jamaica, where my grandfather was born. But those journeys seemed daunting, and possibly dangerous

According to the guide book, which I skimmed in the bookstore, Pyrénées hiking paths were marked and considered safe. I knew the culture and region, and spoke acceptable -- but not fluent -- French. Quick travel decisions are easy for me: I would cross France alone walking through the Pyrénées. I bought the book and searched the Internet that afternoon to order topographic maps of the region.

From the Atlantic Ocean to the Mediterranean Sea, I followed mountain and rural paths across France. I walked the highland trails through Basque wine country, skirted southern Gascony, touched the high Pyrénées, tramped the rough dry Ariège and beyond to the Roussillon. My path took me through forests, past farms and into sheep pastures. Memorable encounters included the French Resistance fighters, roughened farm women who saluted my independence, woodcutters and hunters with bagged game. I met pilgrims on their way to Santiago, English Vicars on vacation, singing Norwegian hikers and reckless weekend warrior mountain bikers. Everyone was intrigued by my journey and many offered assistance in finding water, lodging or food.

I moved eastward on the GR-10, along regional forest trails, or on the French branch of the fabled Chemin-de-St.-Jacques, the pilgrimage path that culminates in Santiago de Compostela, Spain. I stayed in hikers' lodges, on farms offering a spare room to guests as part of rural tourism programs or at small inns run by French families. I found myself volunteering to take the family dog for an evening run or gathering apples from farm orchards to cook applesauce. Closer to the Mediterranean, I picked up the trail the follows the retreat route of the Cathars, a 13th century religious and political sect exiled and driven to the remote Pyrénées by mercenary soldiers looting and murdering under the banner of the Roman Catholic church. I witnessed a wedding party and a funeral, played with children and chatted with the old folks in rural villages.

The motive for this long solo trek? I wanted to do a physically demanding trip alone and I sought a distance that

I knew I could finish. France was within my cultural comfort zone. I didn't want to deal with completely unfamiliar social conventions or language. I've lived in the region and speak passable French, enough to facilitate conversations along the way. The Pyrénées region is profoundly interesting to me, with the Basques at the western end and the Aragonese-Catalans at the other.

Of course I'd considered hiking the famous Appalachian Trail, which runs from Maine to Georgia. But I did not feel safe walking and camping alone in the United States of America. So I headed to France, where a woman alone is left alone, not seen as prey. Camping wasn't the only option; North America has many hostels, part of the Hostelling International network, but these excellent low-cost lodgings are sparsely distributed.

While I strode along, I thought of the history of the region, the people who worked the fields and tended the herds, and the cultures that survived here. Threads of my previous research and reading intertwined with daily experiences. On a long slow perambulation like this, you need story lines of thought to fill the silent hours and give context to the passing scene. Walkers are outliers; most visitors to the region are rolling around on wheels.

When you hike for weeks and weeks, you have quite a lot of time to look around. I learned the landscape; it is alive in my mind. In 1892, more than a century ago, the British guidebook author Henry Blackburn wrote of the Pyrénées, "How little the French people really know of the Pyrénées, beyond the walks round their favourite watering-place... ." Blackburn's guidebooks were illustrated with drawings that he thought preferable to "mechanical processes of illustration which, from an artistic point of view, disfigure so many modern books of travel." He was referring to photographs.

I mention Blackburn because I share a preference for sketching when I travel. Though I also took many photographs, I drew sketches and painted watercolors of scenes that struck my interest. A selection of those images are reproduced in this book, as are a few photographs, which except where noted, were taken by me. Sometimes, I worked quickly to finish a watercolor before rainfall or sketched a drawing before pushing onward to find lodging before dark. I had enjoyable conversations with people who noticed me and paused to watch a woman committing an act of art.

During one day of this cross-France walk, I had a companion. Though I prefer to hike alone for the solitude of mindfulness and having no one else's pace to match, I agreed to share the route with a local woman who wanted to walk the pilgrim trail but was wary of hiking alone. In one day we covered more ground than I would have on my own, raising blisters on my feet. I didn't give up my independence again on the journey, preferring solitude as my method for inner balance and restoration.

The Pyrénées paths are relatively empty, especially in early autumn. But even when I met characters on the French trails, they were polite and curious about my purpose, never personally intrusive. In France, on the Grande Randonee (GR) and connecting local paths, you're never far from a village, so finding lodging at an inn doesn't represent a detour off the trail as is often the case in North American long distance trails. I knew the food in small villages in France could be superb and would always be better than average fare. When you sit down for a meal at the end of a serious day of hiking, you are completing the sensual experience of the day. In the mountaineering dorms of France, Switzerland and a few other countries, you don't have to subsist on freeze-dry pasta or protein bars.

The pilgrimage walk is a purposeful walk, a walk of alertness. I prefer a simple method using the baseline mantra of breath to measure strides. While my mind may dart through time, space and subject, I return to my physical and spiritual center by refocusing on breath and step.

Walking with intent, to answer problems, heal grief, or resolve options is called prayer walking, according to some authors. I didn't know there was a name for such a meditative process during my own walk. Afterwards, during research in the Library of Congress, I learned about prayer walking and walking meditation practiced by Buddhists, Christians, and other spiritualists.

I don't pray to a particular figure or god image, which I consider idolatry; I send prayer into the universal consciousness. For me, prayer and spirituality are already integrated in my mind and daily life. But there may be others who need to name their practice, to link themselves with the tradition of pilgrimage and processions to assert positive consciousness, venerate the dead or celebrate the mystical. I was pleased to learn about the prayer walkers and their admirable example -- proposing attentive physical exercise and mindful resolution with gentle surrender to the presence of the living spirit.

As I walked, I would breathe and stride, stride and breathe. I directed my attention to peace, not in response to any particular events, just human peace. Other pilgrim walkers do the same thing; we petition the universal consciousness, a process called walking meditation.

A Buddhist friend described this as attaining mindfulness through attention to the entire cycle of breathing. Empty the mind to focus on the moment. To really experience the physical action, your mind must be in the moment. Sweeping mentally through life's challenges and minutia while walking doesn't rest the mind. I focused on walking by returning to my breath, deepening the inhalations and exhalations, as yoga teaches.

It turned out that I needed that focus and physical control. At dusk one evening, I fell while crossing a stream and injured my right arm. Though the pain and swelling told me I might have broken bones, there was no choice for me but to push onwards through the dark forest to find help. Hours later, I was admitted to a hospital in the foothills of the Pyrénées. The orthopedic surgeon told me he'd seen dozens of wrist fractures like this, usually cyclists who flip forward off their bicycles. My smashed wrist was the worst he'd seen in a while, but they could fix it with surgery.

Actually it took two surgeries, one to insert five metal nails about four inches long to set the bone and another operation to extract the nails, followed by six months of physical therapy. The accident halted my cross-country trip. The doctor advised that to reduce swelling and bruising, my wrist would have to be suspended in a sling higher than my elbow for at least two months. And my right arm would be in a cast, from fingertips to elbow. I couldn't carry a backpack with only one useful arm, though for a few days I entertained thoughts of continuing despite this further challenge. It took the better part of a year to regain full use of my right arm and hand. Meanwhile, I taught myself to paint and write with my left.

I resumed the route alone the following September, arriving in Paris on the Eurostar train from London about an hour after hijacked airplanes crashed into the World Trade Center in Manhattan, the Pentagon near Washington, and another was pulverized over a Pennsylvania field. Tragic events of mid-September, 2001 also included a catastrophic explosion at a chemical factory in Toulouse, about 50 miles from Lannemezan, the re-entry point for my trek near the hospital where my wrist was repaired. These morbid events caused me to think about the human condition and I prayed – not to a particular deity, but to the pantheistic collective wisdom. So, yes, spiritual practice was part of my walk across France. Certainly I focused on questions of my spirit's direction and soul nourishment. I directed my intentions towards a peaceful resolution of the recent dreadful events: attacks on working people from 90 different nations in the U.S., the chemical plant explosion in Toulouse, the plane downed in Pennsylvania and the endemic disarray in the government of the country of my birth. But my mind was also at play, skipping through imagined stories, conjectures of history and musings on my past and present. This interplay of the spiritual and the secular is part of my normal way of being.

The history of religious pilgrimage is not unblemished. Greed, misuse of power and scorning the public trust are common today and these traits are not new. During the centuries when religious pilgrimage served as an opportunity for travel, there were opportunists using the arriving tide of visitors to sell chits to absolve sins and admission tickets to heaven called indulgences. There were other baser tricks that are mostly part of the past. The whole notion of sanctioned banditry that occurs at the holy spots around the globe is disturbing. I seem to recall a passage in the New Testament about Jesus of Nazareth chasing the merchants and money lenders from the temple.

Does the walker become holy for making a pilgrimage? That depends on the person. Does the pilgrim have to register somewhere to make the journey a legitimate pilgrimage? The Catholic Church does intervene in the pilgrimage through the pilgrim's credentials that are stamped at refuges along the way and presented for a completion certificate written in Latin at Santiago de Compostela. Mandatory distances for receiving the Compostela certificate were arbitrarily determined, a minimum of 100 kilometers (62 miles) on foot, and pilgrims must answer questions about their purpose, which since the 1990s includes "spiritual" in addition to "religious" motives. Spiritual travelers make their own way and some may need to make it official. After such exercise, muscles are lean and a person may be more psychologically grounded and self-confident. Perhaps the practice of walking attentively engaged in mindfulness blesses the individual. Not wanting to align with religious contexts, I prefer the French word for pilgrim, *pèlerin,* which in the masculine form also means peregrine falcon. As a female, I would be a *pèlerine*, a French word that also means a cape. Thus, I would enjoy the protection of the falcon and the cape. Making a *pèlerinage* resonated with me, felt gentle and watchful.

Spiritual commentator Phil Cousineau has described a pilgrimage that seeks neutral, non-religious context as "the kind of journeying that marks just this move from mindless to mindful, soulless to soulful travel. The difference may be subtle or dramatic; by definition it is life-changing. It means being alert to the times when all that's needed is a trip to a remote place to simply *lose* yourself, and to the times when what's needed is a journey to a sacred place, in all its glorious and fearsome masks, to *find* yourself."

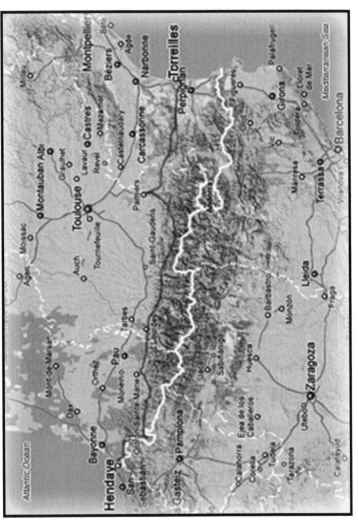

The Pyrénées Region. Author's route is marked with a black line.

CHAPTER 1
Euskal Herria, Basque Land

Hendaye to Aïnhoa

It was September, the time of chestnuts ripening. The farm lanes were layered with the spiked and studded nuts in their green outer casings. Where a car had passed, the crushed shell exposed crumbled white nutmeat. Times past, women used wooden tongs to collect fallen chestnuts in the porcupine-like casings and carried the nuts in oblong baskets, but you don't see the baskets much any more, except as decoration in fancy inns or country restaurants. Women still gather the chestnuts, but now they wear gloves to protect their hands and pop the nuts in a plastic sack. The romance of the ritual seems reduced by the loss of the traditional equipment. Complimenting the bright green of the fallen chestnuts, trees dropped yellow or russet leaves and the crisp feel of autumn met my steps from the Atlantic to the Mediterranean.

That was the color of the season as I set off to walk across France on the Pyrénées trails that run from the Atlantic Ocean to the Mediterranean Sea. The long distance paths in Europe are similar to North American counterparts like the Bruce Trail in Ontario or the Continental Divide Trail in the Rocky Mountains. The paths cross rural or wooded areas and bear regular markings. But on the trails in France and other European countries, hikers bed down in comfortable rooms or dormitories, called gîtes d'etape, with well-equipped kitchens and, good news for the weary, hot showers. Usually, in gîtes that are far from villages, the manager will offer the evening meal for a modest fee, so a hiker can look forward to a fine dinner at the end of a long day. No amenities like that on the trails of North America.

When you must carry your library on your back, serious reading comes before or after the trip. To prepare for the pilgrimage, I searched for writers who had prowled through the region in the past. Library shelves are crowded with books by modern writers who've followed the Camino de Santiago de Compostela in Spain. Fewer have written about walking in Basque country.

Count Henry Patrick Russell, the 19th century Irish-French mountaineer, scaled mountains and wrote definitive guidebooks about his conquests. He also wrote travel books aimed at the burgeoning British middle-class tourist market. You could call Russell a Victorian-era adventure travel writer. In his 1873 guidebook *Biarritz and Basque Countries*, Russell enthused, "there is nothing in France more beautiful than the Basque Pyrénées; and the only unpleasant thing to be said against them is the changeableness of the weather, a misfortune common and peculiar to most countries placed between mountains and the sea."

We can assume that the Pyrénées haven't changed all that much since Russell's day, though roads in the region are now accessorized with cell phone towers, electric lines, and signs indicate landmarks of archeological or historical interest. Roads are paved instead of cobbled or dirt and travelers go by car or bus rather than coach and four. The mountain paths are sign-posted for distance and average time to cover marked intervals, but those of us who venture forth on foot are timeless.

My planned route, the Grande Randonnee GR-10, ran from Hendaye on the Atlantic, through the Basque homelands, on through the craggy Ariège, around Andorra, across the old Comté de Foix, to Banyuls on the Mediterranean in Catalonia. Another marked trail, the HRP, or Haute-Route-Pyrénées covers similar distance at a higher altitude. At times the GR-10 inter-twines with the high altitude path, weaving in and out of the Spanish side of the mountains. In places the trail snaked along country lanes or through farms. Sometimes, the red and white GR-10 markers were far apart, inflaming my anxiety level. Eventually I learned to be comfortable with the path marking system. I also traveled on other GR trails or regional and local footpaths that link to the major long distance routes.

The plan was to walk across France through the Pyrénées Mountains along the GR-10, taking six weeks to two months. I started out with maps scaled one kilometer to the centimeter, maps I had pored over during months prior to departure, inching along the route with my finger, calculating how long I would walk each day, noting gîte locations. I realized that no pre-trip map study offers complete preparation, but it bolstered my confidence to read the marks on paper signifying rivers, inclines defining mountain passes, historic landmarks and archeological sites.

Gîtes d'etape are inexpensive lodgings used by school groups, hiking clubs and independent travelers. The solid buildings, sometimes converted from farm houses or rural schools, are usually under the aegis of the local government, which handles upkeep and pays a part-time manager. In remote areas, the gîtes belong to a mountain hiking club, and the lodges are left open until late fall for use by passing hikers on the honor system. The gîtes are spaced about a day's walk apart, with the presumption that people are hiking during the warm months when daylight extends 14 or 15 hours.

During this pre-trip planning, I wondered what I'd do in the few stretches in the Pyrénées National Park where the gîtes might be closed for the season by the time I arrived. Not a fast hiker, I'd likely be traveling through that region after annual closing in late September. Although there were refuges and other overnight shelters available, they were best suited for trekkers carrying full kit – stove, sleeping bag, lantern, and water purifier. I was going light -- no tent or stove -- a headlamp for illumination and iodine tablets for water purification.

Could I have started out earlier in the summer? Perhaps, but I was winding up a complicated assignment in the newsroom of The Washington Post. I had to recruit and train a staffer to take over my role, and complete various teaching and freelance writing commitments. Tasks piled up and I ended up flying to France a week later than I had originally planned.

So that is why I started the walk in September, the time of the chestnuts and golden leaves. The end of summer brought shorter days and earlier sunsets. Some nights I had no place to stay because I couldn't reach the mountain gîtes. I wasn't covering the daily distance fast enough. After walking for a week and worrying about advancing nightfall, I bought larger scale maps -- 250 meters to one centimeter (820 feet to 3/8 inch), a scale so large you can almost see landscape features on the path ahead as you read them on the map. The extra details enabled me to detour off the path before dark to villages with inns or farms that took overnight guests.

On the train from Paris to Hendaye, the last town in Basque France north of the Spanish Basque border, I considered the reading I'd done prior to departure. In mountain-climber Henry Russell's day, Hendaye was a one-hotel village with fewer than 1,000 residents. During the Nazi occupation, Hendaye served as a last checkpoint for refugees fleeing to ports in Spain and Portugal where boats bound to freedom waited. Some who fled to Spain were captured by the fascist government and interned in prison camps. Downed Allied pilots escaped through an underground route of safe farm houses to Hendaye and secret return to England. But you wouldn't know about that past by looking out the train window. Today, the region around Hendaye is rich, packed with resorts and retirement communities with an ample tax base to support public facilities like jogging paths, marinas, libraries and parks.

A troop of sweaty young hikers from Northern Europe swarmed through the train compartment at one of the few stops on the TGV Paris-Bordeaux route. I eavesdropped and learned they were bound for the pilgrimage path to Santiago de Compostela. They would start hiking at St. Jean-Pied-de-Port, after a transfer in Bordeaux. Soon they were gone, with their soggy cheese, fruit peels and rucksacks with swaying water bottles and damp socks attached. I was guilty then of the pride I took in my tidy little red backpack, polished and water-proofed hiking boots and food sealed in double Zip-Loc plastic bags. But in a few weeks, wet socks and tee shirts hung from my pack which was stuffed with moist cheese and sausage, and water bottles hung from the side pockets.

The lady across the aisle petted a cat, which sat on the fold-down tray most of the five hour journey. Preparing to exit, she stuffed the cat into a satchel with air holes and smiled at me, her eyes perhaps signaling mutual relief that the noisy youths had left. The cat was leashed and relaxed during the journey, but yowled when zipped into the tote bag. I nodded and made a gentle remark about the cat not being content. A few stops later the conductor announced Hendaye station and it was my turn to shrug on my pack and hop down to the platform.

A few blocks to the west lay the Atlantic. I strode briskly towards the ocean, past stores offering deep-discounted flip-flops and kids' toys, beach apparatus left over from August. A craggy-faced guy bummed coins outside a grocery store, grizzled drinkers sagged in front of a darkened bar and I noticed pairs of strolling women with orange or burgundy tinted hair. Maybe it was the style that year.

Elderly couples wrapped in sweaters shuffled along the beach away from the surf line. Sea bathers jumped small waves, though the water was an unsavory brown-gray color, like dirty dishwater in a restaurant kitchen. Surfers in wet suits waited for incoming waves farther out past the gentle surf. A couple of kayakers flirted with the low waves, spitting around in rodeo boats, craft cut smaller than typical white-water kayaks, and made for angling atop crests of waves or river current. A kayaker myself, I took it as a positive sign that kayakers were there to witness my takeoff.

A community bulletin board marked the starting point of the GR-10, with a picturesque map detailing the landmarks near the first few kilometers of the grand cross-country trail. No one noticed my ritual scoop of sand tilted into an empty film container. I wanted a bit of nature's essence from both ends of the journey. There was no one to tell, "Hey, I'm going to start walking across France!" And a good thing, too, since I'd probably be thought daft, starting my walk so late in the day and after the vacation season.

I took a deep breath of the Atlantic wind, faced east and took my first steps on the trail, following the credit card sized red and white path blazes painted on walls, lamp posts, guard railings, and later, every hour, every day, in the forest, painted on trees and rocks, on bridges, fences, and sometimes on the pavement. I was on my way. Under a darkening Maxfield Parrish blue sky, a couple of hours later, I hoofed into Biriatou, a tourist getaway spot in the Pyrénées Piedmont. Three lines of clouds rode low over the valley below. I beat the rain by a half-hour.

The desk clerk at Hotel Biriatou stared pointedly at my knee-length shorts in the way that only a French woman can let you know silently that you are not dressed correctly. I planned to dine at Les Jardins de Bakea, a fancy restaurant across the street from the hotel. "Trained chef, a gastronomic experience," she muttered. I realized I wasn't dressed for a posh resort and rushed upstairs to change into my best outfit, skin-tight black Lycra pants and a black zip-front fleece top with long sleeves. I floated a green and gold silk scarf around my neck. Still sporty, but sleeker than shorts and a tee shirt.

The Lycra and fleece outfit was meant for chilly mountain weather, not a heated restaurant. My face gleamed with sweat as I roasted in the warm dining room. The restaurant was an up-market place, with exposed wood beams and elaborate bouquets of dried flowers, arranged in baskets once used for collecting chestnuts, now tucked into the unlit fireplaces. Next time I'll have to hike with a little black dress to wear in the evenings, a hiking supply never needed on the Appalachian Trail.

A Japanese family of three children and two adults occupied a large table near mine. The children, all younger than twelve, behaved with singular poise. At another table, Americans dressed in polo shirts and sports trousers chatted quietly about the wine. I ordered pheasant, then sweated and ate, pushed up my sleeves and savored another bite. I asked for the leftovers in a doggy bag, an action not widely accepted in France, for tomorrow's lunch on the trail.

The church bell rang at 11 a.m. as I marched away from Biriatou. Gunfire in the distance alerted me to hunters in the woods. Soon, a hunter appeared with a pheasant slung across his shoulder and down his back. When I commented on his good luck, he said, *"En plus, il n'y a pas de but"* which translates roughly to: "And I wasn't even trying." Or, "That wasn't my goal." Something like that. I paused to chat with him about the danger of a stray shot. "The season started two days ago," he said, "but no, don't worry. Hunters pay attention, we don't shoot just anywhere or at anything that moves."

He strode on towards Biriatou and I headed deeper into the hills. Seeing the hunter prompted me to tie a bright orange fleece pullover to the top of my pack and wrap a red bandana around my head, hippie style. The signal-flare orange top was a poor fashion choice, but my purpose was safety. Though only a few guns cracked in the distance, it was still mildly worrisome to be walking through the *terraine de chasseurs* (hunting area) during a hunting day. Suddenly, a female pheasant crossed the trail, then darted back into the underbrush and I cackled with delight that the hunter had missed her, though probably he had bagged her brighter plumed mate. I wondered if that was a good or bad omen.

At this point on my second day, I trudged along without attaching my pedometer because it wasn't functioning properly. The backpack waistband jostled the pedometer clipped to the top of my shorts. The digital display on the pedometer stated no distance covered. Already I was mentally listing items I didn't need and would mail home.

Through the morning, I strode easily around rocky outcroppings to a panoramic view of a lake. Up ahead, there was a level spot that would be a terrific camping area, had I a tent. Onwards to a plateau where a horse stood calmly, not moving. For a minute, I imagined bridling it with my nylon rope and soaring through the sky, but this was a leap into the realm of Ursula LeGuin and Anne McCaffrey, deft authors of fantasy-science fiction novels. I picked up a quill-size black feather from the ground, possibly from the soaring Griffon vultures, and stuck the feather in my hat. Small lizards darted on the rocks and fox scat dried on flat boulders. Yellow sedum flowers poked up between rocks. Sheep, horses and goats grazed in the high pastures.

In the early days of the journey, I consulted a guidebook that included hand drawn maps, with cartoon indicators for places to find food, water, hills and landmarks. Time and again, I found the cute little maps off kilter, somebody's distilled versions of a non-existent reality. If a bridge was noted as a landmark, I would have to decide which of three bridges in the immediate area to use as a turning mark. I spent time searching and backtracking for the next red and white blaze to verify which bridge or turn to follow. After about a week, I ditched the guidebook to the pile of items to be sent home and bought large scale topographic maps.

But I was still using the book at this point and anticipated that the *venta* -- a market selling various artisan goods -- at Col d'Ibardin would be a promising place to stop for a break. Instead, the purported attractions of the *venta* depressed me. A couple dozen warehouses offered liquor, cigarettes, summer sports gear, garden vases, lawn chairs and statuary for sale. Lines of parked cars with license plates from all over Europe spelled out vacationing tourists hunting for bargains among the mass-produced bric-a-brac. Golden-agers lugged plastic tote bags of booze and cheap Spanish smokes. The restaurants catered to crowds from tour buses. Lucky me, I lunched on the leg of pheasant from the previous night's dinner.

I felt isolated. The other hikers, day-trippers who'd parked their cars in the *venta* lot, ignored me, didn't nod a greeting. Perhaps I was expecting the friendly "hellos" typical of hikers passing on the trail in England, Canada, Mexico and the U.S.A. I was forgetting that Europeans usually ignore others, mind their own business. Hadn't I shown my colors as a long distance walker with dusty boots and a bulging pack? These folks wore fresh white sneakers and carried designer day-packs. We were marching to different lifestyles. I hadn't settled into the private hemisphere of the pilgrimage walk yet, and was still striving to be noticed.

I worked out my annoyance during the hard, hot climb up the Col d'Ibardin. The follower of the Tao that I profess to be sought to be present in the moment, finding tree shadows for brief rests and making the right choices about asking directions. So far, on day two, all was flowing well, except for the tawdry commercial scene behind me. From time to time, I'd stop to survey the vistas, looking back on the ground I'd covered, scanning upward towards the thinning trees, and always, keeping an eye out for the red and white blazes that reassured me I was on the GR-10.

During that day, I chatted with an older man out in the mountains. He leaned on a staff panting heavily, sagging around the middle with maybe thirty adipose pounds under his small pack, which he ruefully acknowledged made his exercise difficult. That afternoon, in a mysterious grove of oaks described in the guidebook near a cobbled road dating to Roman Gaul, I spied a white haired woman sitting on a folding lawn chair. She was embroidering. Who wouldn't approach and ask to see her needlework? She told me her grown son left her there while he walked with his kids.

Near the clearing where the woman sewed, I found a Roman-era cart road, cut twenty centuries earlier, mentioned in the hiking guidebook. The road surface was large oblong dressed stones laid out lengthwise to make two parallel tracks for the cart wheels while smaller stones and rubble covered the space between the two tracks to prevent muddy patches and erosion. The small stones in the middle created a choppy surface, so I stepped on the larger flat stones designed to match the standardized axle of Roman carts.

But then, uh-oh. Was that a border marker stating I was re-entering France? I must have stepped over the border into Spain -- I hadn't seen a marker -- who knows when it happened? It's easy to drift over the border without knowing it, like the sheep and birds. Café Inzola, an isolated building on the Spanish Basque side, between a narrow road and the trail, was empty except for a dour and suspicious old woman who looked me up and down. It was too early for the evil eye, but I shivered anyway. The daughter served me coffee and juice while Mama prowled the room flashing glares of curiosity at me. Papa smoked and stared down at the weedy duck pond beyond the parking area. Had I interrupted a family fight?

On the trail near the cafe, I chatted with several golden agers, out for short strolls since none of them wore proper footwear for the rocky, muddy path. The women were hopping along in dance sandals trying to avoid puddles; the men wore soft-soled loafers. They were having a splendid time of it, the women acted out "help-me" smiles and giggles while leaning on their companions.

Though the border between France and Spain, set by the Treaty of the Pyrénées in 1659, roughly follows the Pyrénées Mountains, there are pockets of land where one nation or the other spills across the logical border line. There are independent areas too. Andorra, a patch of mountains and valleys deep in the Central Pyrénées, is a separate principality governed by local representatives and nominally supervised by France and Spain. I later learned of other areas of Basque land where neither France nor Spain are in charge.

The Basque country on the Atlantic is really a separate nation, Euskal Herria, or "land of Euskera speakers," with political and cultural sovereignty that extends back to a time when the Phoenicians ran trade in the Mediterranean. We know that Basque mercenaries fought for the Phoenician colony at Carthage in 240 B.C.E., and several centuries later when the Romans built a network of roads around the Mediterranean Sea, the Basques were trading industriously or hiring themselves out as mercenaries and sailors. Culturally, linguistically, historically and politically, Euskal Herria is unique from France or Spain, though the three Basque provinces in France and the four in Spain report to their respective governments. Basques suffered decades of hostility on the Spanish side, from Franco's fascist myrmidons. Let us not forget that the Germans and Italians destroyed the Basque capital city Guernica in 1937, target practice in the run-up to World War II. Though not a separate nation, on the eastern edge of the Pyrénées lies Catalonia on the Mediterranean Sea, which like the Basque lands, straddles the border and avows intense nationalist spirit and culture, though integrated with France and Spain on their respective sides.

The border lines are drawn, but the fierce spirit of Basques is unassailable. First they are Basque, then whatever other political or national affiliation claims them by residence. Michael Orodoz, a Basque professor I met at an organ concert in Saint-Étienne-de-Baïgorry, circled his finger around a region on my map, a pocket of pastureland where Spanish sheep graze part of the year and the land is considered Spanish, though it is well within the French frontier. Or is it French sheep that graze in an unofficial, but locally accepted piece of France within Spanish Basque? Ultimately, the land is Basque. France and Spain are latecomers by several millennia. The seasonal migration of herds continues throughout the Pyrénées. Sheep know no borders.

I forged on and was soon back in France. Around five o'clock I slowed down to find the gîte on the edge of the village named Olhette. Following instructions posted beside the door, I entered the unlocked lodge to settle for the night. The lodge smelled pleasantly of furniture polish and wood smoke from the fireplace. Not another hiker in the place. Chickens scratched the hard packed ground in an adjacent yard. How different from the moist forest I'd passed through earlier near the Café d'Inzola. There was another note on the porch door of the manager's house stating that she'd return later. I was dipping a brush in the watercolor kit, painting a postcard sized version of a red barn, when a man in his twenties burdened with a massive pack stumbled down the path. He asked in a deep Midi (southern France) accent what the gîte offered. The manager hadn't appeared, so I parroted the prices on the list by the door. Papa arrived panting and sweaty shortly after. Between them they were carrying about 60 pounds – tent, cooking equipment, bedding, food, lamp – the works. Sonny slurped on a water hose from a Camelbak reservoir similar to the rig in my backpack. Assorted gadgets swung from his pack and a huge pedometer hung from his hip. Maybe toting the gizmos of commercialized camping can be counter productive and a physical burden. Papa carried the tent and bragged that he topped off at more than 16 kilos (about 35 1/3 pounds). They thought the tariff too steep at about $23 per person for bed, dinner and breakfast and limped towards a campground down the road.

Later, a couple just out of their teens arrived at the gîte, but they continued on to the campsite, also shaking their heads at the nightly tariff. I was the outdoors version of a gullible American tourist, paying too much, unschooled in local market values. The dinner filled the place where my calories had been, but it was mediocre compared to the roast pheasant of the night before. I ate alone in a small room off the farmhouse kitchen, a dinner of salty ham hocks, pasta, a garden fresh tomato and cucumber salad followed by desert of yogurt and a nectarine. There was a carafe of no-name wine too. The proprietor bustled in and out, bringing each course while I wrote in my journal to pass the time. In the morning her son collected the eggs to sell at the market while I breakfasted on several of those fresh eggs.

Come morning, I learned the mountain climber Henry Russell was right about the Pyrénées weather being changeable.

More than a few mornings in this region opened with light drizzle that passed into the next valley by midday. After wrestling once with the poncho, which felt like an enshrouding wet shower curtain, I banished it and relied on my Gore-Tex rain jacket, which didn't quite cover the pack or my lower legs, but if the rain was a soaker, I'd be cooling my heels indoors anyway. Late summer afternoons brought blasting sunshine. If my energy held, I'd walk through the midday hours and stop later to eat sandwiches, cured sausage or sheep's milk cheese called *ardi-gasna* (local cheese) by Basques.

Once the mist cleared, the morning light improved, but the path changed to a steep upward grade. I stopped to fully experience the mysterious foggy vistas of the craggy rocks and the emerging top of Col des Trois Fontaines. Sure enough, many springs – more than the three mentioned in the place name – made the ground soggy and the grass wet. I found a dry area near a windbreak of pines and sketched the ruin of a stone barn on the next rise. Then I painted the same scene on watercolor paper. The sun now in full blast made it difficult to move on from this splendid prospect. Periodically, tour groups arrived. They ascended on the little tram that runs up the hill from the outskirts of Ascain, then wandered around on the plateau of La Rhune.

Indeed, most visitors to La Rhune -- a relatively modest Basque peak at 905 meters (3059 feet) -- make the ascent in the little tram built for Victorian-era tourists who flocked to the Pyrénées to enjoy clean mountain air and drink the curative waters. With the advent of tourism for the masses, natural features such as waterfalls, caves and mountains became attractions. The nearby Sare cave, one of many cavern areas in the Pyrénées, is under the Pic Atchuria on the Spanish border.

Called the grotto of Atchuria, it drew bourgeoisie and royal visitors alike. Trend-setting celebrities of their day, Napoleon III and the Empress Eugenie toured the caves in 1858.

These nature attractions also brought Victorian-era middle-class visitors who'd read the travel guidebooks displayed in bookstores in London, Paris, Hamburg and New York. Henry Russell's guidebooks were aimed at middle class British bank clerks or textile brokers who planned their vacations along the same routes favored by European royalty whose peregrinations were reported in the popular press, precursors of Style magazine or People.

Between the peaks of Atchuria and Ibantelli, the peasants hung nets between trees to catch ring doves during their autumn migration across the Pyrénées. On my map, there's a miniscule dot midway between the peaks, which are about three kilometers apart. The dot is named la Palombiere, (*palombe* means wood pigeon) which indicated to me a connection with pigeon harvesting. In this era of sensitivity to threatened species, does this 19th century practice described by Russell and other writers continue? Later on in my journey, east of Saint-Bertrand-de-Comminges, near Aspet, long nets were strung from tree to tree across the top of the hills. In the village nearby, when I asked the locals about the nets, they said it was common practice to ensnare flocks of birds this way. Then, as now, the birds were caught for food, divided among the net tenders. How could I, the itinerant guest, criticize their food gathering practices?

In 1931, mountaineer Claud Schuster wrote about Basque mountain travel: "Seen through the eye of the geographer, the mountain chain which springs from the Mediterranean at the Cap de Creus does not cease until it descends into the Atlantic at Finistere. But he who desires a far-thrown vision over the earth should choose the spot where that long line first draws near to the western sea and makes an angle with the great southward sweep of the Gulf of Gascony.

"There…seek the summit of the last of the Pyrénées, a little pyrénée, …Yet, seen from sea-level, the Rhune is a noble mountain. No Alpine foothill stands up so proudly. … The Rhune, small as he is, makes those by the shore long for the mountains… you go through meadows of asphodel; strange birds flit across your path; the wild columbine grows by the roadside; you may find a wild boar just slain at the foot, and diversify the day by counting a covey of vultures circling round your head.

"The rivers which cross the wide plain below you are sacred rivers – Bidassoa, Nivelle, Nive, and Adour; and wherever you look northward a spire or a white hamlet brings back some memory of an English feat of arms.

"In front, as you turn your back on France, the tangled glens of Navarre, tree-clad but desolate; then the rocky coast and the little harbour of St-Jean-de-Luz with toy ships riding at anchor and toy houses by the strand; and then the long line of green, edged with purple and amethyst, melting into the golden sands by Biarritz; and so on into the infinite north. Perhaps it will be last of all that you will look eastward to a wild confusion of silver summits, clad with the impartiality of last winter's snow, which are the Pyrénées."

So goes the elaborate diction of an earlier era, when travel was grand and the going took considerably longer. We can suppose that generations of Britons came to La Rhune, marking the footsteps of Wellington and the horse-guard cavalry chasing Napoléon Bonaparte's troops down. Wellington defeated the French at La Rhune in October of 1813. Tourists arrived soon after the end of that war in search of mountain air and the curative waters.

As I watched and mused, clusters of visitors wandered around the top of La Rhune. In the same way that citizens who've not had the opportunity to read the historical documents of the U. S. Civil War, or the papers of Grant, Lee or Lincoln, will gaze with awe for three minutes over the now green, once fire branded and bloody fields of Antietam or Vicksburg or Gettysburg, then sigh and turn away, the British visitors stare at the wildflowers on the hillside of La Rhune, that "little pyrénée," and give up their minute of silence. Why is following the footsteps of war such a popular tourist pastime?

Henry Russell easily ascended La Rhune. "The country is charming," he wrote in the guidebook *Biarritz and Basque Countries.* "Indian-corn, meadows, and woods alternating with rugged little cliffs, quite yellow with gorse. Two hours ... will take a man to the summit; but a lady takes three."

The morning romp to the summit of La Rhune didn't take this lady anywhere near three hours, less than two for that matter, but I'm probably a lot swifter than Russell, lacking the mountaineer's girth. There's something to be said for modern day light-weight outdoors equipment, which the hikers of Russell's day may have imagined, as we in the 21st century speculate about even more efficient equipment and transportation.

I climbed La Rhune, but couldn't see Saint-Jean-de-Luz or Biarritz on the coast as Claud Schuster described. Perhaps the earlier visitors had x-ray vision or inserted descriptions of what they knew to be in the distance, instead of describing what was actually visible. Or maybe I just didn't find the same look-out point.

Pony on La Rhune, Basque Land

The path was well used, worn bare to hard packed dirt. I descended through the bracken and scurried atop exposed rocks to survey the vistas shrouded in mist. On the way down the mountain, the tourist train rattled past about a quarter of a mile to my left. A couple of *pottocks* (small ponies) rested in the shade of another crumbling stone barn, a ruin easily old enough to have sheltered wounded troops two hundred years ago during the Peninsular War.

During the summer of 1843 the novelist and political activist Victor Hugo traveled from village to village by mail coach or farm wagon. He wrote in sketchbooks, as I do. Pen and ink drawings share pages with his notes and brittle pressed flowers and mountain grasses. I share these habits of collection, annotation and sketching. Victor Hugo took the mail coach from Paris on the 18th of July 1843, bumping southward through Orleans, Blois, Tours, Poitiers and Angoulême. He moved on to Bordeaux by July 21st and visited some of the mountain towns I would pass through. I like to think he paused on his walks to draw the same steeples and stone walls that I sketched and painted for my own pleasure. Drawing a scene fixes it in the mind's eye. There's no better way to remember a place than to draw it. I stopped to draw wrought iron gates and admired the dry laid stone walls dividing the farms along the route. A woman gathered chestnuts in a rutted farm lane. I waved to her when I saw her again in Sare at the village fête.

The harvest festival was underway in Sare. Booths with red awnings were set up to sell food and drink around the *fronton*. Basque village culture revolves around the *fronton* (handball) court, where *Basque Pelota, Rebot* or *Laxoa* or other variations are played. Men done up in white pants with red sashes wandered from booth to booth thumping each other's shoulders, singing and dancing. In a few towns, the handball wall is in back of the church or town hall. The *pelota* court is an icon of Basque society, a place for male competition and jockeying for status in the village.

One lively fellow in a beret grabbed friends and danced a jig, kicking his feet out and hooting with laughter. A group of British bird-watchers – their binoculars and bird books gave them away – clumped together in the lobby, chattering that they hoped their rooms were available, what with the crowds in town. I grabbed a seat on the hotel terrace and sipped a mint syrup and seltzer drink while watching the happy groups.

A car decorated as a large yellow chicken passed by, the driver honking, a straggler from an earlier parade. Townspeople shouted greetings to each other. The women kissed cheeks and the men clapped each other on the back. At another bar thick with festival celebrants, I asked the barman to fill up my water bottles and while waiting, chatted with bystanders.

One hundred and thirty years ago, Sare was a pleasant place with a comfortable hotel in the same building as the mayor's office. Perhaps that hotel was the same one now hosting the flock of British twitchers – as the Brits dub bird-watchers – tapping their hiking sticks impatiently on the stone terrace and stamping the dust off their boots. It seemed possible.

Sare is a compact place. You can walk one end to the other in an easy 15 minutes. But I lost track of the GR-10 markers at the *fronton* on the perimeter of town. After wandering down a steep winding road, I retraced my steps along a stream gully, hunting for the red and white GR blazes. I asked help from a couple of people in a car. They had a detailed roadmap but no sense of direction and suggested the correct route was back towards Sare, the way I'd come. Noticing the number suffix on their car license tag, I realized they were not from the region, and ignored their directions.

I had better luck asking people on foot. A young woman stopped to help. "I want to practice English," she told me, "to prepare for an au-pair job in San Francisco." We chatted about her future job and she pointed out a narrow lane hidden by foliage, which she assured me rejoined the GR-10 path closer to Aïnhoa, the next Basque town on the border. She was right. The lane crossed over a stream where I cooled my feet, enjoying the peaceful emptiness and silence of the forest.

Hoofing along this deserted lane, I speculated about the remainder of the day. A settlement was visible at the crest of the hill; nothing special, just a few houses guarded by hungry curs. Normally I have no fear of dogs, but these barking dogs were ugly and insistent, and instead of backing off and staying their ground as I marched steadily onward, they scrambled and lunged towards me – not a good sign. I wished I had included the Dazzer in my equipment to deal with these nasty aggressive dogs with voices that threatened violence to my person. The Dazzer is a handy tool that sends out an ultrasonic tone that dogs hear, then they cower and run.

But I didn't have the dog repeller and had no hiking staff. So I barked back, stamping my boots and jerking forward to threaten them. I growled and howled and snarled, giving better than I was getting, for the dogs retreated. To them, I was a bigger, louder dog even if I did smell like a human. I was shaking and spent, though, and as soon as I was clear of the village, I rested and ate a Clif nutrient bar to replenish my blood sugar. Odd that no one from the spiffy tile embellished and landscaped houses emerged to call the dogs off. Perhaps if you live on the border, snarling dogs are necessary sentries, especially if the houses are often empty.

The trail paralleled the frontier for a few kilometers and I noticed the carved granite markers, the first I'd seen, though I'd crossed the border several times. In a small valley near a stream, I skirted warily around several large decrepit houses, windows broken out and vines overtaking the doorways. A faded sign on one of the buildings proclaimed *"Venta."* No dogs, no people, just an atmosphere of foreboding enhanced by the isolated setting and advancing twilight. I decided this collection of buildings might have once been a shopping area on the frontier similar to the bustling center I'd passed the day before, or maybe a smuggler's outpost pre-European Union.

Aïnhoa lies east of Sare on the right bank of the Nivelle River. The town commands a well-cultivated plateau. Russell mentions the Opoka Inn and describes the church as "curious." As night fell, I hadn't found shelter. Every inn including the Opoka was booked solid with wealthy merry-making travelers, judging from the parking lots filled with Mercedes cars and the brisk waiters popping corks in all the hotel dining rooms.

Sweaty and smelling rank, I bungled into hotel lobbies asking about a room. These were nice places, comfortable lodgings decorated with fresh flowers, fine carpets, paintings. None had a vacancy. I contemplated sleeping in the small walled graveyard surrounding that "curious" church perched in the center of town. I considered my options at a nearby bar.

Soon I confided my lack of lodging to Mme. Ezkurra, the proprietor, and she volunteered to help, calling around to friends in nearby towns, eventually finding a room in a campground-pension right on the Spanish frontier. It was a few scant kilometers south of Aïnhoa at the junction of streams feeding the Nivelle River. A retired postman holding up one end of the bar offered to drive me the three kilometers to the lodging, Camping Xokoan in Dancharia Frontiere. We all agreed I would not try to walk there alone in the dark. But first, the British woman at the other end of the bar insisted, would

I join her for another beer. She wanted to tell me all about the ex-patriot lifestyle in Saint-Jean-de-Luz on the Atlantic coast and a fabulous restaurant called La Galupe in Urt near Bayonne that I really must try one day. In turn, I told her about the roast pheasant served at the restaurant in Biriatou. The postman nursed his drink and listened to us chatter in English.

It will be a later date when I have the pleasure of eating at La Galupe. In the meantime, I turn to Elizabeth David's *French Provincial Cooking* for French regional recipes. Like many culinary enthusiasts, I accumulate cookbooks, but I actually use this one. The paperback edition dates to 1981 and though the pages are foxed with age and kitchen tarnish, the page corners are not dog-eared because my habit is to place shopping or guest lists to mark recipes tried. The binding is cracked and the pages jammed with mementos spanning some twenty years. This is the first of several recipes that celebrate the memorable meals enjoyed during the walk. Some of the recipes were given to me by cooks I met on the journey.

Basque Pheasant with Spiced Rice
Adapted from Elizabeth David, "Faisan au Riz Basquais"
French Provincial Cooking

- one pheasant, 2 to 2 1/2 lbs, plucked and trimmed for cooking
- 4 small Basque sausages (or use chorizo)
- 6 to 8 oz thick slices of bacon
- 1 carrot, peeled and sliced
- 1 medium yellow onion, sliced
- 1 bouquet garni - a mix of fresh or dried Mediterranean herbs securely wrapped in a small piece of cheesecloth and tied with string to form a seasoning packet about the size of a golf ball
- zest of orange peel
- 3 to 5 cloves garlic, crushed
- olive oil
- 1 lb. fresh tomatoes, skinned, seeded and chopped or 1 large can of stewed chopped tomatoes, drained
- 1 sweet red pepper, seeded and sliced in thin 2" strips or 1 small jar of oil cured Spanish pimentos
- 3/4 lb. rice
- 6 -8 cups veal or chicken stock or water
- pinch of crushed Basque red peppercorns or paprika

Heat olive oil in a heavy pan large enough for the pheasant. Saute sliced onion and carrot, then the pheasant, turning it several times so the bird browns evenly. Cover with liquid -- half stock and half water. Add the bacon, bouquet garni, zest of orange and crushed garlic. Cover and simmer gently for 20 minutes. Add sausages. Cook another 20 minutes. Test the pheasant for tenderness. Put rice in a large saucepan of boiling water with two pinches of sea salt. Boil 12 minutes. Strain the rice and put in the top half of a double boiler with a half-tablespoon olive oil. The bottom part of the double boiler holds hot water. Strain and pour 1/2 cup of stock from the cooking pheasant into the rice. Place a folded kitchen towel over the double boiler, then cover with the lid. Steam for about 20 minutes until rice is tender and add a little more hot stock to the rice if needed. Meanwhile, saute the tomatoes and peppers in a small pan with a tablespoon of olive oil. Cook on medium high heat for about 10 minutes. Season with crushed sea salt, black pepper and coarsely ground red pepper. If using paprika instead of the more highly charged Basque red pepper, add about a tablespoon. The tomato-pepper mixture will be thick, but not a purée. Strain and reserve remainder of the cooking stock from the pheasant for soup or other sauce.

To serve, arrange cooked rice on a heated platter. Remove the sausages and bacon from the pan and cut into pieces, cutting away any rind or fat. Arrange sausages and bacon around the pheasant. The pheasant may be carved and arranged on the rice or presented whole. The tomato mixture may be served separately or poured on the rice. A chicken may be cooked in the same way, adjusting cooking times to suit the weight of the fowl.

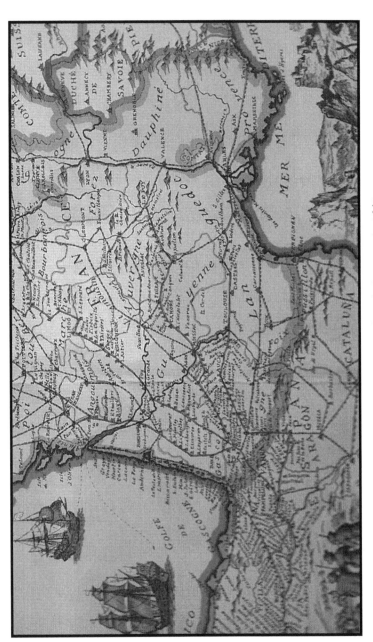

Pilgrimage Routes to Santiago de Compostela, 1648

CHAPTER 2

Chemin de Saint-Jacques-de-Compostelle

Aïnhoa to Saint-Jean-Pied-de-Port

In the high Pyrénées, the winters bring snow and ice, and spring signals the pasturing season when the sheep are moved from winter pens near villages back to the open hillsides for a summer of grazing. In autumn, the sheep are moved back down; this annual process is called the transhumance. Lower down, in the Pyrénées Piedmont, between the rivers that fan out from the mountains west to the Atlantic and east to the Mediterranean, the cold season rarely brings weather more serious than light snow and biting rain. Spring and fall are glorious while the summer months are hot and dry, perfect for grape production in Irouléguy, an *appellation d'origine contrôlée* (AOC) east of St.-Étienne-de-Baïgorry and near Pau. As I walked through this region, I often saw vineyards in the distance. There are mass-market wine producers and small cultivators, local cooperatives and time-honored domaines, but wine from this Basque region is usually consumed locally. The export market focuses on the producers in Bordeaux and the Languedoc Roussillon *terroir* to the east.

In French Basque country, the provinces are named Labourd, Basse Navarre and Soule, but they are lumped together under one official department, the Pyrénées-Atlantiques. The French system of regional departments under the federal center in Paris was an administrative brain-child of Napoléon Bonaparte and later refined by assigning classification numbers and initials to each department. To organize hundreds of small fiefdoms, principalities and regions into manageable state-like units reporting to the federal government in Paris was a brilliant strategic policy that endures today. The western Pyrénées – the Basque homelands in France – bear the identification number (64) for postal codes, telephone numbers and license plates.

Pau is an old noble city that figured during the *ancien régime*, when kings – and a few queens – ruled the country. It was the birthplace of Henri IV, a contemporary of England's Queen Elizabeth I, and still spoken of fondly in France for enacting laws to support the progressive idea that people of different religions had the right to live in harmony. Today, Pau is the regional business and government center. This area around Pau was once officially known as Gascony, and is still called that by many who live in France. Charles de Batz-Castelmore d'Artagnan, of Alexandre Dumas' *The Three Musketeers* novel, was a scion of an estate near Auch, east of Pau.

My route followed higher ground, through the Basque mountains rather than the Piedmont. Though cultural artifacts and social practices in rural Gascony are similar to the Basque way of life, there are distinct differences. In Mark Kurlansky's engaging book, *The Basque History of the World*, I learned that in Euskal Herria (Basque Land), the family house and land form the center of daily life. The culture stems from the family home.

The family house passes to a daughter or son who expresses a willingness to work hard and to cooperate with the extended family, to marry and to remain in the house. Sons may establish their families in dependent houses on the family land. In Basque churches, the women occupy the main pews and the men file in upstairs through a separate entrance to sit in galleries. The opposite, one must note, to certain other traditional religions where the men occupy pride of place and the women are hidden in galleries or screened off in side rooms.

Basque unity has endured longer than that of any other group in Europe. Much has been written about their ancient unique language, which is the oldest in Europe, their highest concentration of type O blood in the world, their fierce political independence and just plain cussedness at the incursion of any interloping power. "This Basque unity is, no doubt, tending to decrease, and will ultimately disappear," Victor Hugo wrote at the end of the 19th century. It's now the beginning of the 21st century and the Basques have held firm for 40,000 years, some scholars estimate. Hugo continued his reflection, "it is strange that this unity, so slender in appearance, should have endured so long. France took one side of the Pyrénées, Spain the other. But neither France nor Spain has succeeded in disaggregating the Basque group. Beneath the fresh layers of history that have been piled upon it during four centuries it is still perfectly visible, like a crater beneath a lake." Basques have held their political and cultural unity through many more than the four centuries of history that Hugo cites. He was referring to the time period after the division along the Pyrénées that established a border between France and Spain.

Aïnhoa, a traditional agricultural town now mostly dedicated to serving the weekend getaway crowd, lay just up the Nivelle River, which lulled me to sleep the previous night. Now it was morning at the campground and I had to figure out a route from Dancharia back to the GR-10. The numbered paths in France are well-established and appear on Michelin road maps. Perhaps in times past, descriptive local names were applied to the same footpaths. Certainly we know that much of the mountain trail system in the French Pyrénées was part of the network of paths that connect to the Chemin-de-St.-Jacques (Way of Saint James) on the southern side of the mountains that leads to Santiago de Compostela. Even if locals aren't hikers, they are aware of footpaths near their town, in the same way that North Americans who live near the Appalachian Trail, the Bruce Trail in Ontario or the Pacific Crest Trail might know about those paths.

I needn't have worried. When I asked about connecting paths back to my cross-country route, the proprietor of Pension Etchartenea pulled out a photocopied hand-drawn map for visitors seeking day hikes. The campground-pension near the Spanish frontier had been a comfortable way-station for me, particularly since the alternative would have been the graveyard of the church in Aïnhoa. Fueled with coffee and brioche from the bar, I also bought snacks and a freshly made ham sandwich for lunch on the trail.

"Don't cross the river," was the proprietor's last advice as I hoisted the compact red mountaineering pack and checked my water supply. With her words in mind, I strode through pine forests on the trail marked with yellow blazes, following the sketched map. But cross the river I did to follow my nose up

Pic de Gorospil and the GR-10 beyond. I made many mistakes before I learned to heed advice from local folks.

Was it ten minutes later that I abandoned the yellow blazed path to pursue dead reckoning? I used the compass and had an inclination where I was headed. Plus, it was broad daylight. What could go wrong? The sun shrieked across the bare hillsides. I plodded from bush to tree, tree to thicket, seeking shelter from the sun.

The distances were longer than marked on the creased and crumpled photocopy map from the campground. My insufficiently detailed regional map used a scale too large to be useful on foot. I needed maps of one centimeter to 500 meters for greater detail. While I rested in scant shade, I contemplated options and scanned the map for a better route, but it was clear that I had to press overland, across the plateau, using the compass to guide me. I couldn't bear the idea of backtracking the harsh distance I'd gained. This was stark country – no vineyards, no farms, no grazing animals. Just scrub brush, scrawny trees and sun. No, I was not lost; the compass would align the route, but this detour was chewing up energy and time to traverse baking plateaus. I could rejoin the GR-10 footpath at Estaben Farm, a refreshment spot described in the guidebook.

Through the midday hours, which played like an Indiana Jones movie, of anxiety, sweating armpits and soaked bandanas, I sloshed water down my throat, mopped sweat from my head and pushed onward. Finally, I crossed the saddle, or col, where a granite upright stone the size of a fire hydrant was marked with an R carved above the number 75. This told me I was again at a national frontier. In the distance, in the direction where I thought the GR-10 path skirted the next mountain ridge to the north and east, I barely could make out a line of humans.

Were they the British bird-watchers from Sare? Another group of hikers? An hallucination? I stopped to swab my dripping face on the stained tee-shirt sleeve. Hadn't I just seen a similar line of hikers moving along the Spanish side on a distant mountain? The vision was surreal, of people in long white robes with staffs in their hands. It's possible the heat distorted my vision because they seemed to float along the path on the mountain across a valley. Could they be a group of pilgrim ghosts marching on air to Santiago de Compostela?

The cluster of horses in a cool gulch below me were certainly real. I could smell them. Two foals with their dams, plus three other horses. A stallion watched from the hillside I'd just passed. They stared at me as I edged along the embankment towards them, the best route around the gulch as the other side was severely eroded. Murmuring gentle "nice horsy" sounds which transcend language, I crept past the group, taking pains not to startle any of the mares with foals as I mingled with them and passed behind their rumps. Why did they stand on the path? I resisted the impulse to stroke the horses as I shifted past them, though I was close enough. I didn't want to startle the animals with a stranger's touch.

After checking the makeshift map again, I trudged towards the Estaben Farm, but I was moving across the land at the wrong angle. With visual checks from time to time on the distant farm in the valley, I soon realized I'd overshoot the farm if I continued on that trajectory. So I shuttled across the side of the hill and followed the road through the valley.

A man and a woman, both dressed in white shorts and no hats, carrying no visible water bottles, were setting out past the cattle barn as I entered the farm lane. Maybe they were part of the other group dressed in white that I'd seen in the distance.

We exchanged greetings and they told me they planned to hike to Aïnhoa, on the marked path. I explained how to avoid the cross-country detour I'd just done. I cautioned the couple that the day was seriously hot and urged them to take enough water for the 12 kilometers. They smiled, unconcerned. Maybe there was water in the woman's purse?

Could I be seriously over-equipped? All the outdoors experts say you can't have too much water on a hot day in the mountains. But water is heavy. The 1.5 liter Camelbak reservoir, which stowed in a customized pocket inside my pack and had a handy sipping hose attached, weighed 3.3 pounds full. I also carried two other one-liter flasks, for a total of more than 7.5 pounds of water. I filled or topped off the water bottles at any opportunity for fresh water, because there aren't spigots in the mountains. In higher altitudes when the heat eased and I needed liquid encouragement, I dedicated one container to wine. Call me timid and risk-adverse: after all, this isn't remote back-country desert. Possibly I didn't need to carry so much water, but I reasoned that if the water was with me, there would be no need to purify stream water with nasty tasting iodine tablets. I'd seen too many long-distance hikers on the Appalachian Trail rationing their water, never able to quench their thirst, not knowing where the next pure water source might be. I had no interest in hiking under that kind of physically-debilitating austerity. I'd done back-country trekking where drinking the local water meant hauling out a purification pump rig or mixing an iodine brew that needs to cure awhile to be potable, anxious chores when you're thirsty. Having to wait for water when you're thirsty is a form of torture in my view, just as terrible as too much water down the gullet and up the nose, so the mild sacrifice of carrying a little more than just enough water was an easy trade-off.

As an authorized hikers' gîte, Farm Estaben takes lodgers and serves meals, but it was too early to stop for the night. I guzzled water to quench thirst followed by a Coke for the sugar and the rapid re-hydration effect. The waitress agreed to refill my bottles. While scribbling in my journal, I eavesdropped on the other customers, a group finishing a meal. They were chatting in French and English about gourmet food, while sipping wine and resting in the heat of the day. I smelled of piss and sweat, like a horse. Like two horses. I was working too hard, marching instead of walking; gulping the experience instead of savoring it.

When I left the farmhouse, the punishing heat smacked my sweat dry. The hillsides sizzled where the GR-10 followed a road for a couple of kilometers. Further along, a camouflage covered jeep jammed with soldiers scrambled up a dirt track towards the communications facility on Artzamendi peak. When I paused to survey the valley behind me, I didn't see movement on the trails or hillsides.

The sun blared down; Egyptian vultures wheeled overhead. Booted eagles too. Onward, past towers and satellite discs which marked the military vehicle's destination, I moved towards a distant picnic area where cars were parked and children played, running down the inclines with kites and balloons. This stretch of plateau was tricky underfoot. Clumps of long grass covered the ankle twisting holes in the terrain and I had to leap over narrow trenches. Had it been used for military training? Were the holes in the ground made by grazing animals or training ordinance?

Red and white blazes led me to a sharply angled downward path from the top of the plateau, down a crag 670 meters (2198 feet) deep, according to the map, with open exposure. Exposure means you're moving along a steep narrow ledge or path with nothing to break a fall. The open face followed down a path with steps arranged from the scattered rocks on the side of the mountain. I was wary of the void below.

There was no alternative route; I had to continue, though I am fearful of vertigo. Instead of thinking about where I was, I focused exclusively on the footpath and the next two or three meters ahead, not the void below. Two booted feet just fit side by side on the path along and down the ledge; that's all the room there was. My knees were shaking as I stepped down and down on the exposed face. My heart rate mounted and the incline created an illusion that I would pitch forward into the chasm. I avoided looking down and slowly continued. I couldn't see the bottom anyway, more than half a kilometer below.

Get off the mountain was my mantra. As soon as possible, in one piece, with no scraped skin. I pulled the whistle that hung from my backpack around to the front, in reach if I slid or fell, not that there were any people around. A rescue helicopter – bright red – happened to roar past as I was inching down, close enough for me to see the profiles of the mountain police at the controls. Was it a coincidence? Had they seen me on the exposed face alone and swung by to check? My guess is the mountain rescue teams pass over the crag several times a day, just in case a hapless hiker has slipped and plunged.

Paging through the guidebook later that night, I learned that this particular stretch of the mountain trail is "one of the narrowest and most vertigo-inspiring on the GR-10." Streatfeild-James goes on to praise the vistas and cautions hikers to take lots of time and descend slowly because, "this particular section has caused more than its fair share of injuries." Well, this hiker tried to ignore the spectacular views and just watched her feet and the path ahead, mindful of loose stones and slick spots. I probably had read the description several times in preparing for the trek, but the printed words didn't quite cover the acute reality.

I did notice soaring lammergeiers that whooshed above. With a nine feet wing span, these bearded vultures cruised easily on thermal columns of rising air. I heard their wings cut the air after the chopper swept by. It was difficult for me to descend such a crag, but by concentrating on the path, and not looking into the void, I didn't stumble. At the bottom, there was a farm house, then the GR-10 path.

According to the guidebook, the blazed route turned at a bridge a few kilometers outside of Bidarray. Though this was not the ominously named Pont d'Enfer (Bridge of Hell) in the center of the town, it proved hellishly difficult for me to find the continuation of the path. I poked around in the woods, looking for the path marker on the far side of the bridge over the Bastan River, but the opening in the trees that should mark the continuation of the footpath was blocked with brush and cut firewood.

Later on during my journey, I met members of a group who set up a segment of the pilgrimage route, known as the GR-78. Discussing obstacles in the paths and other oddities I'd noticed along the routes I'd taken, I learned that some landowners deliberately hide or obstruct official marked paths that cross or follow the borders of their property. Legal right of ways for footpaths are complex and differ in various countries and jurisdictions. However, an established national route such as the GR-10 or GR-78 cannot be arbitrarily blocked by disgruntled landowners. Maybe the brush pile was just a normal accumulation of summer vines and undergrowth, but it appeared that the logs and brush were deliberately positioned to hide the path.

When I knocked at the glass patio doors of a rural farmhouse – the green and white emblem on the gate signified they offered certified lodging – the guests at table eating dinner smiled and looked up. *"Non,"* the host said, *"pas de chambres libres"* (no rooms available). At the rustic hostel-gîte there was plenty of space. I picked a little room upstairs and made the bed with clean sheets rented from the hostel manager. A skylight in the ceiling opened to improve the airflow.

In gîtes and mountain refuges, like hostels, travelers are encouraged to carry their own sheets, sheet sack or sleeping bag. Blankets are included in the lodging charge, so a sleeping bag is unnecessary. I didn't have a sheet sack, having long ago lost the silk one I used on my first hosteling trek through Europe. I assumed that clean sheets would be available for rent at gîtes and that turned out to be true most of the time.

Two college students from Bordeaux were staying at the hostel. "We plan to go up the mountain tomorrow," the woman said. She had a slight build and a huge smile. They intended to ascend the crag I had just navigated down, then cross the angle of the crevasse at the top, to wander on unknown sheep paths on the other side of the rock face. The man pointed excitedly to the tight inclines on his topographic map. "Looks like this is a strenuous route," he said. "Yes, it's really steep," I replied. And I told them about my descent, how the path narrowed into steps cut into a vertical rock face. "I'm older than you two, so my knees might give out sooner," I joked. "I hope you don't suffer vertigo." I nodded to her cute little fashion sneakers, saying that her footgear might not offer the best support. It struck me that some hikers I'd met weren't particularly concerned about carrying water, wearing sturdy boots or sun hats or preparing for potentially dangerous routes. Was I overly cautious? I like to be prepared for the worst.

Leaving the two in the equipped and spacious gîte kitchen, I poked around town and found a nearby auberge. Though it was after 9 p.m., a little late to be starting dinner in rural France, the server cheerfully brought a salad, sausage in a Basque red pepper and tomato sauce with fried potatoes, followed by a Basque tart made with rich egg pastry, part of which I saved for a snack. I drank a half bottle of a 1998 Irouléguy varietel.

At other tables I eyed a group of four women, a couple and a solo man. After watching Lonely French Guy quaff multiple coffees and uncork a second bottle of red, I overheard the women at the other table gossip about a tragedy. My overactive imagination wove a story using the characters in the room. I spun a yarn that lonely guy's sweetheart had been killed in a car crash on one of the curving roads, so he revisits the restaurant to be in touch with her. Or he is a poet, a writer like myself, looking for inspiration in the foggy mountains. Or he's a local, but an artist, alienated in this insular village with the devil's bridges.

Perhaps emboldened by the muscular Irouléguy wine, I took it upon myself to visit the table of chatting women and ask about the solo man. I was wondering, I said, about why he was drinking so many coffees. Has he eaten? And the two bottles of wine? They told me he'd eaten earlier and no, they didn't know him. I explained I had imagined him a displaced poet in the mountains drinking coffee and red wine. They laughed and I laughed with them. Silly me; sharing my imaginative musings with strangers. Part of being a traveling fool is to release tension after the day's struggle with mountains and cliffs.

A colleague at the Washington Post, Michael Cotterman, put it this way when we chatted about my journey before I left. "Walking the earth is your quest. You fill a need out in the world." We resolved that I was like an itinerant Buddhist warrior who goes forth and walks the land, responding to situations and encounters. A myth, but not far from my personal reality. The moments require response in a purely sense-based imaginative way; my imagination crafted a story and I acted upon it. Maybe the lesson for me is that no one really needs me to interfere, but if I want to be the clown, it can be a useful role.

My thoughts turned to the intense work environment that I'd left so recently. I handled a fulltime job, taught night classes in writing at several colleges and wrote articles for other publications. Three jobs, really, all at the same time. Now, I was finding it difficult to believe that I didn't have to return to a desk job in a few months or even a year. On unpaid leave of absence, I was free to see what the world brought me, living quietly and staying focused. Each day goes by as a unit rather than as a clump of time known as the workweek or the weekend. Paying attention in the moment meant dealing with the immediate reality, and that urgent reality was to reduce the weight in my sack so I could move with greater ease.

At the post office in Bidarray I stuffed sleeping bag, clothes and equipment into mailing boxes. Though I sometimes make fun of gear-heads, I had brought too many gadgets. The pedometer used for training all summer didn't work in the field when I wore a backpack. Waterproof matches and a collapsible drinking cup were not required. I certainly didn't need two lipsticks or the second pair of shorts. The quick-dry Patagonia shorts that I washed each evening when I showered were always dry by morning. I rotated two sports bras, hanging the damp one from my pack to dry, like hikers I'd seen on the train. Self-deprecating comments to the postal clerk about taking too many things on my hike fell flat; if the fellow had a reaction, he kept it to himself, wrapping the bursting box with string and stamping the bright yellow cardboard all over with purple cancellation marks. A taciturn Basque, he simply asked for payment and said the boxes would be sent out later that day.

Repacking and selecting the superfluous items to send back to Paris ate into the morning. By the time I started climbing the nearest peak, Iparla, it was noon. On the low part, I was humping up an established path, but on the rocky faces the blaze marks vanished. Sheep trails branched off in all directions. Out of the corner of my eye, I spied a Pyrénées chamois on the rock outcroppings of the Crêtes d'Iparla, but it could have been a stray goat. I pulled out the map and guidebook and studied my position, then surged onward and upward, eventually finding the red and white trail markers painted on the sides of mini-van sized boulders.

The sky was pellucid, the air mildly perfumed with mint and blackberries. Other hikers, day-trippers without hats or water, passed by, headed to where I'd started the day. Some of the older couples were panting and red faced. There was even a shepherd wearing the traditional dark blue beret with a sheep dog at his side. He was breathing normally, moving steadily downhill on the steep narrow path. Finally at the top, I pitched down my pack and lay on the grassy plateau in the shade of a massive menhir that stood near other boulders of similar tapered rectangular shape.

Menhirs, also called standing stones, are upright boulders found throughout Europe and part of early human culture. Speculation about their function, ranges from ceremonial to territory marking to calendars. It's thought that much later, followers of modern religions pulled down many of the upright stones. Not knowing how to evaluate the pattern of the boulders on Iparla, by turns upright or lying sideways, I simply enjoyed the fresh mountain air. Studying the map, I did note that easterly sight lines from this peak led to dolmens on the Nive River and its tributaries. Dolmens are chambers made by placing large flat stones at right angles and thought by researchers to be used as burial barrows. I've sat inside the stone huts and they would make quite adequate shelter for humans who only possessed what they carried. Researchers who have analyzed the structures and markers erected before written history define them as grave sites based on the remains found in the barrows. Other writers suggest the stone structures are related to cults of human sacrifice, which would be the inclination of people themselves influenced by the death centric religions of the modern era. Differences between those ancestors and ourselves are negligible. If I were walking around this area thousands of years ago, as humans were, I would use the topographic features to serve my need to locate shelter, water, food and my community. The high points, rivers, and permanent indicators like upright boulders visible to a sharp-eyed person would be the useful signposts for hunters. And if I were a clever human used to the rigors of the outdoors, I would erect small strong structures between communities for shelter while tending herds or hunting and to sit out bad weather.

Basque Sheep Barn near Col d'Harrieta

On the summit of Iparla, at 1044 meters (3425 feet), gained in the heat of the afternoon, I encountered no other people. Pairs of little birds flitted about. On the edge of the cliff, there was a cross about knee-height made of metal worked into curled hearts at the ends of the cross bar and on top. It was planted in cement and a notation in French embossed in a metal plate told a story: Jean Baptiste, died July 4, 1948 at age 100. I asked residents of the nearest villages about this memorial and was told the cross was for a local man who loved that view from the mountain.

This time with no vertigo issues in play, I savored the views in all directions. Pic du Midi d'Ossau at 2884 meters (9462 feet) crowns the landscape in the central Pyrénées, where

I would soon be walking. I wanted to see Vignemalle, the highest mountain in the Pyrénées chain, rising above the high altitude lakes south of Cauterets and Pic du Midi de Bigorre at 2872 meters (9439 feet) which is capped by the famous Pic du Midi Observatory built in 1878. And Mount Canigou, 2784 meters (9137 feet), is the last grand mountain before the Mediterranean. It wasn't part of my plan to climb each of these mountains on this journey, but I would hike portions on side trips, staying in the towns below, if the weather held. Pyrénées tourists on foot and horseback have long used the strategy of establishing a base in a town and making day hikes.

On the mountain, I'd noticed birds and many little lizards. Hikers need rewards to carry on. Spotting wildflowers up ahead or an oddly shaped rock, I would use it as an incentive to plod upward. Rest at the rock. Pause at the flowers. On Iparla, I spotted a huge worm, twisted and dried out, lying on the path. Bigger than any worms I'd ever seen – almost 12" long and resembling an earthworm, not a snake. The rock it lived under had been moved or kicked. So I picked up the worm with a stick and moved it into the grass and flowers. The trail passed over an area of caved-in rocks where the earth had sunk, perhaps caused by snow compression.

After the crest, I strode on for several hours and the daylight started to fade. I passed a stone *olha*, a summer hut that shepherds use during the transhumance when sheep graze on the pastures above Basque towns. Vultures soared on thermal bursts overhead. The day was shutting down for night. I came to a crossroads in the path where there was a hunter's shelter the size of a trash dumpster with a fire ring and dry wood stacked nearby. I weighed options for the night. I could camp up here at Col d'Harrieta, but without a sleeping bag, I'd be cold wrapped in long underwear, a jacket and a rain poncho. What about dinner and coffee in the morning? That decided it: I strode down the mountain to Urdos.

The Hargain Farm at Urdos

Summer leaves a long colorful imprint on these Basque villages. Wildflowers, yellow, pink and purple, still bloomed. Ripe blackberries bulged on prickly stems. At a farm above Urdos, men and teenage boys harvested corn, trundling tractor loads of husks under black plastic cover for winter animal feed. Urdos was hardly more than a hamlet, dominated by the largest building, a solid stone house with armored tower and fortified entrance. From a distance it was imposing. Up close, the heavy stone walls and slot windows set very high for archers, spoke of adversity under siege and a time when the nearby populace took refuge with the land-owning gentry.

I turned the corner to face the front of the stone mansion and discovered the emblem of French rural inns. The door was open. Calling *"Il y a quelqu'un?"* (Is there someone?) I stuck my head in the vast entry hall stairwell. I studied a collection of blue and white china lined up on a rack in a carved wood cabinet and waited.

A gnome-like woman shuffled out from a series of dark rooms, her bright black eyes shining under a crest of snow-white hair cut short. She was bent over – osteoporosis had gotten the best of her bones and a cookie-sized puffy black mole on her arm begged for a melanoma examination. They do take guests, she said as she led me up the stairway which after a week in the woods seemed to me as wide and gracious as the main staircase at the Library of Congress Jefferson Building, wide enough for several horses to climb side by side. The old mansion open to travelers was a lucky find for me. I chose the largest room, since all rooms were the same price, and sunk into the huge bed. The room also had a sofa, lamps for reading, exposed wooden beams and an ultra modern bathroom *en suite*. Even though the cost was in excess of my daily budget which was about $40 a day for lodging and food, I craved a comfortable place to rest my feet and lay low for a couple of days.

The elderly hawk nose proprietress, Agnes Hargain, a tough old matriarch with Spanish, Basque and French ancestors, sent me to the restaurant down the hill, cautioning that harvest would continue all night under the light of a full moon. The rhythms of country life rule these valleys of the Pyrénées. Raising and harvesting, putting by and planting a winter crop, each task according to the season. Animals fell under that cycle of raising and slaughtering, husbanding and birthing. Agnes' grandson Daniel explained that a calf born the night before under the mid-September moon would be on the table in two years. The pheasants and quail scampering through hedgerows had a future as winter dinner, roasted with the chestnuts stored in the special baskets.

The day behind me, it was time for dinner. I sat alone at a table in the Manechenia Restaurant, inhaling the scent of country *potage* about to be spooned into my dish from a pottery tureen. People arrived to take seats at other tables, nodding "*Bonsoir*" to all.

Dare I say: there are no bad meals in Southwest France? Early on in my travels in France, I learned to read menus displayed outside of restaurants and search for "*menu complet*" listings, which indicate three or four course meals – excellent value for hungry hikers. Here, the four course meal cost a little over ten U.S. dollars and included soup, fish, foul and desert. I ordered a half bottle of Irouléguy 1999 Domaine Ilarria, a drinkable red wine.

The trout was raised in a local hatchery and it arrived from the kitchen with a topping of almonds and parsley. The quail in a sauce thickened with a small amount of cream in the gamy flavored cooking juices completed the meal. I couldn't really pick the bird clean because I was ready to sleep. Dinner started with *potage*, an old fashioned heavy soup composed of leeks, carrots, potatoes, a bean or two. Some versions are made with cabbage or yellow lentils and nearly all Basque dishes feature strips of red pepper.

Garbure or *potage* is standard Basque fare, made every season, with ingredients changed to include produce currently available. Fall and winter versions include root vegetables. Spring *potage* includes ripe fava beans, while a summer version contains green beans, tomatoes and new potatoes. The soup base is the ham, white beans and cabbage. This recipe is my version of the many variations of *potage* I ate during the pilgrimage.

Potage

- 4 quarts water
- 2 cups dried white navy beans, soaked in water for 8 to 10 hours
- 1 bouquet garni (mix sprigs of fresh herbs or about 1/4 tsp. each of dried tarragon, oregano, basil and sage and tie in a small circle of cheesecloth)
- 1 pound ham shank (omit for vegetarian version)
- 2 medium carrots, peeled and coarsely chopped
- 4 to 6 medium potatoes, peeled and chopped into 1 inch cubes
- 1 medium onion, coarsely chopped
- 1 small cabbage, cored and sliced into short strips or 1 inch squares
- 3 leeks, thoroughly washed, trimmed and coarsely chopped
- 4 red peppers, cored and sliced into julienne strips
- 1/2 cup garlic, minced
- 1 tablespoon sea salt, or more to taste
- 1/2 teaspoon freshly-ground white pepper

Place 4 quarts water, the white beans, the bouquet garni, and the ham shank in a large, heavy-bottomed saucepan over high heat. Cover and bring to a boil. Simmer for 15 minutes. Add the carrots, onion, potatoes, cabbage, leeks, garlic, and red pepper. Season. Return to a boil, lower the heat, and simmer, covered, for 30 minutes. Add more water if necessary. Taste and adjust seasoning. Cook until the vegetables are soft but not mushy. Remove the bouquet garni and ham shank. Discard the bouquet garni. Remove meat from shank and add to soup or serve alongside.

Strolling back in the dark, content with the fine meal in my belly, I stared at the stars and moon. The night sky is different here in the mountains, where there are no streetlights and people don't illuminate their yards. Faint lights crisscrossed the fields in the distance – the tractors finished the harvesting that took a week or more in times past, but only a day and a night now.

Crêtes d'Iparla

The mountains I'd climbed the previous day – the Crêtes d'Iparla – were shrouded in mist the next morning. The farmhands worked late, past midnight, yet were up early and busy. The breakfast room signaled cheer and serenity. Yellow and blue dishes, yellow table linen, blue handled bistro-style cutlery and a blue and white butter dish to match the milk pitcher waited for me. Decorative details in the room were artistically arranged and thoroughly charming.

The granddaughter-in-law invited me to take vegetables from their garden. She and Daniel with their toddler son established their own household in a former schoolteacher's house across the square. She explained that her husband Daniel, Agnes' grandson, renovated the old house to prepare rooms to rent to tourists. Daniel's mother owns the big stone house where I was sleeping. Each morning the younger couple manage the farm chores, fetch fresh bread from the village and brew coffee for their guests. I ate slowly at breakfast, enjoying the bread, butter and fruit preserves. I read, rested my feet and napped.

In the garden, enclosed by high stone walls, I picked plump red tomatoes and surveyed the other plants. Red peppers are a signature ingredient in Basque cuisine and in this garden, pepper plants filled a sunny patch. Since cooking a meal on the hot plate in the breakfast room was more work than I bargained for, I left the ripe peppers in the garden and sliced up a salad of fresh tomatoes and basil.

Agnes told me about the Nazi occupation, murmuring in my ear as she escorted me through the village chapel adjacent to the family house. A stone marker over the door dated 1666 put the whitewashed stone chapel at the time of peace and prosperity, after the religious freedoms established by Henri IV and centuries before the turmoil of the Spanish succession and the Carlist wars in the 1800s. While studying my maps, I'd noticed another, larger town with the same name – Urdos – outside of Basque country many kilometers to the east, but Agnes didn't know of any connection between the two towns.

When I was back in the U.S. again, I explored the place names of Basque manors and towns. I came across *Les Noms de Maisons Medievales en Labourd, Basse-Navarre, et Soule*, by Professor Jean-Baptiste Orpustan. The author explains Basque language and customs, a well timed book for the popular and scholarly renaissance of interest in Basque culture. Orpustan discusses the compounding feature of Basque words. "Syllables, each with specific meaning, are tacked together to create words and names." *Mendi*, for example, means mountain or hill. Similarly, references giving a concept of height include the syllable *gain* to convey height, an elevated position, or a position above something else. This concept shows up in Basque composed words like *bidagain, gainxuri, mendigain*, or *argain*. I guess my pilgrimage walk featured *mendigain* (mountain elevated position) nearly every day.

Professor Orpustan mentions Urdos: "On the same basis, the name Urdos, names the hamlet and the house of Baïgorry (1366, la salle d'Urdoz) on their plateau clearly visible and a house of Osses (1344, Urdoz) is placed at the "end of the plateau" on account of a very different height and other characteristics." Knowing that -oz and -os are interchangeable suffixes in Basque areas, maybe the building described as Urdoz on the plateau was a precursor of the stone mansion in Urdos where I stayed.

La Bastide, a hamlet about twenty minutes by foot up the hill from Urdos and about a mile from the Spanish border, was dominated by a large building with the name L'Hospitalet over the door marked with a date in the early 1800's, but I could have mistaken the carved numbers. Indeed, at the Chateau d'Etxauz in St.-Étienne-de-Baïgorry, the year marked over the door was either 1555 or 1666. And the numbers over the door at the chapel next to the manor house where I slept could have been 1666 or 1555.

I didn't like the atmosphere at the tiny settlement of La Bastide and quickly returned to Urdos. A traveler learns to heed the internal instinct. The lanes were dirty with litter and scabs of ordure, not the honest fresh mud of a farm village, but the accumulated refuse of neglect. Children stared out of doorways. Cars blasted past on the rutted lanes. It was strange that this settlement, so close to well organized Urdos, looked like it was populated with unhappy folks. When I asked the Hargain family about the downtrodden appearance of the neighboring village, they shrugged me off. Basques would not comment about neighbors to an outsider.

This particular Sunday was a day of patrimony in France, and many historic buildings were opened to the public without charge. My promenade to St.-Étienne-de-Baïgorry followed an orange blazed trail downhill from Urdos. Waiting for the chateau to open, I sketched the mountains in pencil, my mental voice repeating instructions remembered from classes at the Corcoran College of Art. "Dark recedes, light advances," instructor Leslie Exton would repeat. She established the Corcoran's program for botanical art and over the years, I took many classes with her. "Shade gradually, blend the tones. Remember your distinct tone values," she told me and my drawing ability improved.

The gates opened and I sallied forth. Inside Chateau d'Etxauz, a guide led the group to a granary to view the magnificent vaulted wooden ceiling, hand hewn by master carpenters. The primary floors of the chateau were converted for use by paying guests, but I never considered staying there. The farm in Urdos offered a more authentic experience at an affordable price.

The centerpiece of St.-Étienne-de-Baïgorry is the cathedral. In 1999, the town commissioned one of the few organ makers left in the world, Rémy Mahler, to build an organ in the style of the 17th and 18th century organs of Southern Germany. Each July, the town holds a classical music festival, and the day I visited, a free concert was scheduled. A Basque professor gave me a lift from the chateau to the church and explained the cross-border migration of sheep to pockets of Basque territory in Spain. Transhumance, or seasonal migration of herds, had been practiced in Provence from a very early date. The 13th century growth of towns, with their heavy demands for meat, increased the economic importance of the custom.

I took a long break, staying several days with the Hargain family at Maison Jauregia, the name of their mansion. When I left Urdos, Mme. Agnes shed a few tears and hugged me, saying, "We've grown so accustomed to you!"

Gateway to the Chemin de Saint-Jacques-de-Compostelle

Finally I tramped into Saint-Jean-Pied-de-Port, the gateway to the Spanish portion of the long pilgrim trail known in English as the Way of St. James that terminates at the Galician city of Santiago de Compostela. I was no longer footsore. The path and I knew each other by now.

St.-Jean-Pied-de-Port is a famous place, known throughout Europe as the crossroads for various pilgrimage routes to Spain. The many Santiago de Compostela access routes stretch south from Northern Europe, funneling through England, Poland, Germany, and the north of France. Paths also trace across southern France into Spain to hook up with the path that ends at Santiago. Many pilgrims travel from Saint-Jean-Pied-de-Port to Santiago and consider that they've done the entire route, but that's just the Spanish segment. The pilgrimage path is much longer. Some people follow segments of the route each year, returning to pick up where they left off. Others ride the pilgrimage route on bikes or horses, or even drive it. I heard of a family that brought along mules to carry equipment or the children. It's said that the Codex Calixtinus, the 12th century pilgrim guide commissioned by the Abbot of Cluny, might be the first tourist guide book in history.

Saint-Jean-Pied-de-Port, which means "St. Jean at the foot of the mountain pass" is the last town of any size in France before the western Pyrénées crossing at Roncesvaux or Roncesvalles, as it is called in Spain. This is where Charlemagne was reportedly defeated in 778, later celebrated in the epic poem La Chanson de Roland (the song of Roland) in the 11th century. St. Jean is an old, old town but Charlemagne is not a big draw these days. The town is a popular meeting point for hikers and tourists. Some headed to the Spanish Camino, others enjoying the Basque culture and cuisine. Pilgrims – the tourists of Medieval times– have been trekking through for many centuries. The dull gray stone walls of the houses and streets were embedded with the grit of ages. St. Jean sits at 180 meters (590 feet) above sea level and the pass over the mountains is at 962 meters (3156 feet) above sea level, the easiest crossing point on the western Basque region. Most of the other peaks in the French Basque region top at 1000 to 1500 meters (3280 to 4921 feet). The magnificent snow-capped Pyrénées mountains are farther east.

Irouléguy Vineyard

The day burned bright and hot; I sniffed the purple grapes ripening in fields owned by Irouléguy and Brana wineries and planned to sample the wine at dinner. The Irouléguy domain was planted by Roncevaux monks in the 11th or 14th centuries, depending on which source you consult. After the 19th century phylloxera crisis and several bad production years, wine production in the region declined. Production improved after 1945, and by 1970, Irouléguy attained the coveted A.O.C. (*appellation d'origine contrôlée*). The varieties are cabernet franc, tannat and sauvignon.

Near the ramparts of Saint-Jean-Pied-de-Port, the privileged few maintain houses and gardens within the old city walls. Many old buildings serve tourists as hotels, restaurants or shops. Outside the stone ramparts of the historic center, suburban houses belong to those who maintain the tourism services. Prosperous local folks own historic houses inside the walls as well as estates in the countryside.

With a thirst that wouldn't quit, I took time for refreshment at the Hotel de Ramparts, where Daniel Hargain said they'd treat me right if I mentioned his name. They were nice enough, but had no rooms. At the bar, I sipped a mint and seltzer water which was a better refreshment than sweet cola or headache-inducing beer during these hot, physically demanding afternoons.

Next to me, a man told me he'd lived in California for some 28 years near Stockton, where many Basques settled. His wife, now dead, had been a cook at Villa Basque restaurant there. We talked about Basque history and traditions for a while. At the tourist office, a clerk phoned to reserve a room in a suburban house, a kilometer or two outside the city walls. The place was a modern ranch style house with a private bath for each room. Other guests were motorcycle riders from Yorkshire, a cheerful pair who've visited Basque country eight times. The man pilots the big Beamer and the woman rides pillion. That night, I prowled the top of the ramparts open to the public, and by chance spotted the motorcycle couple sweetly nuzzling over a candlelit supper in a restaurant built into the city walls.

The town receives a steady parade of northern Europeans and a few North and South Americans following the pilgrimage route by car and tour bus. Backpackers wandered around the town, slumped at café tables and scribbled postcards home to Germany or Ireland. I settled for a mushroom omelet and a half bottle of Irouléguy at a busy restaurant on the main drag and watched the stream of vehicles and young travelers writing postcards or using their mobile phones. I missed the silent isolation of the mountains.

In this gateway town, my mind shuffled through images and imaginings of thousands and thousands of pilgrims through the centuries, people who walked, or rode – if they were rich – on their way to the fabled cathedral in Santiago. Scallop shells, the symbol of the Way of St. James, were carved on gravestones, or on the walls above doorways. I noticed scallop shell door knockers and shell emblems decorating cornerstones or arches in the old parts of town. Market stalls and boutiques offered scallop shell souvenirs. Too bad about the Made in China sticker on the back.

There was a time when making a pilgrimage guaranteed entry to paradise, according to the religious bookkeepers of the Roman Catholic Church. Forging holiness and establishing one's character on the pilgrim trail is nothing new. Larking along for the sake of something to do isn't a modern idea either. Surely pilgrims then and now walk to forget painful realizations, change their perspective or use the experience as a path into possibility.

I was building my rationale from all of those reasons. True, I was hoping to become stronger, both physically and mentally, maybe reinforcing my soul in the process. And I was out on a lark, waiting to see what the road brought me, passing time entirely focused in the present moment, which is always the most intense experience in life. Time spent expecting or reminiscing does not shimmer. I was walking my way forward from one era in my life to another. Leaving the Washington Post behind was not an easy decision and I recognized a need to push other aspects of my life into fresh arenas. Someone had left me behind; now it was time to walk away from that period. I hoped for a challenging idea or person who might shift my thinking and action to a higher plane.

Though I know that hopes prayed over sometimes meet a resolution, possibly through coincidence and serendipity, possibly just because, I made an attempt to stay neutral about whatever might happen on the path. I was looking for affirmation of my journey through serendipitous encounters – the stranger who arrived to give needed directions, the water spigot at the town fountain just when the water bottle went dry, the bread store that stayed open even though the town was shuttered for mid-day repose. To my way of thinking, all of these small events and many more strengthened my resolve, affirmed my pilgrimage. This particular day's encounter assumed mythic proportions, however, probably exacerbated by near sunstroke.

The day I left St.-Jean Pied-de-Port stretched long into the night, complicated by rain, mistaken paths, a locked pilgrim church in Ostabat and overshooting in the dark the farmhouse destination at Arhansus. At dusk, Mme. Veronique Etchegoyhen had sent her husband out looking for me on the main road, but I had cut across fields and missed him. Though the distance was 24 kilometers by the road, I'd guess my route that day played out to be much longer.

During the rainy gray morning – a thunderstorm after midnight broke 20 days of drought – I'd encountered a Belgian pilgrim, his map encased in plastic hanging around his neck on a cord. Draped in a dark poncho that hooded a tonsured head and carrying a tall staff, he looked to me like the reincarnation of a perambulating monk. He greeted me enthusiastically in French, "You've been there!" The 'there' being Santiago de Compostela near the western coast of Spain. Because I was heading northeast on the scallop shell blazed GR-65 from St.-Jean-Pied-de-Port, his assumption was understandable. This was the first time I was taken for a real pilgrim, and I felt obliged to stop and explain my reverse route. No, I hadn't been to Santiago and didn't wear the scallop hanging on a cord around my neck or emblazoned on a backpack as many of the pilgrims do. He looked a little crestfallen that I was actually heading away from Santiago, but we saluted each other and I urged him onward with the same luck and strength that had sustained him all the way south from Belgium.

Late in the afternoon, beaten by the sun, I sat under a wayside cross drinking water. The cross was weather-beaten, but not so old as the pilgrim heyday in the Middle Ages. I was puzzling about the age of the cross when a trio approached – two men and a woman. The shorter dark haired man was local – I could tell by his clothing that he wasn't a pilgrim or a sporting hiker. I learned the woman was a friend of his out for an overnight hike. They'd met the tall blond pilgrim from Nancy in a hostel and were now traveling together to Saint-Jean-Pied-de-Port, where the group planned to split up. St. Jean was behind me at that point. I was heading east and they were moving west.

We took funny photos of each other around the cross. I can't recall if we exchanged addresses, but I have none of their names in my journal, so I guess not. We rested, drank water and possibly sipped some wine carried in one of those soft goatskin flasks by the dark haired man. A shepherd arrived on a tractor leading a flock. His son shunted the herds across the road while the wife stopped traffic by waving a red flag. Their dogs charged the laggards and the hundreds of sheep moved in a white wave along the farm lane up the opposite hill.

Soon it was time for us to hoist our packs and continue on our separate ways. The charming man from Nancy invited me to go along with him to Compostela on the pilgrim route southwest through Spain. I was stunned. Sure, I'd imagined that it would be cool to meet a like-minded companion. Naturally, I had flirted with the idea of following the Spanish route, but after reading Shirley MacLaine's book, *The Camino*, I decided the Spanish section of the pilgrim path offered too much contact with other humans. Lodgings promised to be crowded or dank and the food in the hostels was said to be mediocre. These were not the thoughts of a genuine pilgrim. Let me be honest: my pride urged me to follow a route that was unusual, not the one favored by the tourist hordes.

Why was this encounter agitating my plans? Because this man who appeared on the route was the very image of a Canadian doctor I had traveled with back and forth across Canada and around California years ago, an "On The Road" comrade now out of touch. For a while I considered the prospect and questioned the universe: what to do? Was this the sign, the surprise I had asked for? I extended my arms, imitating the cross and said to the sky, show me a sign. The man – I never did catch his name – was probably in his late twenties, sturdy and apparently sunny-natured. Best of all, he seemed to have a sense of travel as an experiment in serendipity. He said, "I guess I'm the sign."

I almost said yes. But then I declined, not wanting to backtrack the route, in this self-defined exercise of onward, eastward motion. True also, embarking on a journey with another meant surrendering independence and would involve daily compromise. I wouldn't be alone, would have to alter my pace and be required to talk. We'd be strangers getting to know each other, pleasant enough, but not the journey I wanted. Perhaps I was learning that I didn't have to follow every eddy in the flow of the moment. I could be stalwart in the passing stream.

Pic du Midi d'Ossau

CHAPTER 3
Walking to Holy Water

Ostabat to Lourdes

Steady on my way, onward through darkening twilight, I found the pilgrim church at Ostabat. There was a time, back in 1350, when twenty or more hostels in the region provided shelter for pilgrims. Pilgrims stopped at the church, gave thanks for safe passage and sought a place to bed down for the night. The pilgrimage route was the place to see and be seen. But this modern day pilgrim found Ostabat's chapel doors locked and no directions to nearby shelter posted on the doors.

A group of men smoked and drank a *pastis* on a nearby bar terrace. I asked them about the route to the farm at Arhansus where I'd arranged a room for the night. Smirking slightly – how could they not, confronted by a sweating middle-aged American women stooped under a pack, so alien from their gender divided culture: women toiling at home, men relaxing in public – they waved me farther along the GR-65 path, toward the two-lane paved road heading south.

Ostabat behind me, I soldiered onward towards the Etchegoyhen farm, which Madam of the farmstead had told me during our phone call lay a couple of kilometers past the village of Arhansus. Suddenly, I was aware of a car trolling behind me. A grizzled guy in a white work van rolled down the window and asked if I wanted a lift. "Arhansus is ten kilometers more," he said in the local lingo, then pointed to the ridge in the distance. "That's the farm you're looking for, way over there. You'll never get there by nightfall." It sounded like he was taunting me. "No thanks, I don't need a ride," I told him and hitched up the dangling straps on the shoulder pads of the backpack, moving it higher up, hoping I cut a hefty figure. He wasn't really menacing, I decided. Surely, he was just trying to be helpful.

Tucking into generous servings of braised beef and potatoes at the farmsteads' solid dinner table, I listened to the other guests – a quartet of travelers on a driving tour – trade quasi-fascist commentary on what was wrong with France (the immigrants) and how to fix France (kick the immigrants out). The host egged them on. If the stuffed heads of wild animals that adorned the walls were any indication, he was a card carrying member of the French equivalent of the National Rifle Association.

While a casual observer might think dinner commentary about politics is passionate because of the volume or velocity, conversation of this type among strangers in France isn't really taken seriously. Dinner is not a forum to educate or convert; table talk is a way to pass the time between courses. Besides politics, the other topics bandied by strangers randomly gathered at the dinner table are the best markets to shop for fine food and memorable meals prepared or eaten in the past.

The content may have been weightier than cocktail chatter, but I knew to treat these encounters with a relaxed and cautious tone. Americans can be set up for verbal targeting and I just didn't have the interest or energy to explain the current political situation in the United States. So I didn't advance views that countered theirs, and inserted wry assertions that they sounded just like certain American radio commentators.

The next morning, as I set off through farm fields, I remembered the head of a five-point buck, antlers with three feet of horn growth spreading on each side. The trophy was mounted on wood and hung high up on the plaster wall in the main room at the farmhouse inn. Would I see deer and other wild animals on my route through the Pyrénées woods? So far, I'd seen wild horses and ponies, a pheasant and a distant fox, along with many sheep, goats and cows.

Something was following me, or maybe I was jumpy after the white-van man the night before. It was a farm dog from the Etchegoyhen place. The dog fulfilled for a while another fantasy I'd entertained – acquiring a dog for company on the road. But the young German shepherd played in puddles, shook its wet fur on my legs and trod on the map when I rested.

The lady of the house had encouraged me to use their phone to make a room reservation in Mauléon, an historic town that I estimated I would reach by nightfall. Just as I stepped out the front door, sprinkles of rain tickled my face. A tractor moved out of a nearby barn towards the fields and I waved at the driver, a son of the family or a hired hand. The dog followed me, lifting its muzzle and grinning in its doggie way, as if to say, "We're skipping out into a great day in the mist." I soon discovered that it was great fun for the young German shepherd to trot in the puddles, then wipe his muddy fur on me and my gear. Slogging along with a poncho slapping my bare legs and sliding down the sides of my face like a monk's cowl annoyed me. I stripped off the poncho, which is not a suitable garment for trekking, no matter what the camping guides tell you. A touch of mist covered the crags in the background. Soon the mornings and evenings would be cold, but not yet.

In the deserted misty fields, I lost track of the blazed route. I needed to assess which way to go towards Pagolle, the next village of any size, so I pulled out the compass and took a reading, ate an orange and muttered to the dog to get off my map so I could study the topographic inclines. Using the compass reading, I decided to follow a country lane that climbed the next hill instead of the path marked on the map which continued on bottom land parallel to a creek. Though the rain was light, walking along a waterway could pose problems; I'd encountered rain-swollen creeks on other hiking trips. It turned out that both routes led to Pagolle.

In one field, I spied a farmer waiting out the rain under a grove of trees. He said he'd seen me through the trees hiking down the mountain and thought the dog was mine. I told him the dog was from the Etchegoyhen family farm called "Karikaondoa" a few miles back, in Arhansus. The farmer, who wore the long blue canvas coat popular with workers throughout France, told me he'd be going indoors for lunch and would call the Etchegoyhen family to come pick up their dog. "It's too far away from home. That young pup won't know the way home," he said. Which direction did I plan to go next, since the driver had to meet me and the dog on a road? We decided that I'd proceed along the same country lane so he could tell the family where to catch up with me and fetch their dog.

Less than an hour later, a car pulled up behind me. It was the young guy who drove the tractor back at the farm. The dog didn't want to get in the car, so the young man picked it up by the scruff and hind flesh and shoved the pup in the back seat. I felt bad for the dog that might well get a hard whup on the hindquarters because of this excursion. The man of the family, whom I'd seen and heard at the dinner table the previous night, exuded a vibe that he'd turn mean if crossed. I petted the dog's head and whispered farewell to my first companion of the journey.

Slowly, the days and weeks passed one step at a time, footfall after footfall. My feet were toughening and I grew comfortable with the rhythm of walking daily. I rested when I felt tired, for about fifteen minutes after two or three hours of marching. Fueling my body was a challenge, and a daily menu evolved: coffee and croissants, jam and half a baguette for a breakfast heavy on carbohydrates, low in protein. Eggs and hash browns weren't on offer anyway. I'd stash protein and other rations in my pack for a late morning snack and lunch. When I could, I'd forage in local markets or *épicerie* (small grocery stores) for bread, cheese, sliced ham and wedges of quiche. I tried to carry a small larder – a can of sardines, olives, *sauccison* (dry sausage) and fruit because there are no markets out on the trail. Then it was time to fill the two water bottles and the storage tank inside the backpack, adjust my cap and step outside.

From 10 in the morning until 2 or 2:30 I walked, with a break to paint a picture or visit a church or cemetery. Occasionally, I'd take off my boots and bathe my feet in a stream. During these weeks of walking 20 to 30 kilometers a day, sometimes longer, my feet developed no blisters, primarily because of a system I learned from my Montana friend Les Ojala during back country treks in the Rocky Mountains. Wear two socks on each foot, a thin liner sock and a thicker sock for padding, a method that prevents friction on the skin.

Continuing on towards nightfall, I'd find lodging, bathe and then stroll around the towns, or, more likely if it was a rural gîte, talk to the manager about the evening meal. At the gîtes, conversation and shared stories with other travelers provided social interaction after a day of tramping alone. I'd finish up the day by writing in my travel journal.

Like many people, I travel in order to have experiences outside my routine life. I travel to meet and talk to strangers, see different landscapes and investigate other cultures. But the regular patterns we set as humans support us, I think, make daily life more fluid, provide a background stability that enables adventurous forays. Setting routines could suppress the possibility of noticing and experiencing surprise, which is always around us, waiting to be discovered. Yet I needed structure to help keep me motivated to continue a difficult physical undertaking. Without the daily routine, I might have taken a couple of days off, then more days, and soon I'd be reluctant to return to the rigors of the daily foot-slogging trek across France. Apart from the three-day rest at Urdos at the end of my first week on the road, I stuck with the plan and kept moving.

With the dog gone, I concentrated on the surrounding landscape. The green fields illuminated by the rain and mist stretched out ahead, the patchwork of shades of green stitched with bushes and trees, dotted with sheep. I stopped in Pagolle and meditated briefly in the chapel. Nothing fancy, the prayer consisted of acknowledging with gratitude the absence of real trouble in the journey so far.

In some of the hamlets I trudged through, churches have stone benches outdoors. Or the church might be left open, offering traditional respite for pilgrims. In the mountains, I'd rest under a tree or brace my back against a boulder. In rural villages, a small church or chapel offered a place to sit down. It was mid-afternoon when I passed through deserted Pagolle.

This area of the Pyrénées is called the Soule and the Béarn, the old names for long-established regions that suffered bloody religious persecution roughly 450 years ago. During the Wars of Religion which lasted decades, Catholic military troops attempted to stamp out French Protestantism (the Huguenots) throughout the country. In turn, the Protestant forces of Jeanne d'Albret, invaded Catholic Soule. The strife ended when Henri IV, Jeanne d'Albret's son born in Pau, the capital of the Béarn, issued the Edict of Nantes in 1598. Protestants gained religious-political equality in France, at least in certain cities, though this freedom was revoked by King Louis XIV in 1685. The new wave of religious persecution made emigration to North America a viable choice for many Huguenots, who also left France for colonial South Africa, England, Ireland, and the Netherlands.

A human on foot moves slowly, with time to notice small signs and architectural details. When I passed through a town in the region, I looked for the unadorned Protestant church, called *le temple*, not *l'église*. I couldn't help but muse: Is it significant that the French word for a Protestant church is masculine, while the word for a Catholic church is feminine?

Centuries ago, the region was also the locus of the long crusade against the breakaway Cathar sect. Catharism emerged from Albi, a city north of Toulouse, about the year 1140. Research places the Cathar philosophy evolving from Persian gnosticism or Manichaean philosophy. Just as the Middle Eastern gnostics were persecuted for centuries before them, the Cathars endured vicious persecution from an army under the aegis of the Roman Catholic Pope until the last Cathar refugees were burned alive March 16, 1244 near Montsegur in the Ariège, a province on my route.

It isn't a long stretch to note that the Cathars and the Protestants had similar complaints about the dissolute Catholic hierarchy. The Cathars broke away long before the Protestant Reformation of the early 1500s. Though both movements objected to the Roman Church as a distortion of the simple non-hierarchical precepts of Jesus of Nazareth, Protestants subscribed to monotheism - a single deity - while the Cathars construed a dualist presence of good and evil in one deity, considered heresy by Rome. Despite the differing interpretations of good and evil, some trace a continuum from Cathars to the Protestant movement.

The much older nature-centered pantheon may have more entrenched roots in the region; standing stones, megaliths, menhirs and dolmens are identified as artifacts of spiritual practices or burial rituals before recorded history. More recent records show numerous local folk who saw the vision of a woman surrounded by light near natural springs of healing water. That these apparitions at Lourdes, the Grottes de Bétharram, Saint-Pé-de-Bigorre and elsewhere were labeled with the names of Catholic religious figures doesn't diminish their origin in natural magic.

Pasture Gate in Basque Land

At the top of a ridge a few kilometers past Pagolle, an elderly man on his daily constitutional greeted me. His eyes had a light-hearted glow and he launched into personal anecdotes. He and his wife used to walk together every afternoon when she was alive, he told me. Now he trod the same routes to enjoy memories of her company. I told him about my cross-country trek and he expressed no surprise, gesturing with his cane to the small communities on the way to Mauléon. "You'll notice harvest season is upon us," he said. (Note to skeptical readers: I wrote down our conversation immediately, so this is not fanciful recall years after the event, nor made-up dialogue. Quoted speech in this book was written at the time spoken or shortly afterwards.) "First you'll walk through Musculdy as you descend. Then through Ordiarp where the church is," he told me, pointing with his cane. "Over there to the north across the way, that's Ainharp." I noticed the similarity of the names of these settlements, wondered if Ain and Ord signified direction or size, or whether local lore was embedded in their meaning. But instead of pursuing my own thoughts and asking him, I followed his lead and talked about how farms are abandoned when the elders die. "The young people aren't staying on the farms," he said. "They work in the cities." "*C'est la même chose chez moi à Maryland.*" (It's the same thing at my place in Maryland.) I answered with my habitually imperfect French that everybody graciously understood.

"But look, the cornfields are ready for harvest," I said, "so somebody must be farming the land." He agreed: yes, enough farmers for the present. Again, he pointed his cane towards the church steeples, the chateau towers and the towns, distant blips between vast stretches of open countryside for me, places filled with meaning for him. Perhaps he remembered other walks and conversations on the ridge, sighting a line with his cane the seasonal changes in the valley. For me, encounters like this gave my walk meaning, made the days more interesting; provided tangible increments to measure my journey.

Then conversation turned to sheep. Cheese making and sheep tending are primary occupations in these parts. I recited some of the villages I'd passed through in Basque country. This man explained that the sheep, which he called *brebis* ("breh-bee") are a sturdy lot. "Other sheep may produce more milk," he said, "but these *brebis* are accustomed to the climate and the rough pasturage of this mountain region." *Brebis* means ewes, rather than a particular breed, but local idiom may use the words interchangeably. Clearly, it was important to him that I understand I was in the Béarn, with its own distinct culture and history. The ewes' milk is made into L'Ossau-Iraty cheese, a specialty of the region, which I savored often in Basque country.

Moving onwards to the east, I pursued the route planned by Daniel Hargain, grandson of the Basque matriarch at the farm lodge in Urdos. Young Monsieur Hargain was fulfilling the traditional Basque family role, securing the family house through the generations, which depended on an heir or heiress who was "of the house" (*etxenko*), the child of a blood relation. Daniel was carrying on the efforts of his father who moved into the stone mansion when he married Agnes' daughter. Four generations lived on the farmstead and worked the land. Having married and remained on the family compound instead of heading to a city to find a better paying administrative or technical job, Daniel Hargain was living in harmony with the stalwart tradition of Basque family unity. He also led mountain hikes and consulted with local tourism officials.

I was still happy about that spate of good luck; I'd happened upon a farmstead with a certified mountain guide who hauled out a box of maps, highlighted a route and marked directional changes for me. I'd explained my difficulty reaching lodging before dusk and Daniel advised following less arduous terrain on the Piedmont path of the Chemin-de-Saint-Jacques, through Mauléon, Oloron-Sainte-Marie and Arudy, and to Lourdes of the famous holy water along the Gave de Pau, a tributary of the Adour River. From there I could head south to Cauterets in the Hautes-Pyrénées.

The rolling hills were planted with corn, winter silage for the sheep and cows, horses and pigs. Harvest brought the men of the quarter together as they cut the corn and stowed it under vast plastic tarpaulins in preparation for winter. It wouldn't be good form to walk through or even along the edge of the corn fields. So, for the last six kilometers, I walked nervously along the busy two-lane departmental route, the D918, into Mauléon. It was country rush hour, between 5 and 6 in the evening, when folks motored home. Vehicles rushed past. Women carrying sacks of groceries and a cyclist with a wire basket stuffed with provisions, ambled along, their backs to traffic. We nodded *"Bon après-midi"* (Good afternoon) as we passed.

Several cyclists labored past me on the road to Mauléon. They were German or burly British, men over 40 and breathing hard, pumping bikes burdened with panniers fore and aft. Their faces were red, their lips whitened from exertion. I hoped I wouldn't have to stop and administer CPR, which I'd learned the previous spring. Several holiday caravans with license plates from other countries rolled by as well. It may be the tail end of the vacation season, but as in the United States, European golden-age travelers schedule road tours after *la rentrée*, (the return) as the traffic-congested final week of August is called.

In the Mauléon tourist office, I asked for help in arranging a stay at the next gîte, south of Oloron-Sainte-Marie. The busy tourist region attracted visitors competing for few beds. Though I could handle these arrangements myself, when there were tourism office employees available I relied on their outstanding assistance. In the highlands, there were no tourist offices, and in some zones, no gîtes.

Mauléon is famous for producing espadrilles, canvas shoes that tie around the ankles. Nearby, Ney is known for the fabrication of classic berets. The small Mauléon museum presented an exhibition about the history of espadrille manufacturing. Photos showed women at sewing machines posed to smile for the camera. Their faces displayed hope and pride, curiosity and indifference, depending on the woman. One man in the men's group photo stuck his tongue out, very pointed and rolled tight.

The espadrille factories brought wealth and fame to a few of Mauléon's families. Then another type of shoe became popular in the 20th century, the Pataugas, a combination boot and moccasin. Photos detailed a foot race with participants wearing the Pataugas 'Iowa' brand mocs. The men scowling in a photo taken during a product promotional tour were clad in short shorts, white sleeveless undershirts and the moccasins, staring at the camera, being stared at by villagers. Pataugas sells select fashion boots these days.

I didn't walk to Ney, the hometown of the beret, because it was off my route. The beret is standard headgear in many military units around the world, but it remains a symbol of French culture. Leaving Mauléon with paper sacks of market fruit stashed on top of clothes in my backpack, I struggled under strong afternoon sunshine through the Mauléon suburbs to a little village named Uhalt, a name that reminded me of Jane Ahalt, a girl in my high school class. I wondered if she was Basque. My thoughts were pedestrian.

It's my habit to browse cemeteries because reading headstones sparks my curiosity. Earlier on the walk, outside of St.-Jean-Pied-de-Port, at a picturesque stone chapel and cemetery in the hamlet of Saint-Jean-le-Vieux on the pilgrimage route, a town decimated by Richard the Lionheart, I found a gravestone for one Evan Salles. When I mentioned it to my friend Serge Salles, he wasn't impressed; said the name was common in this part of France, like Smith or Jones in the U.S. – not his relatives. Here in Uhalt, I noticed the name Jean Salles carved in the granite monument to the dead soldiers of World War II, 1939-45, and Lieutenant Salles on the monument commemorating the first World War, 1914-18. So I guess my pal Serge was right – the name Salles was tied to the region, evidenced also by several towns with that name.

The war monument figures in these small villages are similar – the same battered man, not a kid, more like a 40 year old, beaten by the times. I suppose the smaller communities used the same mould to cast the statues. I found markers on mountain tops where pilots had died, monuments on the edges of fields where Resistance supporters were shot, and in the center of towns, the formal steles listing names of war dead. I had family history on my mind too.

My father's uncle, R. Tait McKenzie, sculpted the Scottish-American War Memorial in Edinburgh and other war memorials. The sculpture in Scotland, titled "The Call, A tribute from men and women of Scottish blood and sympathies in the United States of America to Scotland" was built on the upper promenade of West Princes Street Gardens and honors soldiers sacrificed in World War I. Tait McKenzie's English-Scottish model soldier is young and fresh faced, not as weary as the man depicted in France's war memorials. My great uncle's models were students at the University of Pennsylvania as well as injured Great War veterans in England and Scotland, whom he treated with a pioneering program of physical rehabilitation through exercise.

My maternal grandparents had also been active during the post World War I period, raising funds in North America for war bonds, as well as lecturing and writing about the inexcusable lie of all war and the seductive advertisements glorifying war through news photographs, patriotic assemblies, medals, and even the heart-felt memorial statues such as these. My grandmother's male cousins, two men left in a dwindling family line with a preponderance of spinsters, had died in WWI and my grandfather, who met my grandmother as she nursed the wounded and searched for her missing cousins, escaped the trenches with fragments from a dum-dum bullet in his lungs. Those were bullets that exploded inside the human target. World War I started nearly a century ago, but I considered it very close and took the losses personally.

The memorials held meaning in the small towns and villages of France. World War I had a huge impact on agriculture in France. In 1913, nearly five and half million men were active in agriculture – peasant farmers, hired hands, harvesters – a range of 500,000 to 700,000 were killed or disappeared during the war. And far more significant for the long term care issues were the 360,000 to 500,000 men who were wounded and returned to farming. Villages were especially affected because rural settlements had supplied the infantry regiments that had suffered the greatest losses.

When I stopped in the shade of a tree, a woman in the country house opposite came out and glared at me. I called out *"allô"* to be friendly, but she turned her back and closed the door firmly. Was she concerned that I'd sit down on the grass or ask for money? To some people, a backpack symbolizes irresponsibility, poverty and careless flight. Who knows what she thought of a strange woman with feathers in her straw hat and carrying a backpack!

A stark block of stone in a wooded area east of Mauléon south of Hoquy marked the death of an officer in the Resistance. "Assassinated by Germans, 14 August 1944." The words were carved in French, but the meaning was clear to anyone. Earlier, at the side of a country lane, I'd picked up a wedding decoration, the frilly net pom-pom that Mediterranean grooms tie onto car aerials for the horn-honking drive from church to reception. As an offering for the murdered fighter, I tucked the wedding souvenir next to the dead man's name carved on the block of stone, where several pots of blooming Impatiens malingered in the heat.

The camaraderie at the gîtes and hiker's lodges gave me a sense that I wasn't entirely alone out on the trail. In contrast to the woman who stared at me and slammed the door, folks at the gîtes understood the lure of long distance treks. At rural gîtes the guests gather around the table for a hearty dinner served by the manager or owner. Hikers and cyclists need to eat well to fuel the journey. Conversation focused on weather conditions or distances covered, and then segued into travelers' tales, and I'd join the jolly talk. Occasionally, people touring by car would be staying at a gîte and they'd share stories about landmarks and lookout points easy for them to reach but too far away for a foot traveler.

Hotels in the Pyrénées region – and elsewhere in France – offer dinner and breakfast at a reduced price for guests. When I lodged in a town, I usually ate dinner where I was staying the night, which also permitted me to pad around in socks instead of boots. There were evenings when my overworked feet caused limping pain. A few restaurant guests stared at my shoeless feet – I had no other footwear with me. Pilgrimage walkers were fairly rare east of St.-Jean-Pied-de-Port, so word would get around that there was a pilgrim in residence.

If I found myself in a mountain hamlet for the night, I'd seek a modest hotel, a place where truck drivers or families on holiday stayed. Besides observing neighborly interactions during dinner, I sometimes engaged in conversation with other guests. I actually enjoyed eating alone, reflecting on the day's experiences and writing. The local fare featured vegetable soups, roast chicken or pork with sauce, lamb chops, heaps of potatoes and carrots or beans, followed by salad and homestead cheese. Wine from the region was always my first choice. The walk burned more calories than I ate, so I ordered desert too.

My notebook was a fine dinner companion during the wait for dishes from the kitchen. Curious people asked what I was writing or drawing; most ignored me. Evening entertainment options were limited to reading Natalie Angier's physiology study, *Woman: An Intimate Geography*, the only book I'd brought along, writing in my journal, or touching up sketches made during the day. In the rare instances when I stayed in commercial lodgings with televisions, I greedily surfed the channels for news.

During one breakfast, I chatted with a British cyclist who was wheeling through the back country of the Pyrénées. He posed a question I had thought about: how do the French handle vacationing Germans. The Second World War is remembered as a 'black period' because many of those who served in the French army were captured by the Germans and spent years in prisoner of war camps. Civilians also remember the Nazi occupation, the slave labor camps, the kidnappings, interrogations and murders. I commented on the memorials and place markers for the executions of members of the French Resistance.

During the journey I had the opportunity to engage in several conversations with people I met about this question of France during the occupation. It is not a subject for hasty direct inquiry. I talked with several men and women in the region who had been youths during the occupation. A few were active in the Resistance. One man's brother had been executed by German military police. Another was forced with other villagers to watch a neighbor shot dead in the town square. The answers I received were subdued, not actively bitter, as if to say, why pick a painful scab raw again. Though tempered by time, the suffering of that era has not gone away. No tribe or nation that endures occupation by another nation's military force forgets quickly or easily.

During that week, I broke self-imposed rules and accepted a five minute ride. Because the lift shaved five kilometers and saved my feet more than an hour's effort that day, I had time to paint a couple of small watercolors of the Pic du Midi d'Ossau. The ride was offered by an Englishman who was repairing an old mansion. I'd met him when I stopped to snap a picture of the renovation project, and he walked around a fence. I called out in French, asking about the chateau, and he replied that he'd rather speak English, being English. Soon I was quizzing him about the property and the renovation. Peter said the chateau was small, bought as a "ruin" with land, for 45,000 British pounds ($60,000 at that time). When I explained what I was doing on the road, he said anyone hoofing across France deserved a drink and offered me a bottle of beer. He pulled out photos of house renovations he'd done with his brother and mother. They'd learned on the job, replacing the roof on a crumbling stone relic elsewhere in France. Though that project caused no end of trouble, he said, the interior walls were repaired and now his family lived there. When he heard that friends bought this ruined mansion, Peter's experiences with the first renovation project landed him a job. "When you think of it," he said, "all the features that make a building fabulous, stone walls for example, have to be covered up to fill in the structural cracks."

Draining the bottle, I admired the photos of the renovation work, said goodbye and continued on my way on the country lane. About an hour later, he drove past, tooted the horn, and offered me a lift. I dithered for a few seconds, and then accepted the ride to the inn where I had a reservation, thanking the spirits of the road for this end of day reprieve for my feet. I suggested he come in and I'd buy a round, but he shook his head, said he had to be getting home. He repeated, "You're so brave to be walking alone." What did he mean by that? I didn't think walking alone in France required bravery or was dangerous.

I liked the women at the inn at Geüs d'Oloron. The oldest one welcomed me with a pat on the back. The young one swathed in a big apron sang while she worked and the teenager in training showed off fashion trendy inclinations with hennaed hair and a retro-print polyester mini-dress worn over slim jeans. The place was an uninspired two-story barrack providing shelter to truckers, traveling salesmen and tourists. I slept in a forgettable single room and ate downstairs in the smoke filled restaurant while a soccer game blared on the television. Centuries ago the nearby village of l'Hôpital-Saint-Blaise was an important gathering place for traders and pilgrims before trekking over the Pyrénées, but I don't think today's commercial travelers at this way station have much interest in the Romanesque structure. The twelfth century chapel is crowned by a Byzantine style cupola made of sandstone quarried in the Pyrénées.

This part of France doesn't merit the big infrastructure projects that glorify Paris, Lyon and Bordeaux. In Mauléon, where I'd been the day before, some of the sidewalks were unfinished, the roads were pocked with potholes and cement around bridge supports was crumbling. Just like in the United States, the infrastructure needed repair.

On the way to Oloron-Sainte-Marie, I passed through a mature forest. The route was wider there and a group of cyclists plowed past me, all day cyclists with calves of steel, retirees perhaps, former sportsmen. They were tipping the odds in a different direction than the plump fellows who pass their days in cafes chewing the fat with their buddies. The cyclists were moving too fast for me to hail them for a conversation, and in any event, what was there to say, except we were all over fifty and using our strength before life got the best of our bodies.

Long ago, Oloron-Sainte-Marie was two towns and it was further divided into segments attached to three great cathedrals – Sainte-Croix, Sainte-Marie and Notre-Dame. Now the settlements are joined, but each retains its own hilltop cathedral and traditions. Pilgrims headed to Santiago de Compostela made their way south from northern Europe and passed through Oloron, leaving donations at the church, buying supplies in the town. With the economic boon of the pilgrim trail during the 12th century, the Cathedral of Sainte-Marie at Oloron could afford to pay stone cutters who carved three dimensional musicians, animals, grotesques such as gnomes and mythological figures, saints and sinners into the arch over the main doorway. The portico frame is ornamented with carved stone figures – people cutting bread or collecting apples or performing various trades of the time. Other figures retrace the life of Saint Grat, patron of the city. The cathedral is unusual in that it survived the Protestant wars during the 1500s and continued to receive and serve a congregation.

In the Cathedral of Sainte-Marie, I happened on a tour and joined it. Our small group – all French speaking – was invited into the sacristy to view vestments stored flat in an enormous armoire with shelves that rotated out into the room. Bishops, emperors and cardinals, perhaps even a Pope for all I know, had worn these silk religious vestments embroidered in silver and gold thread. The embroidery depicted scenes from the Old Testament. One brocade vestment, given by Catherine de Medici to Henri IV for his marriage, was given by the king in turn to his friend, Arnaud de Maytie, on the day of his consecration as bishop of this cathedral. This was a fabulous treasure for me, a seamstress, to see.

The two towns were reunited in 1858 by a decree of Napoléon III. In the sister town on the east side of the river, I strode uphill to the quarter of Sainte-Croix, the oldest in Oloron. Place Saint Pierre, the heart of this section, suggests Spanish influence. In the old days, vendors from Jaca, directly south across the border in Spain, would arrive in the old quarter of Oloron, sell goods in the plaza and then in the evening sing and dance in the plaza or play *jotas tapageuses* (cover the jacks) in dark alleys. Perhaps some of that musical tradition survives in the tradition of choral singing that animates Oloron, and the region where there are music festivals during summer months.

Scrutinizing the buildings around the square, I discovered one was a Protestant temple with plain construction. The cross over the door, peaked bell tower and other emblems I'd come to recognize signaled its former use, later verified in a guidebook. Oddly, this church is now a car repair shop, its silent bell tower testimony to the changes. Sainte-Croix cathedral was closed, so I sat in a nearby garden and watched lovers walk arm in arm under the plane trees.

With no time to spare, I hopped to my feet and reached the tourist office just before it closed. Martine, who'd been alerted by phone by the tourist office staff in Mauléon the day before, set me up at the local gîte in Soeix, (pronounced "swex") several kilometers to the south. The gîte turned out to be a former school converted to dormitories with a commercial kitchen on the ground floor. Martine had given me a key to the empty gîte. I guess she trusted me not to lose it. Visitors were coming for the weekend and she was vague about whether I could stay a second night. "It's a group of kids," she said, "there might not be enough room for you."

Throughout France, and especially in the mountainous regions, communities sponsor low-cost lodging for hikers, cyclists and other travelers. The lodgings, or gîtes, as they're called, are converted schools, civic halls or other public buildings no longer in use. Classmates, scouts and organized hiking clubs sometimes reserve all the beds in these facilities, so independent travelers with no reservations might find themselves without shelter. As with hostels, sometimes you can rent laundered sheets and blankets, but sometimes bedding isn't provided. As I prowled through the rooms in the old school house, and selected a bunk with a futon mattress near a window on an upper floor, I found no blankets. I needed a sleeping bag; I'd mailed mine home.

Across the lane from the gîte, neighbors gathered on a terrace. With a smile, I explained the problem – I didn't have a sleeping bag. The family – the Pierrons (the name means, 'of rock', they told me) – loaned me a sleeping bag and also asked me over for drinks. After the drinks and cocktail chat went well, Madame Pierron extended an invitation for dinner.

Despite their apparent domestic comfort, they told me stories of hardship and unemployment, subsisting on social insurance. When I heard about the experiences of Eddie, Fabrice, Dominique and others – all the guys at table – I could see how easy it was to fall into perennial unemployment. They received a monthly stipend for being out of work. The older talkative guy didn't work, though he drove a Mercedes in fine condition and said he was a forester. In these parts, being a forester could mean a government sinecure that doesn't involve showing up anywhere specifically for work until trees need to be cut or fires put out. The situation resembles the under-employed in the United States and Canada who eke out a living with several low-wage part-time jobs providing no pension or health insurance. At least an unemployed or under-employed person in France has medical coverage, shelter and a small monthly check. The question arises: does access to a dependable stipend during unemployment, as the socially advanced countries of Europe offer, foster a disincentive to search for work? I also knew that jobs for minimally skilled young adults in France were nearly impossible to find except in urban centers.

Into the night, we talked and drank. I ducked outside periodically to escape the cigarette smoke. The young men in their twenties lived on the dole and on handouts from their mother, Annie Pierron, who told me she drove down from Paris occasionally with bags of groceries. She dished up a tasty meal, and afterwards, they wanted me to try traditional Basque sheep cheese, Brebis Pyrénées, served with cherry jam for dessert. We discussed the complimentary nature of salty and sweet flavors. I had to agree: the Brebris cheese with cherry preserves offered a satisfying and provocative taste.

Cherry Preserve and Brebis Pyrénées Cheese

This is my own recipe for cherry preserve which I've developed over the years using the sour cherries harvested from a dependable tree on my family's little homestead. Peak production usually occurs in mid-June.

- 2 pounds firm ripe dark sweet cherries, or use sour cherries and add more sugar
- 1/2 cup water
- 3 to 4 cups sugar, depending on preference
- 1/4 cup strained fresh lemon juice
- zest of one lemon
- 6 drops almond extract

Stem and pit the cherries. Save the juice. Cut large cherries in half. Cook cherries and water over low heat. Stir occasionally until the cherries have shriveled, about 30 minutes. Strain the cherry juice and set the fruit aside. Cook the cherry juice in the same pan with sugar and lemon juice, bringing to a boil over medium to high heat until the sugar dissolves. Boil hard for 3 minutes. Add the cherries and stir. Remove from heat. Cover with a cloth and set aside overnight or up to 24 hours. Return the fruit to the stove over a medium high heat. Bring to a boil and stir gently until the syrup is 220 degrees F. on a candy thermometer, about 3 to 4 minutes. Do not overcook. Remove from heat and add the almond extract and lemon zest. Skim off any foam and stir gently. Spoon the preserves into hot, sterilized small canning jars leaving 1/2 inch at the top. Seal jars with new two-piece canning lids. Place the sealed jars in a large pot of boiling water and process for about 15 minutes. Remove the jars from the water. Cool, label and store. Alternatively, spoon the preserves into hot, sterilized jars and after cooling, store in the refrigerator for immediate use. Serve with Appellation d'origine contrôlée (A.O.C.) Ossau-Iraty Brebis Pyrénées Brebis cheese.

During our long night of conversation about the state of the economy, I remembered the group of loiterers I'd spotted in Oloron-Sainte-Marie. Clusters of tattered and scruffy adults and their dogs had taken over a few benches in a corner of the city gardens. I approached them deliberately, rather than avoid them, because I wanted to act in the role of the stranger coming upon the estranged. I had decided to ask them for directions to the post office so I could send papers home. They were notable for etiolated bodies, ragged clothes, and listless demeanor – dog and human alike. Could this be a flashback to Haight-Asbury in 1969? No, different drugs now. The dog's breath blew hot on my hand as I asked directions to a post office. They radiated a cloud of defeat and shrugged towards a building behind a row of trees. An enterprising member of their tribe held the door to the post office open, paper cup in hand waiting for tips. I could see how elderly folks might be afraid of them, taking over the park benches and letting the dogs lie drooling on the pavements, blocking the way. To me they seemed harmless people bored with their lot in life, trying to make a living by hanging out for hand-outs. Maybe they too received a stipend from the government. Maybe they were junkies who used to be enterprising citizens.

I lay awake for a while, happy after the party atmosphere with the neighbors. Crickets chirped long into the night and I hoped I could stay another night. The next morning, I was looking somewhat disheveled myself. The day before, near Moumour, my hair combs fell in an irrigation canal. I had paused to eat in the shade and the combs dislodged when I adjusted my cap. When I tried to retrieve the combs from the water, my hand broke through a spider web. Soon the web strands stuck to my clothes, pack and hair. Alone in the schoolhouse gîte, I washed the organic muck out of my hair and brushed my pack. I twisted my hair into a ponytail now that the combs were gone.

It was time for me to call home and let family know how the walk was going. I found a pay phone after back-tracking a couple of miles on the road to Oloron and slipped in one of the pre-paid phone cards sold in newsstands. It was good to describe my experiences and hear familiar voices. The ever-vigilant Martine from the tourist office spotted me on the way to the small grocery store. She told me there definitely was no room for me at the gîte that night. The students, scouts and adult leaders were arriving for a weekend environmental education event and all beds were taken. But, she smiled, "Let me help you find lodging since you have to leave." She jabbed numbers on her mobile phone, calling Hotel des Vallées in Lurbe-Saint-Christau, a thermal spa town in the shadow of Pic Mail Arrouy. "Madame la pèlerine will be arriving." she told the innkeeper. I'd become a pilgrim by default because I was on the route.

Along the way, old farms overgrown with weeds and left to decay caught my attention. Pausing to study the vine covered barns and boarded up houses, I imagined buying one of these ruins and inviting all my friends who knew building trades to a massive work party, like a Shaker barn raising. The fantasy fuse blew out when the numbers on sales agents' signs indicated prices well beyond my reach. It's common knowledge that fixing up French farms can cause a frustrating money hemorrhage. Peter Mayle's books about refurbishing old houses in Provence explained that wealth was a requirement to successfully undertake such projects. Farms were bought by moneyed ex-pats eager to live in rural France, I'd been told by Peter the fence builder and roof mender a few days before. I'd seen evidence of other renovation projects en route – old mansions, chateaus and farm enclosures being re-bricked, roofed and occupied.

In my dreams there are scenes and images of confusion, but I can't recall specifics. In waking hours, if asked where I've walked, I'm hard pressed to remember the names of the villages. I have to refer to my journal or the map to see where I've been. Perhaps I should move more slowly. Take time to detour and see the sights along the way. But on foot, a detour to visit a pre-historic dolmen or 19th century religious shrine can consume a day. What is my hurry? Is it an element of my nature perhaps, to press on, to run in high gear that moves my inner self? For all my desire to move at the moderate pace of a Zen monk at meditation, I'm a speed queen at three to four kilometers an hour.But I still have an inclination to report the nuances of daily life. I want to collect local cookery recipes, attend village festivals and learn a few words of Basque or the patois of the Béarn. What is it like for a girl to grow up here? How do the women run their houses and businesses? This walk brings me to earth, keeps my feet on the ground, eye-level with local life.

The girl who hungrily grabbed the peanuts that I brought to share with the Pierron family looked lonely in the crowd of adults drinking and smoking through the evening. I thought I should give her something, like a hair clip or scarf or one of the postcards from my hometown that I carried in case there was somebody in the world who didn't know what the White House or the U.S. Capitol looked like? But the youngster was gone the next morning and by then it was too late and what did I have for a child, anyway? I remembered the teenager at the inn near Geüs d'Oloron who lived and worked under the older woman's thumb, her mother or boss. These girls grow up in the family business, with motherhood and commerce their role models. For women, educational and professional choice – the freedom to follow one's own direction through life – remains a viable option only available to few.

The spirits of the heroes of the Resistance shadowed my thoughts. So many cold stones marking murder on the edge of town, like the one east of Mauléon on the death site of men killed by the Nazi security police. I paused at another memorial with a similar somber message, outlined with elaborate rows of perennial flowering plants near Soeix on the road to Lurbe-St.-Christau. I started writing notes for a novel about the Resistance, using the memories of the Nazi occupation that Agnes Hargain at Urdos told me, stories from my own relatives who'd lived through the period and information culled from museums and markers along the route.

The walk from Sioux to Lurbe-St.-Christau was just six miles parallel to the Gave d'Aspe, a peaceful mountain stream. I was moving in low gear after the late night of drinking and talking with the Pierron family. In the fields, a tractor or two rumbled along. South of Eysus, a farm woman looked up from tending her garden and waved. She invited me in for coffee and cookies, a treat of unexpected hospitality. Alice's bright blue eyes twinkled with a youthful air, though her careworn face spoke of decades in the sun. With her upswept white hair and blue eyes, she reminded me of Dorothy Brown, my friend Rosemary's mother, so her aura seemed familiar. While she heated the coffee, Alice asked me about my journey and how my feet were faring. I was touched by her spontaneous care and I was starting to feel like *la pèlerine* that Martine had named me.

Since she tended gardens, I asked Alice about plants that I'd noticed in fields and ditches along rural lanes. They appeared to be Elderberry, but I learned from her, confirming what I'd heard from Fabrice Pierron, that there are two types, the genuine *sureau* (Elderberry) and false *sureau*. The real *sureau* (Elderberry, genus Sambucus) is taller and bushy, producing the flat-topped clusters of small red-purple berries that fruit in late August, roughly the same growing season as the Mid-Atlantic region of the U.S. False *sureau* ripens in late September. It has a short stalk about three or four feet tall and is not bushy, with one or two fruit clusters per plant. The false *sureau* is poisonous, I was told, or at least tastes bad. Just before starting this journey, I'd gathered elderberries for jelly. Syrup made of this fruit is used as an elixir to strengthen the immune system, but the raw berry doesn't have a pleasing taste. When my siblings and I were children we crushed the berries and pretended we were sipping wine, or painted the smallest sister's skin purple. Elderberry is a totemic plant for me.

As I prepared to leave, Alice and I stood outside and watched farm hands in the distance as they cut the corn and chopped it into a green mélange. She said silage today wasn't as good as what they fed animals in times past. Alice hugged and kissed me on the cheeks like a kind grandmother before sending me on my way. This encounter made me feel blessed by the road.

The manager at the inn at Lurbe-St.-Christau led me to a room in the back, saying, "Madame la pèlerine will be happy as a princess there." Was I really becoming the pilgrim lady? Next week, she told me, there will be a grand wedding with 200 guests. Lots of dinners to cook and she's pleased to have the clients. Tonight there will be a traditional wedding dinner, but a small one. "You won't hear anything," she promised, waving her hand toward the dining room.

As usual, I scrubbed my clothing as I showered, but no amount of washing freshened the artificial fiber tee shirts that wick sweat. I scrubbed them and hung them from the shower fixtures to dry overnight. Cotton doesn't retain odors after washing, but once you start sweating, you're wearing a wet shirt all day, not a healthy scenario in early autumn in the mountains. Normal sweaty odor doesn't bother me because I know the surface bacteria will be washed off. But this particular evening, though my clothing was freshly washed, something stunk. I sniffed the insides of my boots, thinking that was the problem. But no, the inner liners were damp, but there wasn't a particular odor. The rank odor was like dirty socks, or the inside of a wet gym bag. My armpits? No, I'd just showered. I laughed at myself, worrying about smelling bad. Is it a peculiarly North American habit to be so concerned about body odor? Eventually I tracked the smell to the thick foam cushion on the pack that rode against my sweaty back. I scrubbed the pack with a tiny disc of pink hand soap, and let it dry in the open window all night.

I fell asleep to chants and choral response by the wedding dinner guests, a Basque tradition, followed by a deejay's mix of disco and polka. Sleep was fitful for this princess of the pilgrimage. I awoke many times in the night to the thump of the drum kit pounding out a polka or the Gloria Gaynor anthem, *I Will Survive*. Although I'd earlier been downstairs to have a look at the festivities and was waved to come in, I didn't join. I was too weary.

Stone walls covered with moss marked the entrance to Lurbe-St.-Christau thermal baths about a half-mile past the hotel. Rusted signs pointed visitors to empty pools closed for years. A gatehouse with gingerbread cut-out trim hinted of genteel city dwellers who came south in search of a cure. The abandoned spa, with its windows boarded, paint chipped and broken glass on the pavement nearby, was part of the string of Pyrénées cure towns that once attracted visitors from all over Europe in search of relief from joint pain, depression or boredom. Now people sought spa facilities in luxury hotels and the quaint mountain thermal baths of the past were closed.

Trees thick with moss shadowed the path in the Bois du Bager (Badger Forest). The hunters were out. When I stopped to paint a landscape at the entrance to the forest, a guy in camouflage hunting clothes was standing by a small truck, listening to a two-way radio. Later, I noted a similar Citröen *camionette* (small truck) with hunters in the front seat following baying dogs running through the woods on a fire road. It was impossible to determine if the men were tracking the dogs for sport, or actually out shooting. It was Sunday, so it likely was a real hunt, yet I saw no game pulled, heard no shots. Perhaps I had happened upon a test day, with guys and dogs loudly mucking about for fun.

Soon enough, I entered the portion of the Bager forest where hunting was prohibited. Hikers and hunters share the public lands in France uneasily, I'd heard, though the hunters were always cordial to me. The mountain bike (vélo tout terrain or VTT) trail suffered erosion and muddy patches. Rutted and turned up clumps of wet grass indicated where boars had snuffled under the soil, leaving telltale spike holes from their tusks and their cloven hoof marks. Though it was a VTT trail marked for mountain bikes, there were no knobby tire tracks in the dirt.

Bois du Bager is a lovely forest to walk through and I was all alone now. The hunters were behind me. I aimed my feet away from the purple autumn crocus on the pathway. This was a favorite flower of Margaret Hand, my dear friend who'd passed away a few years before. Margaret had a special grasp of remaining positive in the face of adversity, and cultivated an attitude of enjoying life no matter what happened. She would have been pleased about this trek, my "outward bounding" as she dubbed all outdoors activity after going on several official Outward Bound adventures herself.

I surveyed the trees deep in the forest. Why were ladders leaning on several tall trees? What was the purpose of the ropes hanging down from the branches, weighted with lead counterweights? Might be for trimming branches, or maybe the ladder rigs ascend to perches for hunters, but I didn't see platforms above the ladders. Maybe the weights on the branches encourage trees to grow straight. A few trees bore numbers inside painted borders. Was that "99" painted on the trees indicating a year? Was there a registry of trees? I was curious about forestry management techniques in France because my brother is an arborist.

Forested land in France derives from the royal preserves that reverted to the people after the Revolution of 1789. During the period of nationalization from 1790 to 1815, there were vast transfers of forested land from clergy and noble families to communities. When the Bourbon monarchy returned to France from exile in England in 1815, some land was returned to the previous owners. During the 19th century, towns and communities claimed portions of the forest domains for fuel and lumber harvesting. By the 20th century, portions of forests were owned by commercial entities. Corporate financial interests view forests as an asset on deposit for the future, a crop to be harvested. Despite the proliferation of commercial owners growing trees for harvest, many forests in France are publicly owned and set aside for recreation, hunting, mountain biking and hiking.

Hunting is one of the traditional uses of forests in France. Conflicts arise between polarized sectors advocating different uses for forests and the community of two million active hunters. Mixed use of forests has been reviewed in some areas of France, but in the southwest, away from the regulatory eye, there are more hunters than cyclists, more hunting dogs than hikers.

Deep in the Bois du Bager, I found a "No Hunting" sign hidden under some brush. It was brand new. Did a hunter rip it off a tree, or was the sign tossed in the bushes by those who were supposed to install the signs? I debated with temptation, decided another sign would turn up if I was meant to have one. Sure enough, later that day, another *"chasse interdit"* sign slightly bent, was lying by the side of the path. I decided to take that sign and give it to my brother the tree man. I also found an unused sheet of sand paper, which was useful for refining the lead points on my art pencils.

Small farmers live by the old ways, planting, tending, harvesting and nourishing the soil for the next round. Sheep dominate Basque lands, but this was slightly north and traces of sheep pasturage are few and far between. Through history, the norm in the Béarn was that every community had its permanent arable land and hillsides covered with bracken and grass where peasants cleared space for extra fields. This practice of sharing land cemented community relationships.

Cows grazed in the distance; I heard their tinkling bells (*clarines*) which are also placed around the necks of ponies, sheep and goats. Far more prevalent during harvest season in this part of the Pyrénées Piedmont are sounds of tractors cutting the corn, grinding so loud that it seemed a train passed.

Discovery filled my thoughts. Each moment, step by step, breath by breath, I was looking around and absorbing scenes and impressions. The slower pace allowed me to see the landscape unfolding. My dream last night was of a blind child leading me around and into various troubles, under dark skies, up dirt hills, and always searching for lodging. The search for a night's bed is a part of each day, but am I the blind child? Or does the blindness symbolize not knowing or seeing the real meaning in this walk?

I'm planning to stay the night in Arudy on the Gave d'Ossau (pronounced "gahv d'osso"). Victor Hugo wrote during his journey through these parts that " 'Gave' is the local name for a brawling river, the word being derived from the same Celtic root as the English word Avon." The terrain was steeper and a few miles to the south was one of the giants of the range, the Pic du Midi d'Ossau. Arudy offers a venerable old inn, Hotel de France, on the town square. Music from 45 or 50 years ago played faintly in the dining room. I'm struck by the fragility and durability of the women who look after these hotels, usually a senior woman with two or three younger ones helping or in training. The manager assigned me to room 27, my birth date, and outside the door hung an engraving of an owl, my emblem animal from two years prior when I'd found a dead baby owl during a cycling trip, took the carcass home and taught myself taxidermy to preserve it.

From Arudy, I hiked beside the Gave d'Ossau south to Louvie-Juzon, which was shut up tight at midday. Down by the train tracks, industrial warehouses simmered in the heat with slabs of marble and polished stone stacked waiting for shipment. I asked quarry workmen taking a lunch break in the shade of their bulldozers about directions to a path up the mountain looming ahead. They shrugged, as people here do, indicting you're on your own, they don't know the answer. Marble is a big part of the regional economy and I hiked past several quarries on the route that I intended to be a shortcut.

Some shortcut. I read the map incorrectly and ended up lost in a forest on the wrong side of the mountain. I climbed straight up the steep backside of the 1,645 meter Montaigne du Rey (King's Mountain) and struggled through underbrush that scratched my face and caught my pack. I was bushed and dripping sweat, but eventually came to an open pasture where a herd of horses grazed. I continued to wander around looking for a path down the eastern face of the mountain and sunk into a muddy stretch which sucked my boots to the eyelets. The 'thwock' sound of boots gummed in mud echoed each footfall and mud spattered up my bare legs. Just then, a man carrying a sack of feed across his shoulders emerged from the forest. Bottles of water roped together balanced on the feed sacks. Aha, he must be headed for the horses. With him was another guy and a dog. They both wore knee-high rubber boots. Horse man said he'd give me a ride down in his 4-runner, which was parked on a fire road farther down the mountain. Dog man chatted with me, said the switchbacks down the mountain led to where I had started at Louvie-Juzon. I told horse man that I'd take a ride down the mountain to save my knees after hacking the day away slogging in a steep circle through mountain brush.

He told me to carry on ahead while he fed the horses and that I should wait by the vehicle about five minutes away. Dog man was headed in the opposite direction. Horse man returned, fired up the Toyota 4-Runner and told me the short version of his life story. A retired truck driver who keeps 55 horses in various pastures around the area, he'd just been traveling in Wyoming and California looking at horses, perhaps to buy them. I thanked him for the lift to the base of the mountain and slid gracefully away from his invitation to dinner because I felt fairly certain that dinner would end with another kind of invitation. Women can foresee these dramas without needing to let them unfold. The indicators are subtle and unspoken, easily read by those with a bit of life experience. I had no interest in finding out that I might be wrong, that he was just an amiable, lonely soul eager to chat about the western United States and practice Franglish. I thanked him again, dodged the requisite cheek kisses and walked onwards. Montaigne du Rey was finally behind me.

Would the most unusual place I slept be in a parked camping caravan on the outskirts of Bruges-Capbis-Mifaget? The campground-gîte was locked when I arrived. I saw nobody inside but rattled the closed door. Alarmed, I covered the kilometer to the village in record time and found a snug food shop just about to close for the evening. I asked the proprietor to call Camping le Landistou for me. After confirming that the campground was indeed open, the shop owner sold me food. I strolled back slowly while chatting with a farmer and his wife out in the warm twilight.

Thin and nervous, the campground proprietor fished a key from a wall rack, rented me a clean set of sheets and towels and said that she'd prefer payment immediately, not in the morning. She escorted me to the bathhouse, waving a feeble flashlight and demonstrated how to turn the hot water on and off. Then she showed me how to turn the hot water off again. Probably the establishment's profit margin was slim. While I signed the guest register and collected my change, the woman told me that often pilgrims on foot arrive with nothing – no food, sleeping bag or money – and ask to stay without paying, sleeping on the floor or on the porch, or they beg for food. I forgot that in my sweat-soaked clothes and dusty boots with mud caking my legs, I looked first cousin to a vagrant. It didn't matter that I had cash and Visa cards in my wallet; I appeared to be a credit risk.

The cozy trailer was permanently parked in the campground, one of several campers gathering layers of leaves on their roofs. The bed was short and lumpy, but the evening was calm and the silence divine. To pass the time, I pushed two folding chairs together so I could put my legs up and unfolded the International Herald Tribune newspaper which I'd been carrying for days. I slugged back cheap wine and boldly inked in the crossword puzzle. Bugs slammed into the light bulb suspended over my head in the screened mini-porch attached to the camping trailer. Ducks gaggled noisily past in the river, and I was quite pleased for the long rest.

That night I experienced an odd dream of going to a restaurant on Connecticut Avenue near the bike trail crossing just north of Chevy Chase, the same trail I'd walked on the day last March when I formed the idea to hike across France. In reality, the restaurant is Italian, but in the dream it was vegetarian and you reached it by sliding down many vines, Tarzan style. At this dream restaurant, surfer hippie guys and gals lounged around, all silent, mildly accusatory in their glances. I had something I wanted to complain about, but couldn't find anyone in charge. In the dream, one man looking at me wore a 1975 vintage Indian v-neck embroidered cotton shirt in blue. Were these phantoms in my dream the spirit emblems of deadbeat pilgrims who once hung out in this camping park? I had a strong, eerie feeling throughout the evening, and wondered about the nervous proprietor who vanished into the trees.

By the bright morning, all the rustling spirits were gone. I set off at a jubilant pace through farms, past orchards and wheat fields. This was the best kind of experience for me – rested, fed, feet in condition – on a sunny day. I took photos of a sweet donkey and a colt in one field. In Asson, I was stunned to find a dead adult owl in my path. Its white breast feathers and gold and brown back markings were clean and fresh with no blood or damage to the feathers. Its claws curled backwards so I deduced the bird may have flown into a live electric wire and been electrocuted. I picked the owl up, carried it wrapped in my map to a churchyard and placed it in the crook of a tree. For a moment, I was tempted to add the owl to my taxidermy collection, or maybe cut off and save the wings, but that would have been disrespectful.

Rain drove me to quit early the next day, when I sheltered at Hotel des Touristes in Lestelle-Bétharram. I chose the hotel from a rather grim selection of down-at-the heels lodgings. At least the building had touches of its former status with Art Nouveau curlicue iron work on the façade, wrought iron balconies and high ceilings with antique lighting fixtures. I tucked into the slice of a room that might have been a servant's closet a century before when the place opened for business.

A Thomas Cook guidebook from 1905 describes Bétharram on the "left bank of the river above Lestelle, a pilgrim resort dating from the time of the Crusades, and a prosperous village of 1,500 inhabitants with paper mills and lime kilns. Bétharram has a seminary and a 17th century church, highly decorated; a Mount Calvary, with chapels, in one of which the shrine, containing an image of the Virgin, is visited by pilgrims from every part of Béarn and the Basque country. About two miles distant is a fine grotto, with stalactites; fee for guide, 2 francs." Not much has changed since the guidebook was published, except that the pilgrims head to Lourdes and there's a little train for tourists that creeps through the big caves, which now cost far more than 2 francs to enter.

Legend has it that many of the chapels and churches in the region once contained statues or images of the black madonna, thought to be an ancient symbol of pagan fertility couched as a Catholic icon. Although I didn't go there, I read that south of Oloron-Sainte-Marie, in a church at Sarrance Basse-Pyrénées, rests a much repaired black stone madonna put in the care of the Premonstratensian religious order in 1345, and now in the care of the Bétharram Fathers.

Lestelle-Bétharram was already a pilgrim site when Bernadette Soubirous experienced her visions of a barefoot fairy-girl in the grotto near Lourdes in 1858. Bernadette even visited Bétharram's shrine, according to Shyne Denys Lawlor's 1870 book *Pilgrimages in the Pyrénées and Landes*. For 700 to 800 years prior to the start of the Lourdes spectacle, pilgrims had been traveling to Bétharram to partake of healing waters and seek the blessing of a tender and diminutive female presence that evolved over the centuries from a Pyrénées nature spirit into a Roman Catholic icon, the Virgin Madonna. Bernadette's vision also changed from her original description of a small fairy spirit dressed in white whom she called *aquéro* (a local word meaning an indefinable being, neither human, nor divine), to a maternal figure that resembled the well-established images and statues in Catholic churches.

The Bétharram sanctuary had been destroyed by order of Jeanne d'Albret, the queen of Navarre from 1555 to 1572, who made austere Calvinist Protestantism the official religion during her regency. The reign of reformist extremism was ended by her son Henri IV. The actual destruction of Bétharram sanctuary was carried out under Count Montgomery, one of the chief Protestant men of war during that time. Yet Bétharram and other areas maintained the traditions of Roman Catholicism even during the Protestant period. And indeed, the Old Religion born in nature has not faded away. The Pyrénées traditions of honoring forest spirits, creating flower shrines at megaliths or caves, and frolicking in communal ecstatic celebrations timed to lunar cycles – as well as the planting and harvesting – continue. These ancient folk rituals endure unimpeded by the machinations of religions driven by power and politics in the written historical era.

Lourdes' rise to fame and tourist popularity hinged on the visions reported by a poorly nourished and tubercular teenager. Bernadette's apparitions at the Massabielle grotto in 1858 brought international attention and great prosperity to Lourdes. At the time, other towns in the area already served northern Europeans and French visitors in search of healing waters and recreation in the Pyrénées. Gout, rheumatism and diseases such as eczema and syphilis drew the lame, sick and frail to Cauterets, Eaux-Bonnes, Eaux-Chaudes, St. Sauver and Bagnères-de-Bigorre. It is understandable that Lourdes wanted its share of the burgeoning 19th century tourist trade.

Who is to say what Bernadette saw or thought she saw as she wept in stupefaction at the grotto? Who can comment on the intentions of the pilgrims who took hope into their lives after visits to the shrine? Perhaps the sense of purpose and community encouraged the sick to carry on with their lives. Surely the water and mountain air were beneficial, though the crowded baths and shared fountains sparked a 1906 rumor campaign by the journalist Jean de Bonnefon and others that Lourdes could be a breeding ground for cholera.

Bernadette grew up hard, was malnourished and sick before the visions and shunted off to a faraway convent in Nevers as soon as the authorities decided to promote the vision as a visit from the Virgin Mary, a useful tool to unify and reanimate attention to Catholicism in an increasingly secular society. Surely the officials were aware of the economic benefits to the region that followed a vision. Bernadette died in 1879 at age 35.

E. M. Cioran, the great Romanian-French philosopher, writes in *Tears and Saints*, "The Church was wrong to canonize so few women saints. Its misogyny and stinginess made me want to be more generous. Any woman who sheds tears for love in loneliness is a saint. The Church has never understood that saintly women are made of God's tears." The pain and sacrifice felt by holy women has long been expressed through ecstatic prayer. Excluded from the Eucharistic rite before Jesus was cold in the tomb, is it any wonder that women over the centuries found communion and meaning in visions?

Lourdes enjoyed rapid ascent of prosperity with the help of the enthusiastic journalist Henri Lasserre who produced *Notre-Dame de Lourdes*, in 1868, transforming Bernadette's shadowy vision of a tiny figure her own age into a mature woman. Ruth

Harris describes Lasserre's work as "the most romantic of stories" in her 1999 book *Lourdes, Body and Spirit in the Secular Age.* The bishop overseeing the diocese steadfastly steered the religious political machine. Lourdes prospered and Lestelle-Bétharram fell on hard times.

There were no other travelers in Lestelle-Bétharram's Hotel des Touristes, no line of waiting visitors for the little train that runs through the grotto. The Bétharram shrine where the vision of the gentle lady occurred long before the water spirit appeared to Bernadette was locked on a weekday morning, as was the gate to the nearby monastery.

There is no shortage of grottoes in this part of France and quite a few reportedly were visited by fairies or beautiful ghostly women. Older than the Alps, these ancient granite mountains formed between 100 million and 150 million years ago. Caverns and deep tunnels are common. One of the best known chamber tombs, at least to archaeologists, lies between the Adour River and the Gave de Pau, north of Lourdes, east of Pau. For an area of about ten miles north to south, three miles east to west, bordered by the towns of Pontacq, Ossun, and Ger the terrain lies over cave barrows, which are graves from prehistoric times. A military reserve occupies much of the area, alas. In some of the barrow graves, seated skeletons were found leaning against the cavern walls. A notable dolmen at Poùey-Mayou is north of the community of Bartrès. Artifacts recovered from these sites are retained at the Musée d'Archéologie Nationale at Saint-Germain-en-Laye near Paris.

During the long morning walk from Bétharram to Lourdes, with stops at Bétharram's basilica, bridge and grottoes, all modest attractions by contemporary tourism standards and lacking tourists, I was touched by the simplicity of these sites compared to the showy development of Lourdes. In the Bois de Subercarrere, I speculated about the lay of the land before Lourdes became an international tourism and pilgrimage site. Light played with tree shadows on the path. A few sports enthusiasts jogged or led their dogs through the suburban woods.

Once inside the city limits of Lourdes, now an administrative center for the region, I tromped rapidly along the Gave de Pau to where the river bends south. I moved onto paved footpaths used by those who've come to Lourdes for a cure or to be pushed in wheelchairs or in the peculiar black hooded perambulators endemic to Lourdes, which resemble adult-sized baby carriages. I dodged through skeins of pedestrians weaving slowly along, eyeing the displays of souvenirs, holy water bottles, statues and other cloying religious paraphernalia. I didn't see a bottle opener with the vision printed on it, but that doesn't mean it wasn't for sale. Hoping to find an element of simplicity, I strolled through the area dedicated to prayers, where crowds lined up as if for passport control, past the fountains where the faithful filled their own bottles, past the old basilica and up the hill towards the train station where I boarded a bus bound for Cauterets. In this famous pilgrimage zone, I didn't feel any holiness.

CHAPTER 4

Women and Mountains

Cauterets

Anne Lister, a self-assured 19th century English woman with relentless energy and a fat inheritance, made mountaineering history here. In 1838, she was the first non-local person to climb Vignemale in the high Pyrénées. Lister lived on the income from family farms in England and could afford to hire guides to organize expeditions. Guides that had scaled these mountains often; and probably their daughters, mothers, wives and sisters had done the same.

After a walking tour in Switzerland in 1827, Lister decided to try mountain climbing. By 1830, she had climbed a few peaks in the Pyrénées and in 1838, returned to the region for more mountaineering. She hoped to tackle a mountain not yet conquered by an amateur climber. Shepherds and hunters hiked these mountains, and once the foreigners with heavy purses arrived looking for climbing adventures, the shepherds were scouting new routes up the daunting peaks. A guide Anne had hired during previous journeys in the Pyrénées, told her about a new route up the 3298 meters of Vignemale, the crown behind Cauterets.

The new ascent route was discovered by local mountain guides Henri Cazaux and Bernard Guillembet who had climbed Vignemale the year before via the Glacier d'Ossoue. They fell in a crevasse, but made their way across the glacier in a free-form descent to Aragona across the frontier in Spain. This circuitous southern route was used by Anne Lister to make the first ascent by a visiting amateur climber.

Though it was August, Lister prepared for cold weather, which is always wise in high altitudes. Like me, she wore layers of clothing. Unlike me, her garments were cloaks, shawls and petticoats, with a complex arrangement of tapes and loops adjusted to tie up her skirts. The guides brought along crampons for crossing ice. According to her diary, Lister left Cauterets with the guides before dawn on August 7, 1838, and pausing only for brief rest stops, the group reached the summit of Vignemale by 1 p.m. They wrote their names on paper enclosed in a bottle left at the summit. That should have been proof of the accomplishment.

But the next day, Lister's lead guide escorted to the summit Joseph Napoléon Ney, known as Prince de la Moskowa, an honorary title inherited from his father Marshal Michel Ney, a barrel maker who was honored by Napoléon Boneparte for exceptional military leadership during the Russian campaign, and was executed by the Bourbons after Napoléon's ultimate defeat. The guide told Joseph Ney he was the first amateur to reach the top. When Anne discovered the guide's deception, she refused to pay him until the matter was rectified. The guide admitted that he'd lied and signed a certificate asserting Anne had conquered Vignemale first. The proof was the bottle with the signatures and statements by the other guides. Recognition for the first ascent of Vignemale was a point of honor for Anne Lister, but her achievement faded from public notice. More than a century later, when women mountaineers were looking for role models, Anne's diaries were published, revealing the details of her intriguing and adventurous life.

At Lourdes, my feet took a rest on the bus to Cauterets. Without a direct pedestrian path and unsafe pedestrian conditions along the narrow snaking road, the bus was a prudent choice. Another option was a circuitous detour of two or three days walking, but I'd promised friends in Paris a visit on the weekend. From my perch in the tall bus, the twisting two-lane road bored south between walls of slab rock, almost like a tunnel. At times this perspective and the momentum of the bus summoned an illusion that the bus would hit the exposed rock, as the driver spun the steering wheel and the bus lurched from side to side through the curves. I snuck covert glances at a bull-necked guy covered in tattoos with a shaved head that called to mind late night Comedy Central television entertainers or a hackneyed idea of a French Foreign Legionnaire. Soon the driver halted at Argeles-Gazost, where passengers left the bus to head east for the ski station of Luz-St.-Sauveur, or St. Luz, as some call it, with its illuminated runs, high-tech ski lifts, snowboarding from paragliders, and all night après-ski entertainment. It was too early in the season for skiing, but St. Luz draws visitors year round.

In the past, Argeles station served as a tourist railway hub. Visitors from the north stepped onto the platform, collected their bags and bargained with coach or taxi drivers for the overland passage to the high Pyrénées. Now, the train station was boarded up; visitors arrive by bus or drive themselves. From my vantage inside the bus, I saw broken windows and a schedule pasted on the door of the former train station. The area was grim and deserted. A taxi waited for an silver haired couple slowly descending the bus steps. Perhaps the abandoned Argeles train station was doomed by the same changes in transportation that curtailed train travel in the United States. Rising gasoline prices would change that.

Yet Cauterets is still a vacation town. Sleek couples shopped, ate and strolled between spa treatments. The Hôtel des Pyrénées dominated the highest point in town and drew tourists to its casinos. At the Pas d'Ours gîte, (which could be translated either as 'steps of the bears' or 'not bears') the décor replicated a Scandinavian lodge with fireplace, wooden furniture painted with folk designs, and brightly colored cushions. Tureens of nourishing hot soup appeared each night and the other guests were cordial Scandinavians. At dinner, the owner's son, a lad of eight or nine years, asked me questions in French about the United States. "Why do Americans need to own guns," he asked as he worked on lessons for current events class in school. "They're afraid," I ventured, "and a little stupid because they think guns solve problems." I met his parents' eyes and saw that they trusted me to say something useful. "I'm glad I'm walking in France," I said, "because I don't have to worry about that here." I steered the conversation to other topics – mountain caves, bats (*chauve-souris* which means "bald mouse"), and places I'd been on my long distance trek.

That night, I dreamed of my Brazilian friend Clicia. In the dream she introduced me to a man and the nature of the dream included conversation and social interaction. I didn't see her until two years later, when I attended her wedding to a man

I'd not met before, except in the dream, which we determined by comparing calendars took place around the time she became engaged. How interesting it is to speculate on the matter of dreams and know that time and space are meaningless in mental communication with close spirits and friends.

When I arrived in Cauterets on the bus, the post office stayed open for me. *"Frappe sur la fenêtre, on vous attendra."* (Knock on the window; we'll wait for you.) the clerk had instructed when I called from Lourdes to ask if there were letters for me at this mail drop address. It was dark when the bus dropped me off in Cauterets and I wondered if the postal clerks were still working. I knocked on the window and a clerk stuck out his arm, passing me the treasured letters from friends back home. They were curious about my arrangement to receive mail so late in the season, he told me, and wanted to meet a traveler in the 21st century who didn't rely exclusively on e-mail.

Internet connection was easy to find in cities, but in the mountain hamlets I was passing through on foot, there were no internet cafes. Resort towns like Lourdes or Cauterets offered online connections and I discovered public internet terminals at post offices in large towns. I didn't want to carry a cell phone, which couldn't access service in the mountains, so I'd asked friends and family to write me at various points. There were public phone booths, but as in North America, the advent of universal cell phone use has decreased their number.

I prowled around Cauterets, hiking the wooded hills, pausing to watch a helicopter ferry in enormous steel beams that were being installed on a mountain to restrain the cliff facade that had shifted and now threatened the road and paths below. That side of the Val de Jéret was temporarily closed to hikers. One day found me on a long hike along the Vallée de Lutour to Lac d'Estom and the refuge hut at the base of Vignemale, steps that Anne Lister may well have taken during her sojourns in Cauterets, although her news-making ascent originated on the southern aspect of the mountain. It was late September and I was dressed in hiking shorts, a fleece top and a breathable waterproof jacket. Squads of alpinist women armed with hiking poles marched upward around me. Moving slowly, I was enjoying myself and relieved to carry just a water bottle and food stashed in the deep pockets of my rain jacket, instead of the heavy pack.

Lac d'Estom was choppy from the blustering wind and rain. A scribbled sign was taped in the window of the refuge, indicating it was shut for the season. I stared up at the snow covered mass of Vignemale and hoped for another opportunity to hike here when the refuge was open. Then maybe I could attempt an early morning ascent of this well-known peak. Huddling under my jacket hood, I painted a quick watercolor of the brilliant turquoise water and the looming mountain. The husky hiking women advised against going farther up and urged me to turn around soon because of an advancing cold weather system and the unpredictable autumn weather. I was right behind them all the way down.

On the descent, I placed my feet carefully on the rain slick rocks. In the valley where the path levels off, people stop at La Fruitière, a restaurant on the banks of the Gave de Lutour, a tributary of the Gave de Cauterets, which is fed by glaciers and lakes in the Haute Pyrénées. Hikers were shedding outerwear and sipping steamy drinks. Grateful for the warmth, I took a bench near the fire burning in a radiant stone hearth. I downed two mugs of hot chocolate and then continued down the mountain to the gîte.

During subsequent research in the Library of Congress, I turned up this account by another traveler, T. Clifton Paris, who climbed the same route to the Refuge d'Estom in 1842. "The Lac d'Estom is, I think, one of the most solitary and savage scenes in the neighborhood of Cauterets: I paid it a visit yesterday, and found it a bright mirror of the darkest blue, and so transparent that every rock and gelid cavern at the bottom could be distinctly discerned. It is situated at the head of the forest-covered valley of Lutour, and its scenery is well worthy [of] the neighborhood of the Vignemale, which mountain can be reached from its shores, but only on foot, by the laborious pass of the Col d'Araille."

Clifton Paris continues: "At seven o'clock I was entering the Hôtel des Pyrénées, and was shortly engaged at one of the famous dinners of the celebrated Madame Cazaux. Madame Cazaux, who has been graphically and faithfully described as having a waist of a circumference greater than that of her shoulders, and which would have stretched the belt of Falstaff, is universally acknowledged the greatest culinary adept in the Pyrénées, and the dinners of the famed Hôtel des Pyrénées, which can be obtained after ten minutes notice at any time in the afternoon, have delayed many a wanderer on his journey."

After the weekend in the capitol with Rosemary, David and their daughter Acadia, I returned to the Southwest to resume the walk in Lourdes, the point where I'd stopped the cross-country walk. During the night on the train, I slept fitfully in the disposable synthetic fiber sheet sack provided by SNCF (*Société nationale des chemins de fer français*). I awoke several times while the train shunted back and forth at two stations where cars were detached and hooked on a locomotive headed to Irun in Spain. Other train cars continued to Lourdes and Tarbes, including the one I slept on. At Lourdes, I missed the five-minute stop allotted for passengers to get off. I had wakened briefly to the announcement, dozed off and then sat up in a panic just as the train was blowing out of the Lourdes station. This wasn't the first time I've overslept on a long distance train. I remember hasty exists in Malaysia, England, Germany and Austria, but this time I actually missed the connection. I complained to the conductor, but he said he'd announced the Lourdes stop twice. SNCF is so regulated and precise, that I'm sure he did. I muttered an explanation that I needed to be in Lourdes to continue my cross-country walk and I wasn't going to be resuming the walk at Lourdes if the train was headed to Tarbes. With no coffee in my system yet, these small annoyances felt like disasters. The conductor glanced at his watch and looked at me quizzically, "Madame, Tarbes is a few minutes away, just 20 kilometers. What is the problem?" How could I explain to the conductor that I was on my way across France on foot and back-tracking on foot to Lourdes was a big bite to add? There was nothing to be done about it: I was headed to Tarbes, a long way north of the town where I'd left the path.

Fingering a 10-franc piece, I stumbled down the corridor trying to time my steps to the rhythm of the swaying train. In the nook near the doors was a machine that dispensed hot espresso coffee in a tiny cup. The vending machine didn't work; the coin just clanked into the return slot. A group of us grumbled to each other at the end of the carriage. My mood was dark. I decided I was having a bad day and it wasn't even 7 a.m.

At Tarbes, I considered my options. The station was packed with travelers huddled next to their bags. Was there a strike I hadn't heard about? The automatic ticket machine burped out my American Express card and I didn't have the right coins to buy a ticket back to Lourdes from the automatic dispenser. Machines were frustrating my plans this morning. The line at the ticket window lengthened as I tried to decide what to do.

After a stop in a lavatory redolent of bleach and mint air freshener, I ordered coffee and breakfast in the station cafe bar. Hoisting my pack over one shoulder, I tried again to find a ticket dispenser that functioned. All three machines suddenly flashed the out of service message on the digital screen while I stood beside them fishing for coins in my money pouch. The line lengthened at the window, where a single clerk slowly punched out tickets on a computer keyboard. I overheard comments about a strike and employee slow-downs.

That's when I decided to forget about my obsession with picking up the trail at the place where I left off. Strikes, long lines, and no ticket dispensers pointed to fruitless time wasted in the train station. What did it matter in the scheme of my long journey whether I resumed the walk at Lourdes or Tarbes? I would walk a few additional miles by starting farther north.

This new plan meant I'd have to hunt for a map because I didn't have a detailed map for the area around Tarbes and I wasn't confident enough to just wing it and walk on the highways. This region was slightly north of the zone I'd anticipated following on the cross-country trajectory. With the mission to find a map in mind, I strolled around Tarbes for about an hour, and though many places sold maps, most were road maps. Eventually, I found a news and tobacco store with a rack of topographic maps in the corner. The cashier threw in a couple of free pens, a promotion offered by the newspaper of the region.

Though the region is rural and agricultural, the streets of Tarbes are lined with nightclubs, record dealers and musical instrument stores, recording studios and even a store selling equipment for disco light effects. Perhaps they supply equipment to the discos scattered in outlying towns in the region. During other sojourns in France, I'd visited a couple of those rural nightspots in converted barns or warehouses. Aha! I spotted a poster announcing the Tarbes Festival of Jazz, that explained the town's focus on music.

While walking through town, my mood balanced and I decided to explore the most significant landmark here, the Haras National de Tarbes, an equestrian center. At the southern end of town, where the office buildings gave way to big box stores and warehouses, long rows of plane trees (genus Platanus, with leaves like a maple tree's and bark that sheds in patches) defined the entry to the huge training center for dressage and equestrian performance training. Were the stables open or could I watch a class in dressage, I asked the admission ticket seller. "All the horses and trainers are preparing for a festival," explained the cordial receptionist. "Visitors don't have much to see this week." I asked if she knew any hiking paths in the region. She didn't. The group of young women chatting with each other in the gift shop didn't know of any footpaths either. They were about to leave for lunch, so I hastily bought postcards and secured permission to explore the grounds.

The Haras stretches for many hectares and includes stables, riding rings, and fields laid out with jumping courses. But there was not a horse to be seen. They really were away at a festival. Soon bored with the empty barns, I returned to the road heading south. I'd checked the map and found a turnoff for a country path that skirted farms on the southern edge of Tarbes.

But first, lunch. Halloween decorations covered the windows and counters in the bakery where I grabbed a ham sandwich made with a crusty baguette. A toddler-sized doll dressed as a witch and a plug-in witch's face with eyes that bulged and lit up proclaimed a holiday four weeks in the future. The shop counters were crowded with piles of orange paper tablecloths and napkins, ribbons, and candy corn that accompany the American fiesta. My pal Rosemary had told me that her Parisian friends were now organizing Halloween trick-or-treat parties for their children. In the past, the 31 October holiday wasn't yet a big deal in France, where *Toussaint* (All Saints Day) on November 1 is an official holiday. But American festivals were seen as trendy, especially this one aimed at children. When I commented on the decorations, the bakery proprietor told me that provincial Tarbes hadn't really twigged into the Halloween holiday yet, but the decorations stimulated traffic into the store. I suppose the rest of the country will catch up with Paris soon and houses in Tarbes and elsewhere will be draped in fake ghosts and jack-o-lanterns.

The day's walk followed paths between farms, narrow country lanes through small villages and along dirt tracks through fields of corn used as winter food for livestock. At one village, I chatted with a woman tending her roses and she suggested I ask the lady two farms farther along to open the church for me. In these times of vandalism, churches are locked, creating difficulty for pilgrims on the Chemin St. Jacques who traditionally expect to be sheltered in churches if there is no other lodging. Visitors interested in history and architecture have to rely on chance to find the keeper of the keys. The women with the power to open this church said I was the first pilgrimage walker she'd seen in quite a while.

After looking me up and down – the knee length shorts, black baseball cap and heavy mountain boots drew a second look – I guess she decided I wasn't going to clonk her on the head with my water bottle and steal the altar silver. She fetched an iron key the size of a man's shoe. The church door creaked open and I smelled a humid, earthy odor, like a cave or a long-sealed cellar. A wooden Baptismal font with a stone basin stood at the left of the main door. The tall cabinet was curved in the front and a door swung out to reveal the carved stone basin inside. The building was in slow motion decay, with paint peeling, the plaster ceiling warped and cracking, and mold colonies spreading along the walls. This wasn't the first neglected rural church I'd seen during the walk. There are more churches than congregations to maintain them.

The walls were painted in small red and blue figures of the Virgin Mary. Reluctant to embarrass or offend the key keeper, I refrained from photographing the frayed interior. She stated that few residents attended church now, and in any case, the priest visited infrequently on a circuit of rural parishes. Left unspoken was the fact that this part of France tended to be Protestant in centuries past. But I didn't hear or see anything during my walk that signified the energetic born-again evangelical Protestants were proselytizing in this area as they do in Mexico, Central America, China and India. Someone told me that one of the Protestant sects now sponsors American missionaries to recruit door-to-door in France.

Our conversation warmed and she invited me to come in for coffee at their farmhouse, where I'd left my pack. Her husband, lean and bright eyed, perhaps from the abundance of fresh air, asked about my route and they both wished me luck on the journey. "Bon courage," they called as I waved farewell and moved away from the farm compound.

Aircraft droned overhead. A small airport south of Tarbes attracted gliders and recreational fliers. Golden light in the late afternoon led me towards the Pyrénées in the distance. I couldn't resist the light and stopped to paint a field scene, stubs of corn leaning over where the harvester had rolled along. A little animal rustled close by while I painted. Was it a feral cat after mice or a hedgehog searching for broken corn cobs?

After the Harvest - Cornfield near Bagnères-de-Bigorre

My goal for this day was to continue from Tarbes to Bagnères-de-Bigorre. In the days ahead, I planned to head east towards Saint-Bertrand-de-Comminges in the mountains and from there continue on forest paths until the GR-78. Bagnères-de-Bigorre is another mountain town like Cauterets, made famous by Victorian travelers in search of diversion, healing waters and the fresh air cure. In the distance, gleaming in the sunlight, I saw the snow-capped Pic du Midi de Bigorre, one of the highest in the Pyrénées and the site of a world-famous observatory. With the absence of nighttime light from cities, you can almost always see stars in the Pyrénées region.

The farm woman filling her apron with potatoes from the field straightened and stared at me. A momentary wash of uncertainty clouded her face as I approached. So I smiled and waved in greeting and whipped off my sunglasses. I could see that my age shocked her. *"Mon Dieu,"* I could almost hear her say as I marched closer, "she isn't a 20-year-old student."

I paused and chatted about my route and she told me about the harvest and whistled to a cat that prowled the field. The lines in our faces were similar, showing women accustomed to the outdoors. She offered directions on how to continue along the tractor lanes I was following, and even walked beside me for a while, cradling the potatoes in her apron. She smiled broadly and said she wished she could do something like this. As I headed off on the dirt lane, she offered the French equivalent of "You go, girl." *"Bon courage,"* she said, raising a hand in salute.

It helped my morale when people were kind, filling a water bottle, inviting me in for coffee, offering directions, and calling ahead to help me find lodging. I can't recall anyone in France not understanding why I chose to embark on such a demanding trek. I was received as a person, not a representative of my country. Folks here knew that even in a democracy, a nation's government is not the same as the individuals of that country.

Women attached to the homestead have a certain predictable shy demeanor. Though the farm women I met were clearly strong and capable of heroic labors, I saw other women of a certain age who exuded an aura of lonely neglect. Their counterparts in the United States – myself included – embed themselves in self-improvement courses and volunteer activities after raising their families. Some of women in the villages I walked through – those who didn't have farms or country inns to run – looked as if they needed something to do. Once the children left, and in this region the next generation searches for work in cities, the women who worked at home were left with no occupation, no grandchildren to care for. There's not much in the way of continuing education courses. People attend school when they're young, enter a career and stick with it until they retire, strike, are fired or die. It seemed to me from my ground's eye view that women who'd made a career of homemaking needed more opportunities.

Sunlight on the pastures and cornfields promised mild weather, though I could see the mountains were snow capped in the distance. Blackberries were past their prime in the hedgerows I strode past, but I found a few purple berries. Horses ran up to the confines of electric fences, looking for food or a hand of friendship. I whinnied back at them since I had no sugar or carrots. Interacting with the animals was important to me. Between the fenced animal pastures, fields will be planted with clover after corn is harvested for livestock food. The dead stalks of corn are cleared away for winter silage, then clover is seeded to replenish the soil.

A man hobbled towards me along the farm lane. From a distance, his build resembled my father's and for a moment I remembered my Dad, as I do sometimes, believing that the spirit of a deceased loved one can briefly be reflected in a living stranger. This comforting reminder brings the essence of loved ones through the presence of random strangers. A certain gait, gesture, stance or expression will trigger that personal thought. It happens quite rarely, a few times in a decade. As the man came closer, I changed my mind, "This is a rummy with a sack of squashed aluminum cans." Not like my Dad at all.

I could smell the booze on him as he approached. He proffered the plastic sack. "I've been working hard today collecting," he said. I smiled, "Great job! You have a full sack there." That sounds patronizing, but he was like a child asking for approval. I didn't know what he had in the bag. He leaned over unsteadily and opened the bulging sack. Stuffed inside were enormous white *champignons de Paris*, not aluminum cans collected for coins at the recyclers. I smiled again, saying, "Beautiful mushrooms. What will you do with them?"

His bloodshot eyes were glazed over with cataracts or chronic tippling. Yet, I heard a lilt in his voice as he described his cooking method. He said he was a serious gourmet, a real cook. "I cook up mushrooms and freeze them so they are ready for making a sauce later. In oil, not butter. Then you put onion and tomatoes in when you make the fresh sauce," he said. He confided he doesn't like his sister-in-law's cooking because, "she makes up packaged stuff from the store." He preferred his wife's cooking, he said, but she's dead now.

He plucked mushrooms out of the sack to show me how to identify consumable mushrooms. These fungi were large versions of the white mushrooms sold in U.S. supermarkets. He pointed out characteristics to look for: pinky beige gills, no veils or other attachments from stem to gills, pure white top and smooth body and stem. The bottom of the stem is straight rather than bulged at the end. The mushroom top is firmly rolled at the edges, not flared. The Amanita varieties are the killer mushrooms, with veils under the crown and flared edges and a bulb at the end of the stem. I wished him well and we parted company. This recipe is my interpretation of the mushroom hunter's description of the sauce he liked to cook.

Mushroom Tomato Sauce

- 3 tablespoons extra-virgin olive oil
- 2 medium onions, diced
- 1 pound white button mushrooms, or a mixture of various mushrooms, sliced
- 1 pound fresh tomatoes, peeled and crushed, or a 28-ounce can of crushed tomatoes
- 1/3 cup dry red wine
- 1 teaspoon crushed sea salt
- 1/2 teaspoon ground black pepper
- 3 to 6 cloves garlic, minced
- 3/4 cup chopped fresh herbs (such as parsley and oregano)
- 1 cup thinly sliced basil leaves

Heat the oil in a large saucepan over medium heat. Add the onions, season and cook covered, until the onions are softened, about 8 minutes. If using fresh tomatoes, add at this point and cook with cover on, until the tomatoes are soft, about 5 to 8 minutes. Add the garlic and mushrooms and cook, covered, for 6 minutes more. Add the wine and cook, uncovered, for 3 minutes. Stir in the chopped herbs, taste and adjust seasoning if necessary with salt and pepper, and cook for 4 minutes. If using canned tomatoes, add at this point and heat through. Stir in the basil. Serve over pasta or with braised meat.

You know you're in the country when folks stop to chat. As mushroom man wobbled home, I continued to the outskirts of Bagnères-de-Bigorre and noticed a country mansion set back among trees with signs on the front lawn. Pyrénées Club, one sign proclaimed, and the other, posted prominently in front, *A Vendre* (For Sale). Where fields gave way to gas stations and sidewalks, a man stood aside and waved me ahead of him saying, *"traditionnellement en montagne les poids lourds ont la priorité"* (the big weight vehicle has priority in the mountains), referring to my protruding pack. A genial fellow, I thought, until he turned the conversation to the unlucky 12-year-old girl found murdered and probably raped after she disappeared in late September, from a town far away, an event so rare that people hundreds of miles away talked about it. "The news says there was no trace of violence against her," he said, and in the next breath warned me to be careful. The girl wanted to run away, so she didn't have to live with nasty relatives, he told me. I knew such an abduction-murder event was rare in France, and it does happen in the U.S. No one explains why mortal violence is so common in the United States. Is it the guns, the culture of violence and intimidation rather than reason? The latent misogyny? I didn't want to hear about violence and misfortune and increased my pace.

The last three to five kilometers of the day are always hard for me. And the two days of comfort in Paris had put a dent in my stride. Finally, I reached the main drag in Bagnères-de-Bigorre and searched for a quiet hotel. In a trice, I checked into Le Lutecia which faced a swell park. Under cypress and pine trees, the paths crisscrossed a tidy series of flower and shrub gardens. Benches promised excellent people-watching perches. In the remains of the day, I wandered around reading menus displayed outside of restaurants. I settled for the meal at the hotel because I could eat and drink my fill and not need to walk anywhere but upstairs to bed.

During the time when this part of Gaul was a provincial outpost under the rule of Imperial Rome, Bagnères-de-Bigorre was known as Vicus Aquensis. Archeologists have found ruins of a temple to Diana and coins and other fragments provide information of the centuries when Rome's governors and army occupied the region. In the more than two thousand years since then, the mineral waters of Bigorre have attracted visitors from Europe and beyond. Those famous marauders of history, the Vandals, trooped through some 400 years after the death of Jesus of Nazareth and destroyed the Roman baths at Bigorre as well as other Roman colonized settlements in the region. Then the Visigoths, Saracens and Normans plowed through the region wrecking havoc. As with all the old towns along the Pyrénées pilgrimage routes, Crusaders bound for Jerusalem assembled here and pilgrims headed west to Santiago rested here before crossing the mountain passes into Spain.

Flash forward to the relatively settled times of the 18th through 20th centuries and Bagnères-de-Bigorre emerges as an establishment dedicated to curing rheumatic and respiratory diseases. If I'd had an ailment needing attention, I could have checked myself in for a three-week cure, or just soaked in the mineral baths for days.

While the Romans took the waters at Bagnères-de-Bigorre, their provincial headquarters lay to the east at Lugdunum Convenarum – now called St.-Bertrand-de-Comminges – which I hoped to reach soon. Close study of the maps showed that paths through the Baronnies, a network of forests in the foothills of the Pyrénées, would offer the best route. Mountain lakes and rivers throughout the region were said to offer healing tonics to body and soul. The Baronnies offered a range of historic buildings marking centuries of settlement, from Roman era ruins to medieval monasteries, fortified chapels established by the Knights Templars – returning crusaders who'd founded a military religious order around 1118 – and other fortifications dating back to the days when the Bigorre region shifted alliances among the ruling powers and invaders.

In this area so close to Lourdes, there were other, older spiritual centers too. In the Haute-Pyrénées, there's the Cistercian Abbey at Escaladieu, founded in 1142, and the monastery and extensive caves of Médous, where legend has it that a shepherdess in the 18th century saw an apparition of a small female figure remarkably like Bernadette's vision a century later near Lourdes. Could these visions be the young viewers themselves reflected in water? Shapes made by mists rising from the thermal water?

During the heyday of the pilgrimages to Santiago de Compostela, the cathedral towns and abbeys in the foothills of the Pyrénées served as meeting points on the pilgrimage route. After gathering and resting at the cathedrals or abbeys, groups of pilgrims rode or walked farther west to St.-Jean-Pied-de-Port where the mountain passage was less arduous or headed due south entering Spain at the perilous crossing of the Pyrénées at Viella and continued to Huesca and then across Galicia to the Atlantic Ocean. Nowadays, Bagnères-de-Bigorre lacked the bustle and youthful energy of St.-Jean-Pied-de-Port, however. The mature people in the shops and cafes seemed like residents, not tourists.

In the morning, I found the marked route to climb the Pic du Midi with the Observatorie Midi-Pyrénées on top.

Observatory construction began in 1878 and continued for a century, broadening the range of scientific research to include botany, meteorology, and climate change. A sign at the trailhead advised that the observatory was temporarily closed to the public. This was disappointing news. Should I spend the day wandering around the mountain anyway, or should I press onwards towards St.-Bertrand-de-Comminges? After buying a small quiche for sustenance and eating it at the edge of the cheerful rippling Gave de l'Adour that cuts through Bigorre, I stepped eastward across a bridge, headed for La-Barthe-de-Neste.

Strains of a cello caught my ears and I stopped, trying to identify the source of the music. I turned and looked up and down the street, enjoying the resonant melody. In the next block, a man on a bicycle pulled up beside me, asking me if I needed help with directions. He said he'd noticed me walking back and forth, as if I were searching for a street. I explained I was listening to the music and Pierre Gasser introduced himself and announced he'd been playing the violoncello on the balcony. Would I like to come upstairs and hear more, maybe drink a coffee?

The mini-concert was quite agreeable and at one point, I sat down at the piano and played an improvisation, arpeggios and chords pulled from distant years of piano lessons. Soon Pierre brewed the espresso and explained he had to go teach a lesson. "Come by again after you finish your walk," he invited. I said I'd like to hear his trio play in concert sometime and we discussed my route. There was a gîte a dozen kilometers down the road, so I shouldn't have any worries.

It turned out that the gîte at Uzer was closed for repairs. French friends told me later that I should have knocked on the mayor's door, since a town that advertises a public gîte is supposed to provide alternative accommodation. But I didn't know my hiker's rights at the time and chatted with the workmen who were revamping the hostel-gîte. "It's late in the season," one said with a shrug, as if to explain why the lodging was closed. They waved me onwards, saying there was an inn at Bourg-de-Bigorre, a country village farther along, and that it was close enough to reach by nightfall. I felt no particular urgency, for the map was plainly marked. I could follow the narrow road or cut across some fields on a footpath to reach the village faster. I chose the shortcut.

First, the route meandered through several farms and two men on a tractor chatted amiably with me. "Where are you going?" I told them the name of the village. "No, the path doesn't go through," said the older one. "It's on the map," I insisted. "There must be a path." The other farmer, who rode behind, standing on the tractor frame, said, "Maybe there is an old path."

I pushed on, past herds of cows grazing in the late afternoon light. Far off in the distance I could see the Chateau of Mauvezin, also called the tower of Gaston Febus, the hero of Gascony and defender of Foix, a provincial capital in centuries past. I had painted the castle a decade earlier during a driving tour of the region. Immediately ahead, a narrow stream of fast moving water was bridged with small split logs nailed to longer planks.

Each year, the Tour de France swings through this region. In 2005, the Col de Peyresourde and Col du Portet d'Aspet figured in the contest. In 2000, the tour streamed through Bagnères-de-Bigorre on July 11 just about ten weeks prior to my visit. The 218.5 kilometer 11th stage of the year 2000 tour climbed the hill to Mauvezin, the stark square tower in view ahead.

Down a small valley, past a herd of cows chewing their cud in the twilight, I strode onwards, noting that it was now about 5:30 p.m. and I had about 45 minutes before darkness fell. The cart track faded in a grove of trees and I heard a stream before seeing it. Must be a continuation of the water I'd crossed earlier. Surely there will be another little bridge or a built up area where tractors ford the stream.

But there was no bridge and the fording area consisted of large rocks arranged as a breakwater, creating currents around and over the rocks. It was too wide to leap and the water was too deep for me to keep my boots dry. My choices were to remove my boots and wade or step across on the large submerged rocks. I stepped out onto a wet mossy rock and felt my foot slip, so I gingerly retreated to the creek bank and searched for a better place to cross. Should I backtrack, head to those farmers finishing up their work for the evening? A self-imposed drive to reach a town with lodging before nightfall overrode my hesitation. On the far side of the water I could see indentations on the ground through overgrown bushes, possibly a footpath. Light was fading fast. If I turned back and approached the farmers, I'd arrive just as they sat down to dinner. I didn't want to impose on anyone, and these farms weren't taking in lodgers.

Nothing to do but move on, so I stepped forward onto the nearest rock in the stream and slipped backwards into the fast moving water. As I fell, I instinctively flung my right arm behind me to break the fall and my wrist wedged against submerged rocks. My clothes were soaked and I couldn't move my right wrist. Twisting in the water, I reached backwards with my other hand and extracted my right arm. I couldn't move my right hand

and waves of pain hit. More mad than frightened, I tried to adjust my limp wrist, pushing the hand back against the joint, thinking the swollen wrist was just sprained. The icy water numbed the pain as I tried to realign my wrist, shoving my hand into the wrist. Denial of reality makes one stupid. The immediate purple swelling and pain convinced me this was no sprain. I stumbled and splashed across the stream. Rummaging through my wet backpack with one hand, I couldn't find the first aid kit. In the rapidly darkening twilight, I tugged out the first cloth I touched from my pack, a long Japanese wash-towel textured to exfoliate skin, a travel gift from my friend David. The towel stretched as I wrapped it over and around my wrist, like an Ace bandage. I was wet and shivering, a sign of shock, so I shrugged into my rain coat, ate an energy bar and steeled myself for the ordeal to come. I fished out the flashlight. By now it was dark.

With my right arm bound up and supported by a scarf looped around my neck, I limped along with a bloody knee and bruised derrière. I'd hit the rocks hard in the stream. Adrenalin pushed me ahead and I tramped through the overgrown path. It was slow going because I couldn't see beyond my feet even with the flashlight. Catastrophic thinking distracted me: I feared stepping in a hole or ditch and turning my ankle too. I talked to myself: "You can do it. This isn't the worst that could happen. There must be a doctor in the village. It's just a sprain; don't worry." It required effort to restrain negative thoughts and self-blaming. A litany of 'should haves' clamored for attention. It was clear that I'd been negligent in a variety of ways – overconfident, stubborn, inattentive to detail, and the biggest error of all – not listening to the local folks.

It was a long thirty minutes to walk out of the forest to Couyou, the village at the end of the misbegotten shortcut.

Of course, the farmers were right, there wasn't a path, just an overgrown unused forest track. I kept the stream on my right, remembering where the path line appeared on the map. I stopped several times to survey for the best way through the branches and underbrush.

At the cluster of houses where the forest track terminated, I knocked on doors, desperate to find help. When no one answered and I noticed no lights, it dawned on me that the village was a vacation and weekend spot. It was midweek in October, long after the traditional vacation season. I might not find anyone. I scrambled from house to house. No lights; window shutters locked. The town was boarded up. Panic was rising in my gullet. What should I do? I heard dogs barking at a distance, so I moved in that direction, with fear and shock settling in a clammy sweat. A light flashed at the house where the dogs barked and a farm woman came out on the porch. I hollered in French that I needed help, that I was hurt.

The woman pulled the dogs indoors and gestured for me to open the gate and come into the house. Inside the large kitchen, a man was laid up on a hospital bed near the fireplace. Mme. Adeline Mounic introduced herself and told me to sit and rest while she fetched a bowl of ice for my wrist. She explained that her sick husband wasn't able to climb stairs so family life revolved around the kitchen. "Where is your mobile phone?" she asked, pulling out her own to summon a daughter to drive me to the nearest hospital, about an hour away. She thought it very odd indeed for an American not to have a cell phone. I was distracted and irrational, said I should probably keep on going rather than wait, explaining that I shouldn't impose on her. Adeline – she insisted I call her by her given name – shook her head. "No, if I were you, I'd stay here and rest. You should eat."

I realized I'd better start listening to local advice. I needed help and I'd better find the humility to accept my situation. Adeline wrapped my wrist in a towel with ice, and fed me chicken broth, salad and bread. Then she made coffee. "You have a long night ahead of you," she said. I copied down her name with a shaky left hand, Adeline Mounic, planning to write a thank you note, which I sent months later with gifts for her daughter and granddaughter.

Soon her daughter Monique arrived. She was all business and hustled me into the car, drove carefully around the curves on the road to the hospital and waited until the diagnosis was complete and I was admitted. Wanting to be certain that a friend knew where I was and what had happened, I gave her the phone number of my friend in Toulouse and she said she'd call. Lucky for me, the French medical system is the best in the world, according to a survey by the World Health Organization, and my experience bears that out. I was admitted immediately with no discussion of payment or whether I had health insurance.

"I treat people with broken wrists all the time," said Dr. Khoury in English. He was the surgeon in charge of orthopedics and the emergency room staff had phoned him at home. He'd come to counsel *"l'Américaine"* about treatment. "Many cyclists flip over their handlebars like this," he grimaced, gesturing with his wrists cocked backwards at an acute angle. "And skiers break their wrists every winter. This is the Pyrénées, you know." I'd happened upon a regional hospital with an experienced orthopedic surgery team.

He was justified in his mild sarcasm because I'd put up a fuss, resisting the suggestion that I'd need a chest x-ray in preparation for anesthesia during surgery. I told the medical assistant that I didn't want a chest x-ray. Couldn't they just set the bone and be done with it? I was disoriented and frightened, and by now, flying high on painkillers and the powerful natural adrenalin that had been raging through my body for the past few hours. Dr. Khoury explained that he could set the bone without general anesthesia, but considering how much pain I had now….his voice trailed off… did I really understand how the pain would affect me later? He wrote his cell phone number and invited me to call if I was in difficulty during the night. "It's a very bad break," he said, "but we can fix it."

About the pain: it was more than I'd ever experienced. I was alone and worried about surgery. The wrist was propped up on pillows and nurses fed me medication all night, but the experience was sobering. I hadn't known the small hell of a broken bone.

The bone-setting operation was achieved with a laser-optical tool that projected the interior of my wrist on a computer screen. Before the surgery started, the doctor also showed me a device that drills pins into the radius and ulna, the wrist bones which I'd broken. The metal pins held the rather delicate bones together during the healing process, to be removed weeks later during a similar laser procedure under general anesthesia. I appreciated learning about the tools they'd be using; it gave me something to think about while the surgical team assembled.

I came to with my arm in a cast the circumference of my lower thigh. Lonely and frightened on the table rolling into surgery, castigating myself, I was even madder and unruly when I came to. A nurse told me I'd flailed around under anesthesia and the surgery team had to hold me down. I snarled at the recovery room nurse that he enjoyed hurting people and I didn't want to see his face. The attendants in the recovery room – wearing masks and cloth boots, surgical caps and baggy green operating room tunics – looked scary to me. There were other patients in the recovery room, but I was the vocal one. I screamed about my pain and begged for more potent drugs. I yelled at the nurses; couldn't control myself. When I calmed down later and apologized for my rude behavior, the recovery room nurse said he was used to mistreatment. He told me outbursts are common after anesthesia. *"Pas de problème"* (not a problem), he said, "the drugs affected you."

While we waited for a physician to approve another dose of morphine, the recovery room nurse showed me an x-ray of the repair work. Clever man to realize I needed a distraction. The radiography showed a star pattern of five nails in the radius bone, with each spoke two inches long. I had thought the 'nails' would be the size of finishing brads or staples, maybe map pins. Zounds, these were real nails in my wrist!

Back in my room, nurses Mr. Dabat, Mme. Snela and others tended to my needs. In the parallel bed in the room where I slept, an elderly woman moaned and twisted. Her leg was in traction and she was tied to the bed some of the time because she tried to pull out the catheter. One of the nurses confided that my roommate was *"coo-coo"* and circled her finger near her temple. My roommate was a resident of the adjacent mental hospital.

When I woke up, I asked the lady how she injured herself. My roommate said she'd broken her shoulder and leg chasing a turkey at the farm, but it's possible I misunderstood, or maybe that was her version of whatever accident befell her in the nearby asylum. I looked at my encased arm and looked over at her suffering in traction with two major breaks. Her pain must be unbearable.

Once I found out that the Lannemezan Hospital complex was primarily dedicated to care of the mentally ill, I understood the anguished screaming I'd heard at the other end of the hall. When the disturbed patients broke their bones in another wing of the institution, they were trundled over here for repair. That could be the reason why my room was separated from the others by several empty rooms. Perhaps the ward administrators wanted to keep "*la petite Américaine*" away from the really wacky bone repair cases. As the regional hospital, Lannemezan dealt with all kinds of health issues, from births to routine surgery to mental illness. The situation reminded me of a similar travel story. Back in the 1970s, when I'd been traveling with my family in Alberta, I'd asked my father to stop at a hospital so I could receive Tetanus and Yellow Fever inoculations, a series I'd already started in preparation for a future trip to Africa. We picked a hospital at random on the map, following the blue and white "H" signs from the highway. When we found it, at the end of a long road through cornfields, we discovered it was an institution for the mentally disturbed. The receptionist turned us away, saying I'd need to get inoculations in Calgary or some other big city. Here I was again, miles from nowhere, in the middle of a journey, seeking health care at a mental institution.

Dr. Khoury visited to mark my progress. "Hold your hand higher than your chest if you want to heal fast," counseled the doctor in English. "Higher!" The elevated position for my arm was intended to reduce the size of the hematoma resulting from the accident and the surgery. My effort to jam my wrist and hand together while I lay in the stream in a wrong-headed attempt to straighten my arm hadn't helped. My upper arm was swollen and purple to the armpit. I hadn't realized I'd hit my elbow on the rocks, but the bruises showed the tissue damage. The restraint I wore during the surgery must also have caused bruising.

The telephone beside the bed rang. I struggled to pick it up with my left hand. Monique Mounic, who'd driven me to the hospital, had phoned Jean-Louis, my friend in Toulouse, and he was calling to check on my recovery, promising to visit the following day after the morphine wore off. Family members called, as did other friends as they heard the news from Jean-Louis.

The pretty blonde ward assistant swept the floor and whispered something about the nails in my wrist bones. "The pins are called '*broche*,'" she said, "and that's also the word for a female witch in the Béarnaise region." "Then, my wrist is set with witches," I said. She nodded and grinned. She was right, the metal spikes hidden inside my body were doing witch-healing work.

In my diary from that week of my journey along the Pyrénées path, there is a page of shaky printing, an effort to write with my left hand as soon as I could sit up. "Learning to write. There's a blank canvas; I just can't use the brush very well. To develop the right side of the brain, work with the left hand. Painting will be a challenge too. But every new practice improves the totality."

After three days, I could leave, Dr. Khoury promised, if I continued to improve and no infection started. During the final visit he asked me about health care in the United States and I explained that I'd not be able to afford a three-day hospital stay for a broken wrist because the cost would be extreme. We talked about health insurance and the general welfare of the citizens and the differences between the 'tough luck, you're on your own' philosophy in the United States and 'we'll provide at least the minimum and probably more' theory in France. Dr. Khoury understood the economics and politics behind the differences, but he thought a rich nation like the U.S. should do better for its people.

Medical insurance covered the operations because the procedures occurred within the one month of coverage that continues after employment stops. Supplementary travel medical insurance came with my international teacher's registration card, similar to the international student card. Treatment in France cost about $2,000 including x-rays, surgery, anesthesia, and three days in a semi-private room, as well as a subsequent overnight hospital stay, anesthesia and surgery two months later to remove the nails. The entire process was respectful and civilized.

By day two I was on my feet, trolling the drip feeder behind me as I scuffed down the hall for exercise. I had one of the nurses take a picture of me with two of the other attendants. Dressed in the white open back gown, with my good hand I held the rolling drip feeder and in my wrecked hand I held a split of wine, which the kitchen routinely provided with meals. How sensible to realize that a modest dose of wine improves the disposition of an adult in captivity. One morning, I fed the madwoman in the other bed because the nurses were busy. She sang for me, a wistful song about waiting during the war – World War I. *"La guerre de 14-18,"* she said, when I asked. I don't think she was crazy at all, just neglected and hurt. Her family visited and for an hour she was quiet. Maybe she wasn't a patient in the mental ward at all; I probably misunderstood the nurse who told me the lady was *"coo-coo"*.

When time came for me to dress, Denis, the cute nurse with the small silver ring in one ear, helped me tuck into my sports bra and tee shirt. He just happened to be on duty that day and anyway, I didn't mind his help a bit. As he was trying to angle the front zipper of the sports bra upward, the bustling female nurse arrived and made loud jokes that American bras didn't close properly. It was all in good fun.

The accident brought this section of the walk to an end. Though I briefly contemplated returning to the trail after the first operation, Dr. Khoury shook his head. "How will you move your arm in and out of the pack straps with the cast? How will you cope with rocks and climbing?" he asked. "You have only one arm now." I recognized it would be foolish to trek with one functioning arm. The accident was teaching me to slow down and ask for help. The cross-France walk could wait until the following year. Cousin Pierrette picked me up at the hospital and I settled into two months of visiting friends around Europe until the second operation on my wrist. It was prudent to stay in Europe so the same medical team could remove the pins after the wrist bones bonded.

In Ordino, a picturesque mountain town in Andorra, the hidden country squeezed between France and Spain, I passed the time with relatives by painting detailed watercolors with my left hand. Whole days drifted past as I painted pine trees and snow capped mountains, interrupted by pills to counter infection and manage pain. For any two-hand procedure, teenaged cousins helped by tying my boots, zipping a jacket or pushing out medication from plastic packs.

Now I learned about the challenge of navigating through a fast paced society with an incapacitated limb. Opening a door, dialing a phone, writing messages, fishing for coins in a wallet or juggling packages required coordination and I was a one armed person now. Other people with splints and casts caught my eye. Occasionally, a concerned stranger came up and gently touched my cast. Don't worry, your arm will be better, a woman said. It happened to me, a man sympathized. The bones will heal; don't worry. You'll get your arm back. They quelled my worry that I'd be less adept at the two-handed creative pursuits I enjoy – cooking, kayaking, cycling, sewing, knitting, yoga, and gardening.

Hiking in Andorra after surgery
photo by Roberto L. Mera y Sierra

I also stayed with my friends in Paris and visited my life-long pen pal Andrew Stockwell and his family near London. I started writing Andrew when I was eight years old and we each still have all those letters, cards and clippings exchanged over a lifetime.

The French medical wizardry worked brilliantly. When I returned to Washington, an orthopedic specialist in hands examined the x-rays and healing progress. She said the repair was impeccable. Physical therapy lasted longer than I expected, but within six months, I was cycling and kayaking again. Adho Mukha Svanasana (downward facing dog) yoga pose made my wrist ache and I had to soften my air punches in kick-box classes, but as the months passed my right wrist mended, though slightly thicker than it was before.

During the winter and spring, to prepare for continuing the walk, I read narratives by Pyrénées walkers and Resistance fighters. In France, relatives took me to the memorial honoring the Free French Army at Castelnau-Magnoac. As I read about the refugees crossing the Pyrénées, images of their bleak, cold treks crowded my mind. What if I'd been part of a group of refugees fleeing to Spain or Portugal during WW II? Or a downed British flyer trying to escape the occupied zone and return to England to fly other missions? My own Godfather, a Polish pilot, was interned in Romania and escaped through France to fly missions from England with the RAF and USAAF. The fleeing refugees probably fell on the rocks at night and broke arms, ankles or wrists. An injured escapee might be left behind to fend alone, perhaps hide in a cave or a shepherd's hut. There was a story to tell about that era, so I wrote notes and considered the history of the Pyrénées as barrier and gateway.

Memorial to the Corps Franc Pommiès at Castelnau-Magnoac

CHAPTER 5
Back on the Path Again

Saint-Bertrand-de-Comminges

When I resumed the walk across France, St.-Bertrand-de-Comminges, a pilgrimage town tucked between the Garonne River and the Pyrénées, was the first destination. That was my intention, anyway. South of St.-Bertrand-de-Comminges, the map notes mountains, remote lakes and ski refuges all the way to the Spanish frontier and beyond. It seemed to me a realistic estimate that the walk from Lannemezan, where I'd stayed in the hospital, to St. Bertrand, as locals call it, would take a couple of days. On previous driving trips through the region, I'd visited the celebrated cathedral built for the 11th century Bishop of Comminges – the healer Saint Bertrand. I planned to take my time walking the forested terrain and warm up gradually to a daily walking rhythm. Little did I know that the first day back on the path would destroy my feet.

But first, here's a pocket history of Comminges which dates to the era when Roman soldiers and settlers ruled the region. Lugdunum Convenarum was the name of the Roman era settlement. In 72 B.C.E. the Roman General Pompey chose the spot to defend the colonies Rome had established in Iberia from invaders from the north. Eventually the marauders from the north destroyed the Roman settlement in 585 C.E. Five hundred years later, St. Bertrand, known in his lifetime as Bishop Bertrand de l'Isle-Jourdain, arrived in the community with a reputation for healing the sick and gave his name to the place. While Lugdunum Convenarum was still a vital Roman colonial outpost, Herod Antipas, a son of Herod the Great – the same Herod who is mentioned in accounts of the crucifixion of Jesus of Nazareth – and his consort Herodias, lived in exile in Lugdunum Convenarum, sent there by the Emperor Caligula. Meanwhile, over the Pyrénées to the south on the Iberian Peninsula, the Roman troops protected the established manufacturing, mining and trade centers.

Religious legends have had centuries to evolve. It's said that the Apostle James, a witness to the crucifixion, was preaching the new religion in Iberia. Herodias and Herod Antipas heard James preach in the Iberian city of Cadiz, called Gades during Roman times. The Apostle James returned to Judea and was beheaded by order of Herod Agrippa, or in some versions of the tale, Herod Agrippa himself wielded the sword. Angels took the remains skyward. So they say.

The convoluted folk tale that ensues places a casket with the remains of this same James (Iago in Arabic-Spanish) in a shipwreck off Galicia in northern Spain, then moving by unknown hands to a field known as the Compostela (Field of Stars) on the far western plains of the Iberian peninsula. The casket was reburied in the Cathedral of Saint Iago, forming the terminus of the Camino de Santiago de Compostela, the pilgrimage path. The link between Santiago de Compostela and Saint-Bertrand-de-

Comminges is the path deeply worn by the footsteps of tens of thousands of pilgrims through the centuries.

On the way to St.-Bertrand-de-Comminges

photo by Yvette Maurette

The ruins from the colonial Roman settlement of Lugdunum Convenarum are slowly being excavated. In the flat land below the cathedral, stone remnants are exposed to view and you can walk on them, explore and imagine activity in the past. There is a forum, temples, a theater and trenches leading to thermal baths, and who knows what is yet to be uncovered. According to a brochure produced by the mayor's office, Bishop Bertrand l'Isle de Jourdain, of a noble Gascon family, founded the cathedral between 1073 and 1123 in the abandoned Roman city, doubtless reusing stone blocks from the Roman era construction. A cult of St. Bertrand emerged after his canonization in 1175 or 1218, depending on which account you read. Similar churches were built to serve pilgrims and honor holy figures in other Pyrénées towns such as Bagnères-de-Luchon, Cauterets, and St.-Just-de-Valcabrère. And let's not forget the region's biggest marketing miracle, Lourdes.

The personality cults emerged and developed over the centuries. Events were labeled miracles, attracting more pilgrims. Over the centuries, a stream of pilgrims headed to Santiago de Compostela. The goal of the pilgrimage was to wipe one's spiritual slate clean, receive indulgences that opened the gates of heaven, or, I'm inclined to guess, to leave the cold bleak north of Europe and travel to warm and different regions. Some historians pin the start of pilgrim traffic along this route to the 9th century, others mention the 11th and 12th centuries onward. One of the world's earliest travel guides is a 14th century handbook to the Way of St. James pilgrimage path.

St. Bertrand's reputation as a healing saint after his death and canonization put the town on the pilgrimage map, just as events in the 19th century did the same to Lourdes, and Bétharram. During Bétharram's years of fame, predating the visions of Bernadette at Lourdes, another teenaged girl had sighted a mysterious misty figure of a woman in a grotto, which attracted passing travelers to seek cures in Bétharram's waters. The cycle of identifying holy places and attracting pilgrims is a long-standing enterprise in the Pyrénées region. Miraculously, all these holy places were conveniently located near established thoroughfares.

I noted that the delicate goddess carving known as the Lady of Brassempouy or Venus of Brassempouy, found in 1894 (or 1892) , an indigenous icon carved some 25,000 years ago, resembled descriptions of the later visions described as the Virgin Mary. It ceases to matter whether the pilgrims passed through this mountain pass or another one on their way to Spain. They probably wandered on sheep tracks, selecting the path of least resistance. And who can say what drew the pilgrims to a certain place to be healed, which prompted other settlements to establish their own fonts and miraculous caves? When you are actually on the ground walking, you realize that all of the region has been trod for centuries upon centuries and the stone buildings we now call churches or chapels also served at times as overnight shelters, citadels, watch towers, strongholds against attack, and refuges for animals and people. Nothing is particularly sacred because everything is infused with sacred elements. The holy healing places may offer special cures and in the misty grottos of this reliably verdant landscape, it would not have surprised me to see a vision of a goddess of nature. Alas, I did not.

Topography influences where buildings are sited, so communities seeking to protect themselves build on high ground or areas sheltered from wind and secure from floods. People decide to walk this way rather than that way based on the easiest terrain, the way that requires the least effort to cross distances while avoiding obstacles such as mountains, cliffs and treacherous rivers. If a place draws crowds because of a reputation for miraculous healing, typically the site already attracts human traffic because it's near an easy passageway. From all over Europe, pilgrims advanced through Comminges to receive the benefit of Bertrand's intercession and healing hands. The cathedral offered shelter on the route to Santiago, which lay to the west over the crest of the Pyrénées Mountains.

It was appropriate to resume my route near the hospital in Lannemezan and walk to the Cathedral Sainte-Marie at Saint-Bertrand-de-Comminges, which is the official name of this pilgrimage destination. Though my right wrist was mended and I'd undergone months of physical therapy to rebuild my emaciated arm, I welcomed an extra dose of spiritual healing. I was ready to walk, but my spirit was affected by the events of that particular September.

In August, 2001 I had been nervous about flying to Europe after reading a report by Reuel Marc Gerecht, a former CIA operative, in The Atlantic magazine. He warned that the U.S. had insufficient intelligence resources in Pakistan and Afghanistan, where the Taliban and Osama Ben Laden maintained their followers. Even more troubling, the author reported that the U.S. government wasn't paying attention to the information they received from intelligence sources. I had a persistent feeling during August, 2001 that flying in September wouldn't be prudent. In late August, I reserved a single cabin with Cunard Lines on the Queen Elizabeth II, departing New York September 3rd and arriving in Southampton September 10, 2001. The three airplane hijack attacks in New York and Virginia and the fourth airplane that exploded in the sky over

Pennsylvania came as a surprise, claimed leaders of the United States, when in fact, we now know, there was ample warning but inept, and perhaps criminal, lack of communication among the various U.S. security and intelligence organizations. I did not have access to any special information, just newspapers and magazines and standard dial-up connection to the internet. The lyrics of a Bob Dylan song resonated: "You don't need a weather man to know which way the wind blows."

I was under the English Channel on September 11th, in a Eurostar train headed for Paris, insulated from news of the burning towers in New York. At Gare du Nord, my friend Rosemary met me with the horrible news. I tucked my arm through Rosemary's and thought that this prelude to war forces people to be nervous and alarmed. This could be the summer of 1939 or 1914 when rapidly shifting events and incompetent leaders pushed the world into war. Was this what my mother experienced after the attack on Pearl Harbor in 1941 and subsequently prompted her to join the British Women's Army Air Force (WAAF)?

Rosemary and I spent the rest of the day mesmerized by the repeated footage of the collapsing towers on television, eventually turning it off because her child feared the events were continuing to unfold in a global attack on all high-rise buildings everywhere. How many other children were affected by the endless repetition of those dramatic images?

That night we strolled around Île de la Cité. Small groups held candlelight vigils and a counter-tenor sang plaintively near Cathédrale Notre Dame de Paris. We were too late for the hastily arranged official ceremony of mourning inside Notre Dame, so we leaned against the cloister wall listening to the singer and prayed for peace on that sad and somber night.

In a few days, I decided to carry on with my plans. Nothing would be gained by a vigil in front of the television screen or worry about the unknown. I moved south to Lannemezan to resume walking. On the train, at noon, the conductor announced the national pause throughout France in memory of the 2,974 people from 90 countries who'd died in the attacks in the United States. Heads bowed for five minutes.

At Lannemezan, I picked lodging for the night by process of elimination. After walking past each place in the city center, I went to the one that wasn't dingy or unsavory. A smiling woman greeted me at Hotel de Lannemezan with a warm comment, "Where are you walking to?" Soon I was telling her of my mission to finish the solitary walk across France and that St.-Bertrand-de-Comminges was next on my itinerary. Her eyes brightened. I could tell she wanted to say something important. Smiling and clasping her hands, almost in an attitude of prayer, she asked if I minded, could she please, please join me for the first day? She had wanted to make the pilgrimage to St. Bertrand, but did not want to walk alone. With the stark horrors of the 9-11 attacks just days behind us, I reached for this affirmation of human connection. *"Bien sûr!"* (Of course!) "Come along," I said, "we'll make a pilgrimage together."

"I need to make the pilgrimage to St. Bertrand in memory of my brother who died recently," Yvette Murette told me. I sat at the bar and sipped coffee while she doled out the history of her family and the hotel. She had a husband she didn't much like, a grown daughter and an itch to move on. Maybe the pilgrimage walk to St. Bertrand could help shape her thinking. The next day was a Saturday and Yvette couldn't leave her duties as hotel desk clerk and cashier for the bar-restaurant. I suggested that I could use that time for training walks. We could set forth together on Sunday for St.-Bertrand-de-Comminges, some 30 kilometers away. Yvette offered to give me a deal on the room for two nights, since I hadn't originally intended to stay that long. She also loaned shampoo, soap and a freshly laundered terry cloth bathrobe, a gesture I appreciated since there were no luxury items in my small backpack.

The final weeks before departure had been hectic and my training routines faltered during the week at sea. My feet needed toughening and my leg muscles were out of tone. I had rubbed alcohol on the soles of my feet to harden the skin, a trick I read about in mountaineering books, but I hadn't done serious walking in a month and though the ocean air had been stimulating, I was a tenderfoot.

That night I celebrated the return to the path with a bottle of good Gaillac, a robust red wine from Domaine de Mazou. A few of Yvette's friends joined our table and we practiced using my *boussole* (compass). I pulled out my maps, but after a cursory glance to be polite, Yvette said she knew the way through the forest. No need for fancy topographic maps or a compass.

Yvette and I spooned cereal and yogurt in the morning, much earlier than I normally liked to face the day. It was just 7 a.m. About five miles outside Lannemezan, past the hospital where my arm had been repaired, I asked about a shuttered convent with a statue of the Virgin Mary in a weedy and uncut field. Yvette explained the convent had closed down and the nuns were gone. On the road approaching St. Bertrand, there were shrines and crosses at turns or intersections. The most notable was an old wooden cross attached to a brick building. At the junction of the two cross pieces, a metal circle that might have once been a car hubcap was affixed as an ornament. We took photos and sipped honey-sweetened tea from Yvette's thermos.

Though she had a decade more than me on her bones, Yvette set a furious pace. After two hours, I fell a few minutes behind, then, as the hours dragged, ten minutes behind. She wore a daypack; I carried supplies for several weeks. Yvette sustained herself on tea, while I guzzled water and crammed energy bars in my mouth. The supply of energy bars that was supposed to last several weeks was disappearing fast.

Yvette waited for me to catch up, though I'm sure she thought me weak in the feet and soft in the head for urging one misguided shortcut that tacked on an extra hour as we bushwhacked around the ruins of a stone water mill deep in the woods. We both kept our humor, but I resolved not to walk with another person again. I prefer getting lost alone. Some stretches along this well-established route skirted pastures and were paved with stone, while other paths cut through the forests. West of Lombrès, the route was torn up by loggers. Though marked with the UNESCO heritage symbol of the regional pilgrimage route – the yellow shell of St. Jacques symbol and the labyrinth design – heavy equipment had plowed along the hillsides. The path was part of the European network of the Chemin de St.-Jacques-de-Compostelle, but that hadn't meant anything to the loggers. Beyond the ruts marked with bulldozer treads, the loggers left oil puddles, muddy eroded patches, crushed trees, and clear-cut hillsides. I complained to Yvette, who shrugged and said, "It's politics." I grumbled that even here the logging interests trump environmentalists and historians.

Though Yvette was an enthusiastic hiker, she scorned maps and didn't read inclines on the topographic maps I consulted. She was spooked by the bushwhacking that I proposed, even though I pointed out our position on the map, trying to convince her, and perhaps myself, that we were right here, by the stream and a slight hill, beyond which lay the path to St.-Bertrand-de-Comminges. I'd all but reached the trail we sought when she turned the other way, and flew off to retrace our steps and return to the main road. I was obliged to follow, though I was certain we were steps from the shortcut I'd identified on the map. My feet suffered and my pack straps dug into my shoulders.

About an hour after leaving Lannemezan, we'd come across a cousin of Yvette's on a dirt lane barely wide enough for his tiny Renault. He was on his way to check a pasture where pretty beige cows grazed. Yvette greeted a man cutting brush at Bizous, where we had the first brief rest stop. In a farm house courtyard, a woman snuck glances at us while hanging laundry. Later, on a path near a forest, we passed an older hunter in a blue worker's jacket, his gun lowered. He chatted with Yvette as well, their dialect a little fast for me to keep up. A couple of men toiled in the fields with dogs at their heels. Yvette was way ahead of me by then. My first day back out on the path and I was yearning for a long rest and a cold beer.

A stream confounded our progress in the forest. Flowing briskly through hewn rock sides with several channels and stone planks along the top, we were looking at a water channel that powered a mill in times past, or run-off from a grist mill designed to irrigate a wheat field. In the forest, along the stream, we also passed an area of rocks aligned in the ground and covered with moss. The stones formed a trench at right angles to the water, possibly marking another irrigation channel or a water bypass. Following her lead to the waterfall, the source for these old fixtures made from stone, I took pictures and wanted to linger. But there was no time to look around because Yvette was in a hurry. She needed to be at St. Bertrand to meet her daughter at 4 p.m. for a ride back home to Lannemezan. A spirit as big as Yvette's is rare in the world and I'd walk with her again, but not so fast.

The huge cathedral, visible from miles away, must have drawn hope for pilgrims over the centuries. Carry on, you're not far now, the tower called. My first view of the cathedral was before a town named Labat several kilometers distant. I couldn't help but think about Labatt's Blue, a Canadian pilsner that I fantasized quaffing at that hot, dry moment. As it happened, I waited until evening before awarding myself a celebratory *demi-pression* (half-pint) of beer. The sign promised St.-Bertrand-de-Comminges was close at hand, just 4.2 kilometers away, but to me it felt more like 4 miles. I imagined that fatigued travelers were awed by the spire atop the largest man-made structure in the area.

When we approached the Cathedral, our sore feet turned on the bumpy cobblestones in the old town center. Yvette's daughter Sylvie was waiting on the broad stone steps, ready to drive her mother home. Playing for a laugh, I made a mock gesture of kissing the ground, grateful that the day's march was over. It was Sunday, and a flea market set up in the area around the cathedral entrance spilled into the narrow lanes leading to the Cathedral. The vendors chatted with tourists and customers. Tired and foot-sore, I could barely walk to a small café on the town square. After sharing crêpes and coffee with Yvette and Sylvie, we saluted our achievement and parted. I did not see Yvette again. She sent me a postcard during the winter after our pilgrimage enclosing photos from our day of walking. The note stated she'd divorced her husband and left the hotel.

The friend who taught me how to make crêpes was the Canadian doctor with whom I'd crisscrossed North America in the mid-1970s. This recipe is from my own collection and is easy to remember. If you are camping and don't happen to have a whisk, use a fork to whip the batter.

Crêpes

- 1 cup flour
- 1 cup milk
- 2 eggs
- 1 tablespoon oil
- a pinch of salt

Put the flour in a deep bowl. Make a well in the flour and break the eggs into it. Add the oil, salt and a little of the milk. Beat the mixture with a whisk until the batter is light and thin; gradually add more milk until the batter is smooth. Flavor with a tablespoon of almond or lemon extract, vanilla, rum, or kirsch if desired. Let the batter sit one hour and thicken a little. Just before serving, add a little water or milk to thin the batter. Heat a crêpe pan or flat frying pan with a small amount of cooking oil. Pour or ladle a portion of the batter and spread carefully in the crepe pan to make a large thin pancake. Shake or tilt the crêpe pan so the batter extends smoothly all over the heated surface. When depressions in the batter appear indicating one side is cooked, flip the crêpe to the other side by inverting the pan on a dinner plate or another pan. Serve crêpes hot with a sprinkle of sugar, or spread with preserves, melted chocolate, chestnut purée or other filling and roll the crêpes with the filling inside. The crêpes can be filled with savory mixtures such as chopped ham and mushrooms and covered with Béchamel sauce.

It was difficult to absorb that I'd walked from Lannemezan to St. Bertrand in one day. Had I been on my own starting from Lannemezan, I'd have stopped, painted pictures or even quit for the day at a town where there was a gîte. I was amazed and inspired by Yvette's hurricane energy. She said she was 60 and her daughter was 36, and she moved like a tiger, making me feel slow. After all, it was my first day back on the trail and my feet weren't hardened. Could I lope along that fast when I'm 60?

Finally I stirred myself to find lodging. Opposite the Cathedral, I settled into the Hôtel Comminges, managed by the Mmes. Alaphilippe, dark eyed and vivacious sisters who drifted through the salons and bar, checking on customer service or leading guests to the 14 rooms in this old family house. After stashing my bag and showering, I sat outside on the terrace and sipped my reward-for-the-hike beer under the creeping vines and stared at the Cathedral. Surely in this central position, the hotel was the main hostelry in centuries past, as it was today.

A group of visitors left the cathedral, some of them afflicted with palsy or underdeveloped limbs. Their guardians hustled them to a waiting bus. Do the sick come here for blessings and healing prayer? Next to me on the terrace, a woman warmed her hands under the belly of a muff-like miniature poodle while her companion commented on shoppers who fingered the remaining bric-a-brac for sale by antique dealers. A few tourists in shorts or sleeveless dresses were ill prepared for the darkening sky and quickening wind. Leaves skated across the cobblestones. A storm was gathering, might blow tonight, and the air was certainly colder.

The cathedral's architectural hodge-podge shows surviving parts from Roman, Norman, Gothic and Baroque eras. There are so many carved figures in the walls and layers of ornamentation that a visitor can always discover a detail. I'd read somewhere that there's a special carving in the cathedral. "Green men' are nature totems that appear on tree trunks or are carved into walls, or they appear naturally in the way vines climb or bark grows. The jury is out as to whether these faces appear naturally or by some convergence of spiritual energies, or by human hand, but the Celtic phenomenon endures. The choir stalls at the cathedral of St.-Bertrand-de-Comminges also blatantly depict the intertwined nature of the sacred and the profane. Carvings of plump voluptuous women indicated various virtues, while robed and bearded men raised their hands in warning – or beckoning and blessing.

Green Man Carving, Saint-Bertrand-de-Comminges

In the morning, I hobbled around on blistered feet through intermittent rain. I wanted to explore the Roman ruins of Lugdunum Convenarum down the hill to the east of the cathedral on the plain on the banks of the Garonne River. First I stopped at St.-Just-de-Valcabrère, on the flatlands. Its tower aligns with the spire of St. Bertrand's cathedral on the acropolis. The taciturn gatekeeper of the church at St. Just demanded 12 francs (about $2) admission. With my bad attitude enflamed I didn't feel like paying for a look at a church and muttered to St. Just in protest, leaving a tour of the church for a future visit.

After poking around the Roman ruins, despite the exploding blisters on my feet, I slowly trod the road to the old port on the Garonne. The soles of my feet were inflamed. Each step made me wince. Stone levees, possibly ruins of a water mill, remained on the banks of the river. What were they grinding two thousand years ago? Wheat? Millet? There have been settlements in this warm Mediterranean region for millennia. An Indigo Bunting (or its European cousin) flew out of brush just as I arrived at the water line.

I could barely stand up after sitting and resting at the fountain in front of the Barbazan Spa. Elderly residents of a nearby retirement home came to fill their cups and thermoses with mineral water from the fountain. The oldsters didn't have enough to do, so they paraded around and threw mock insults at each other. One tall man escorted a moderately inquisitive dog named Ludo, who bothered another man. Irritated remarks were lobbed at the dog owner. I didn't like listening to these bored and griping old codgers. They weren't much older than Yvette, or me, yet they'd already sequestered themselves, waiting to die.

The thermal baths in Barbazan were closed to the public, much to my dismay, since I'd hoped to soothe my feet in the mineral water. Workers were improving production of thermal water, which has bacteria in it, the woman at the desk told me. Inside the baths area, men in thick work boots huddled over pumps and water reservoirs. If the water had bacteria, why were those grumpy oldsters drinking it?

I didn't stick around to find out. After limping all morning, my soles were throbbing through my socks and boots. I decided to halt at Barbazan, not even ten miles from St.-Bertrand-de-Comminges. A consultation with my inner healer determined an afternoon lying in bed at Hôtel Rocher reading and watching news on television. I examined my feet – two blisters on the right foot and a hot spot on the left foot, the result of yesterday's extended march. How could we have covered 35 kilometers (22 miles) that day, as my maps indicated? Maybe it was more.

The couple who ran the Hôtel Rocher – I came to think of it as the rock and a hard place motel – were cold tempered, not the least bit helpful. Perhaps they were worn out by the summer-long tourist traffic. And what miserly fare: one pat of butter and one roll, one dab of jam for breakfast. An appealing resort up the hill was already closed for the season.

I needed to get away from Barbazan – no spa, mean hosts and I was turning into a sour puss just like the golden agers and their dogs. Struggling into my socks and boots, I started off on the path above the town, heading upwards and south into real mountains. The forest path turned into a stone track flush to a stone cliff. A cave opening was obscured by carefully arranged sticks and branches. The stone pavement was intended for farm carts pulled by oxen, mules or donkeys. The Romans built a network of roads through the province when the regional government was just down the hill on the plains near the Garonne River and the stone paved roads endured through the centuries, across forests or along edges of fields. Nowadays, they're used by hikers and shepherds moving sheep or farmers driving cattle home to the barn. The solidity of the stone pavements just wide enough for a cart and laid with grooves to permit water run-off led me to conclude that the area was commercially productive in the Roman era. I'd walked similar stone cart roads in Tuscany, in Spain and in the parts of Germany where the Roman army established settlements.

When the forest grew more dense and treetops obscured the sky, there were competing paths, some on the map, many not. The stone paved route disappeared and gave way to dirt marked by knobby bicycle tire tracks. Through these mountains, the marked routes were biking trails rather than hiking trails. The VTT (Vélo-Tout-Terrain or mountain bike) trail required four hours to walk and was extremely difficult, according to the brochure I'd picked up in Barbazan. The alternative was a hunting path that followed the spine of the mountains. The mountain biking route offered a sure, marked path, so I took it.

It was remarkably calm up in the mountains. I didn't see anybody for hours. Near the base of a tree along the path, I did notice a face that looked like a classic "green man" carved by time and nature in the bark. Were my antenna attuned to the supernatural? The face in the tree was halfway up Plamajou, which at its summit is 1041 meters (3415 feet), in the Forêt Domaniale de Sauveterre-de-Comminges. The face, perhaps helped by human hand, perhaps shaped by weather, spirit and chance, placidly watched the passing foot traffic, the animals and the men who hunt them. I decided to draw the image and fished for my book and a pencil.

At one high point in the forest, I passed a large depression in the ground. The pit was about twenty-five feet in diameter and used as a holding pen when boars (wild pigs) are rounded up and captured. It resembled other boar hunting pits I'd seen in the outback canyons of Kauai in the Hawaiian Islands and in the forests of Tuscany. I knew the forest was thick with boar and saw the muddy holes the pigs' tusks and hooves leave after they've rooted around searching for food. Wild pigs are hunted throughout the Pyrénées Mountains and elsewhere in Europe. The meat might be grilled or cubed and used in a stew. Many hunters make sausage with the meat, which has more fat than commercial meat, and much more flavor. The animals annoy farmers by turning up soil, injuring farm animals and wrecking havoc in gardens and planted fields. I wondered whether I would encounter a boar face to face as I did in Kauai.

During the morning, I spied a doe and a fawn along one leg of the trail and watched them bolt in fear. Amusing myself with the idea of creating future Valentine's Day cards, I snapped a photo of a vine with heart shaped leaves cascading in an L shape. The vines of heart leaves were draped artfully from tree branches, crafted by nature design, not by human hand. Through the forest, I noted rocks marked with a large letter P, painted in orange. I supposed that meant potable water, since the rocks were wet and dripped as if near a spring, but I do not know if this is a fact. Red blazes on trees and numbered trees signified forest managers at work, and were not intended as path markers. The most reliable markers were the bumpy tracks made by mountain bike tires and impressions of hunters' boots in the mud. The trail passed a ruin of an old stone building, possibly a house or a stable, on the hill above Lourde. Stone fences made by inserting large rectangular stones in a line, narrow ends up, like a smaller version of the standing stone lines in Brittany, defined long-forgotten property lines.

In Lourde, a road worker, barrel-chested with piercing blue eyes, told me to head towards St.-Pé-d'Ardet "where there's a *chemin pédestre*." The pedestrian path was actually an old stone paved road, not used by cars, from St. Pé over Juan Malaut mountain. The road was paved with cut stones and bordered by walls of laid stone that were level with my shoulders providing shelter from wind. Wood-cutters with oxen or mules were probably the original commercial users for the road. I wondered if anyone use these old roads and footpaths besides hunters, mountain bikers and the rare trekker like me? Stone walls, covered with moss, were dry laid, without cement, a lost art since the advent of barbed wire and electric wire fences.

Moncaup

I settled in relief into this Pyrénées hamlet of 25 inhabitants. Pic de Cagire and Pic du Gar loomed over the valley where the sun was shining in a bright sky. The church bell sounded sentry, opening the day at 7 and 8 a.m., chiming noon and ringing day's end across the valley again at 7 p.m. In between, there were bird chirps, cowbells and silence. Even the wind swept discreetly through distant stands of larch. Except for the prominent telephone and electric lines strung across a pole in front of the gîte, this could be a thousand years ago.

Colette Savès-Ducès, the manager of the gîte, told me that in the recent past, the schoolmaster lived on the upper floors of the school, which was converted about twenty years ago into lodging for hikers. The outer rooms on the ground floor of the gîte are now used for a kitchen and storage and the school room is now the dining room-lounge. The old school building had separate doors for girls and boys on opposite ends of the building. As they do in these southern parts, Colette rolled her "r's" in *portail*, the word she used for door. The accent of the Midi – anywhere in the south from Provence to the Pyrénées – emphasizes certain sounds or sounds out syllables that would be unvoiced or shortened by northern speakers. It could be a linguistic throwback to the Langue d'Oc of the south, or it could be a regional quirk.

As I sit in a lawn chair and rest my aching feet, I track the bees visiting the hollyhocks and pumpkin vines. A troop of field cats lurks in the hedge for a plate of old bread and milk put out by Giselle, who is one-half of the other guests at the gîte. Her husband Pierre and their white lap dog Kiki complete the picture. They live near Toulouse in Muret by the Garonne River, in the direction of Foix, they tell me, and I nod, imagining one of the suburban Italianate style developments that I'd seen during drives out of Toulouse when I lived in the city center during the early and mid-1980s. Giselle and Pierre were nice folks, genial and relaxed on their first vacation in a gîte.

A little cat with tortoise shell markings slinks up looking for handouts. Giselle tells me this pattern of fur is specific to female cats. "They're called Isabelle with a coat like that," she said, which was new feline lore to me. This cat from the feral colony living in nearby fields approached the food dish and boldly ate. Roused from my reverie by conversation with Giselle, I decided that I'd better wash the rest of my clothes in the utility sink and take advantage of the sun to dry them.

Lunch arrived when Colette returned in the little van and unloaded a huge straw bag full of provisions. She is a true cook – busy in the kitchen cooking dinner the day before when I arrived at the gîte door and cooking all morning the following day to produce our luncheon feast. First we had country paté and dry sausage (*saucisson sec*) with a glass of Porto, courtesy of Pierre and Giselle, who had filled their car trunk with tax free booze in Andorra. Vegetable *potage* with tiny star pasta was followed by a quiche *aux fruits de mer*. Next, she served fish in a Basque tomato sauce, followed by salad with feta cheese. Dessert was cake with a compote of apples colored with juice from red raspberries. There also was herbal tea and more red wine. I was in my version of heaven - sunshine, mountains and abundant good food.

Quiche aux Fruits de Mer

- 1 (9 inch) prepared pie crust or use 1/2 of a pie crust recipe
- 1 1/2 c. grated Gruyère cheese
- 8 oz. cooked cold shelled seafood (shrimp, crab, lobster, mussels, or scallops - any combination)
- 1/2 cup finely sliced scallions
- 2 tbsp. flour
- 1/2 tsp. sea salt
- 1/8 tsp. white pepper
- 4 eggs
- 1/2 cup cream
- 3/4 cup milk

Roll pastry in a circle to fit the pan. Crimp the crust edges. Sprinkle grated cheese, cooked seafood, scallions on top of the crust. Beat together eggs with milk and cream. Season and sift in the flour. Mix gently. Pour liquid mixture into the crust over the cheese and seafood. Bake 55 to 60 minutes in a preheated 350 degree F. oven. Cool 5 to 10 minutes to set the quiche before slicing. Makes 6 to 8 servings.

Surrounded by mountains on all sides, this town retains the rhythms of times past: church bells, a little work, a break for a long lunch, a short rest, some more activity and by gosh, it's the hour for an *apéro* (aperitive) to prime the palate for dinner. I could easily settle into a regular life like this.

One of the village's 25 inhabitants, curious about the new arrival at the gîte – that would be me – approached. She's a woman of a certain age towing two dogs on leashes. The dogs sniff around her heels and lie down at the side of the road waiting for their mistress to go through her gossip routine. I say hello and we have a fence-side conversation during which I learn that rain is needed, there are fewer cows than in times past, and the hunting season begins tomorrow. The pigeon shoot is held October first, in two weeks. When I allude to my plan to climb Pic du Gar, Madame tells me that the path to Pic du Gar branches off from the forest road I'd walked yesterday. If I want to buy food for a picnic lunch, she explains, the schedule for vendors is as follows: on Fridays there's a man who sells *charcuterie*. The baker visits the village on Monday, Wednesday and Saturday to deliver bread, and the apple season starts at the end of September.

When I wedge a word into the monologue, I mention that my walk started the year before but was interrupted when I broke my wrist near Lannemezan. Gently, she corrected my usage of *dernière année* for "last year" which is incorrect diction. It should be *l'année derniè*re. I had fallen into the trap of speaking French words with English syntax. Her curiosity about me satisfied, she nodded good day and yanked the dogs upright.

In my purple shorts and yellow tee shirt, I passed for an Easter egg or Humpty Dumpty hobbling around on blistered feet. Colette wore tiny socks and feminine sneakers beneath a long skirt with a pleated flounce and a slit to her knees, which looked great, topped by a loose tee shirt, at once practical and dressed up. Though I tried, I never achieved the look of casual femininity that French women seem to have in their DNA. Even their hiking clothes are cute. A horn flashed noisily, like a train whistle. "That must be the baker," Colette said, hastening off to buy bread.

The former school now converted into a gîte features immense windows facing south and north. Upstairs, my bunk opens onto the southern line of mountains. My first view in the morning is Pic de Cagire. I slept nine hours my first night at the gîte and my right foot with two deep blisters is better for the rest, but the puffy skin of a surface blister hasn't appeared. My treatment is soaking, massage, applying Tiger Balm medicinal cream, and keeping my bare feet elevated in fresh air. With a day or two of rest like this, I should recover and be able to continue the route.

The field cats meow insistently. Hunger drives them. Despite the handouts from neighbors and visitors to the gîte, their meager bodies speak neglect. Their fur lies flat without luster. Do they eat songbirds when no one provides handouts at the kitchen door?

During my modest explorations on the trails around Moncaup and on the way up Pic Juan Malaut, I passed frail pink dianthus and the woods were covered with flowers that resembled small orchids, masses of them. Saxifraga granulata maybe? The same flowers were on the banks of the Garonne at Valcabrère near St. Bertrand. These places are minutes away from each other by car, sharing a micro climate; days apart on foot.

South-facing hillsides like this one in Moncaup stay hot and green well into autumn, making them perfect for animal pasturage, whereas the plains at the edge of the Garonne River are planted with corn for winter food for livestock. The region is also known for rustic farm cheese; I remembered seeing a goat farm near Valcabrère with a sign advertising *chèvre* for sale.

The tinkle of the animal bells captivated my attention as the natural music floating through daily life. The animal bells combined with church bells reverberating off the mountains reminded me of gamelan orchestras in Indonesia. The light tones of brass chimes, gongs and bamboo xylophones of a gamelan orchestra dance and blend together like these random bells sounded by the moving animals. When I left Barbazan yesterday, a serenade of sheep bells sent me on my route.

Colette warned us during dinner that this is rutting season for deer, and the bucks scream during the night. We shouldn't be afraid if we hear strange sounds. This phenomenon attracts visitors to the region, who come just to hear the bucks fighting. A group has booked the gîte for the weekend, so there won't be room for me to stay longer. I suppose that's why most travelers make reservations, but I prefer possibilities even if it means disappointment sometimes.

On another day at Moncaup gîte, I hiked up the 1756 meter (5761 feet) Pic du Gar through the hamlet of Calem and pine forests, taking food, water and a painting kit. A stone refuge at the top offers emergency shelter to hikers caught in storms during winter. One room was locked, but there was a vestibule open with a fireplace, some cots without mattresses and an old sleeping bag. An empty wine bottle stood in the window. *"Fermez la porte"* (close the door) was scratched in big letters on the door. About 50 yards away, another small shelter was tucked between shears of granite.

Flocks of birds with cleft tail feathers swirled around the Pic du Gar just as I arrived on top, winged on thermals, then vanished. A huge eagle, or was it a lammergeier, native to the Pyrénées, swooped overhead while I painted a watercolor of the mountain scene. A cow, part of a herd of cows and grazing sheep, watched me from the opposing Pic Saillant the entire time I was up on Pic du Gar painting, about an hour. I'd look up from my watercolor block and there was the cow, staring at me. Lucky for me, it wasn't a bull.

In the forest, I spied an izard (Rupicapra pyrenaica), the normally shy Pyrénéen mountain goat sometimes called chamois. I heard movement and looked in the right direction. The animal has a goat-like brown face with darker brown markings outlining its face and short upright horns. Heading back down, I spotted two more izards. I also saw bear scat, but nobody offered confirmation that bear lived in the area, even though the Ariège is where Pyrénées brown bears were reintroduced after decades of population decline nearly to extinction. Colette said the izards are going blind because of overcrowding. Their situation is not much different than their American white tail deer cousins who are suffering wasting disease from overpopulation and crowding resulting from loss of habitat to logging and development and the absence of natural predators.

After a final lunch on Friday, I thanked Colette Savès-Ducès and paid the incredibly modest bill (about $30 U.S. for several days of lodging and meals). Memories – and calories – from the final lunch of a venison *daube* (a robust stew of meat, potatoes and wine) plus a salad of grated carrots and a fruit salad dessert carried me forward. An easy walking segment lay ahead, just a picayune ten kilometers to Milhas, where a family-run guest house would be my lodging.

Somewhere in the hills near Juzet-d'Izaut, a villager came up asking if I'd heard the news of the explosion in Toulouse. The date was Friday, September 21. Back at the gîte, after lunch, I'd seen the television film clips: a chemical factory in Toulouse had blown up that morning, spewing toxins, leveling neighborhoods, killing and maiming hundreds. Shattered glass covered sidewalks miles from the epicenter. If the terrorist attacks in the U.S. had not happened the week before, this event would be seen as just a terrible accident. Though news announcers were showing restraint, Pierre and Giselle at the gîte muttered darkly about illegal immigrants and sabotage.

When I said I knew about the explosion and revealed my nationality, the villager all but embraced me in sympathy. "Our hearts are thinking about your country these past ten days," he said. "If it wasn't for Americans, we'd all be doing this." And he made the fascist straight-arm salute. Would this sympathy and good will continue if the rumors of a war initiated by U.S. President Bush actually come to pass? The factory explosion in Toulouse worried me. Ammonia gas was drifting towards Auch, west of Toulouse. My walking path was southwest of Toulouse, below the toxic drift.

The villager didn't mention Hitler; the raised arm in pantomime serves as a signal in this region where the Resistance was strongest. "Americans are our closest friends," he said. "Fifty six years ago you saved us from this." Again, he raised his arm. He was gray haired, perhaps in his sixties. Doubtless he remembered events from his youth, or maybe he was older than he looked and had worked in the Resistance network as so many youths did, running messages, delivering food or ammunition, and escorting downed Allied pilots to safety.

The air was heavy under gray overcast skies. Clouds of ammonia from the chemical plant explosion were blowing far from my path, but I couldn't suppress my imagination. Perhaps I was distracted by news events, but after crossing the Ger River, I lost the trail. I followed an animal track, squished through a muddy ravine and eventually slopped through a cow path into Milhas. The path had been recently cleared of saplings and brambles and the brush was piled along the trail edge. The gîte logo on a marker pointed towards a brick house and I knocked on the door.

An hour later, half the village had dropped by Mme. Layell's guest house to confer about the explosion in Toulouse and to sneak a look at the American woman sitting at the kitchen table sipping coffee and hot milk. I drank what she offered, despite no outright desire for coffee late in the afternoon, which might keep me awake. Soon, the son came home, a roly-poly type in his late thirties who demanded, "Mama, do this for me," and gave her some rapid-fire instruction. Then, "Mama, make me a cafe." He looked like the curly haired singer in the Turtles, a rock group of the 1960s. I wanted to smack some manners into him, but I didn't confront him.

Towards evening, I took Rox, the family's blond Labrador Retriever, for a walk. I decided that the over-eager Rox didn't exercise enough. We had fun, racing along the lanes and chatting with one guy in a Land Rover who rolled down the window and asked, "Isn't that Nanette Layell's dog?" Then he told me he was worried that his house in Toulouse, about sixty miles away, was blown up by the factory explosion and slammed the SUV in gear.

I phoned my friends and relatives in Toulouse. There was no answer at Jean-Louis' apartment in Toulouse. Cousin Regine Aragon in Gimont said all the family was fine and I shouldn't worry. She was more concerned about me being outdoors during the day and walking, perhaps breathing toxic fumes. But the worst of the day's threats to my health were the two tiny ticks that I pulled from my body. One was lodged near my left armpit and other on my leg. They hadn't tucked in too deeply and I covered the bites with Tiger Balm, the most effective topical remedy that I know. The ticks were so small that I could hardly see them. Deer ticks, probably, or izard ticks, if there is such a thing. Lyme disease occurs in Europe, but these ticks hadn't bitten yet.

Family relations frayed to rudeness *chez* Layell. Mr. Layell ordered the wife around brusquely and she snapped back just as roughly. The adult son demanded more coffee and a meal from his mom, and sat hunched at the family table reading the football sheet, ignoring his parents. He lived in a separate house on the lot behind the family house, but ate with mom and pop. All this was explained to me by Nannette Layell as she cooked. I guess they were a fairly typical family, the woman serving the men without thanks, both parents treated rudely by the offspring.

The guest room sported brown wood-paneled walls, a beige linoleum floor and easy-wipe surfaces – not my chosen furnishings – but they were serviceable. It was obvious that the shower and toilet had been installed by an amateur builder, likely by a local handyman. At least the plumbing worked. Blue sheets, a colorful coverlet and towels cheered me up after the mannerless drama in the kitchen. I prefer the anonymity of a hotel or the camaraderie of a hikers' gîte, rather than these country guest rooms *en famille*, but there is really nothing else available in rural areas. With a car, I could easily find slick tourist lodgings if so inclined, from chateau inns to chain hotels. But I was on foot.

Oddly, I dreamed of my father, who died in 1982, and I dream of him rarely now. He was dressed in a tuxedo during one episode in the dream, at some grand event with my brother Liam and I. We were surprised not to be having such a great time at the party, whatever it was. But we were happy to see each other. There were other portions of the dream with my old dad, quite clear and present. Seeing my father and brother in the dream gave me courage and a feeling of protection.

Maybe the long talk the other day with venerable Mr. Jean Girard in Moncaup influenced the dream featuring my father. He epitomized Henry Miller's sentiment: "In France the old men, especially if of peasant stock, are a joy and an inspiration to behold. They are like great trees which no storm can dislodge; they radiate peace, serenity and wisdom." Visible at a distance with an aureole of white hair, the tall, robust native of Moncaup had trudged up from the village to the school house gîte and talked with me about the 20th century. Mr. Girard was born in 1909, my dad in 1912. "We had potatoes so large we could feed six people with one," said Mr. Girard, tapping his cane for emphasis. "There are no more crows," he said. I heard several start cawing after he left. "No airplanes here," he said, and one droned overhead. Could old Mr. Girard be deaf or was he pulling my leg?

Mr. Jean Girard in front of Moncaup Gîte

Yesterday, atop Pic du Gar, several military airplanes swooped past the mountain top, one so low I could practically see the pilot. Were the pilots patrolling the peaks? Joy riding, like the American pilots did in Italy in February, 1998, when their thrill-seeking moves severed a ski lift cable and killed 20 people. I'll bet these military jets were patrolling the Pyrénées in response to the terrorism attacks the week before in the United States. I delayed leaving the table in the Layell's kitchen after dinner so I could watch television images of marines heading out and Bush addressing the U.S. Congress. I was naive enough to hope that it was just a flaunt of force and flag waving; surely no war action was contemplated by civilized nations.

Mr. Layell insisted on driving me to the next mountain pass, saying I should avoid the forest paths behind Milhas. "It's hunting season," he said, "and they'll be out today because it's Saturday." I'd learned to heed local counsel. If Mr. Layell thought I should avoid a forest where hunters roamed, then I would follow his advice. At the gîte in Moncaup, Colette had waved her hand over the same sector of the map murmuring a similar warning. "You could get lost here," she said. Best to accept the ten minute car lift, I decided. Besides, by the time the trek ends, I'll have walked far more miles than the straight route, with all the extra mountain climbs, detours and evening forays with dogs like Rox. The Tour de France had swept through here, over the Col de Portet d'Aspet about seven kilometers to the south, as the crow flies. The ten minute car trip bisected the forests that I'd been told were too dense and dangerous to navigate.

I met Colette one more time by chance in the Aspet *épicerie*, where I restocked my backpack larder with fruit, cheese and a half liter of wine tapped from a huge barrel container. "Is it legal to sell wine in demi-liters?" one sales clerk asked the other, holding up my empty water bottle. I bought a half liter of the same wine served at the gîte. We chatted about the coincidence of meeting after I'd left the gîte and I helped carry provisions to the little truck. She planned a big meal that afternoon for the 18 people expected at the gîte for night hiking and listening to deer rutting in the forests. We kissed good-by four times, back and forth twice on each cheek, in the southwestern manner. Depending on the region, people kiss two, or three times, and in the deep south, four or sometimes five times. If you're not familiar with the number of kisses that local custom prescribes, you can find yourself off a beat, thinking the kiss on the cheek ritual is over while the person greeting you or saying farewell is aiming at a cheek. The kiss is perfunctory and is included in all social greetings. Business or commercial greetings are handled with a handshake. As we parted, I said that I hoped to return to Moncaup and stay at the gîte again someday.

After walking downhill all morning, I stopped to eat and rest beneath a cross dated 1864 near the town named Bataille. Earlier, I'd seen hunters' cars parked on the mountainside and heard shots in the distance, so accepting Mr. Layell's lift past the main forest was probably a prudent move. They were hunting pheasant, or boar. A cyclist passed, puffing hard uphill. I watched a farmer driving a tractor with a bovine of invisible gender towed in a huge trailer.

Mist and fog hovered over the Forêt Domaniale de Saleich, which I decided deserved a picture. Mont Aragnoué is the closest peak, and largest in my immediate view, at 808 meters (2659 feet). The mountain forests in the Ariège region remain the wildest, least populated areas in France today. As in the past, the forests provide food, firewood, and timber crops. The stands of trees sustain the habitat, protecting valleys from rock slides and floods. During the Nazi occupation of France, the locals used the forests and caves in this region as a zone for stashing refugees, fighters and supplies. Outsiders wouldn't know their way through the forests.

Hawks cruised overhead and soon the sun edged around clouds in the watercolor I was painting. Mr. Robert Raufast stopped his blue Nissan truck with two huskies in the back and joyfully welcomed me to Chein-Dessus, the town where he lived and a kilometer from where I sat painting. The enthusiasm the locals offer a visitor on foot astonished me. What a contrast to how pedestrians fare in my own country! The prevailing attitude in the U. S. will change – those who walk are also worthy citizens and owning a car is irrelevant, even a detriment to society. Is it a stretch to say that people on foot in France have an easier experience?

"I noticed you painting as I went down into town," he said, "so I had to stop and welcome you." We chatted about the countryside and that led to his telling me about the World War II *maquis*. The *maquisards* were so named because they hid in the brush (*maquis*) or went underground. Resistance members worked out of la Baderque west of Herran, he told me. Germans discovered their secret activities and burned the village. "The Germans brutalized the *paysans*, slaughtered animals and burned la Baderque," he said. Raufast was four or five years old at the time, yet remembered blood running down people's faces when they were beaten by the occupying troops and he saw the dead lying in the street where they were shot.

Mr. Raufast came from a two-cow family. One cow was taken by Nazis and butchered in the main square at Herran. The other, perhaps the less submissive beast, got away from the captors and was found later in a nearby field. Raufast's father, a metal worker, had no employment during the war, so he took to the hills and made charcoal from forest wood, ending up in the nearby village of Couillas. At least I think that's what Raufast told me about his father's history which I wrote down as he spoke.

"When the Germans came to attack la Baderque, the local *gendarme*, a brave man and being a policeman, the only person with a gun, tried to stop them," said Mr. Raufast. "But he was killed and the locals had nothing, no weapons." Raufast told me that it was probably a woman who betrayed the resistance fighter's whereabouts to the Germans. Perhaps it was true, a repetition of what he'd heard as a child. It's an oft told excuse, to blame a woman. We chatted about my walk, the region and local town names. With so many nearby caves, I suggested, perhaps they have been useful hiding places. Raufast chuckled, perhaps remembering youthful escapades as well as the wartime use of the caves.

The town of Herran was Spanish, he said, since there is a town of the same name to the south, over the mountains. In Spanish, *herrar* means to shoe, and *herraje* are iron fittings or shoeing and *herrero* is a blacksmith. Perhaps the town name refers to metal forgers. The land around Chein-Dessus, where Mr. Raufast lived now, was once forested mountains. Hillsides that were clear-cut areas are now reforested, he said, but wood cutting continues. Many villages to the south have *'chein'* in the final syllable, he pointed out, as we studied the map that I used to plot a route.

Before returning to the patient huskies enclosed in the truck, Mr. Raufast told me about the Guerre des Demoiselles in the Ariège. From the 1830s to 1850s, farmers and woodcutters disguised as women played pranks in the night to scare the tax-levying forest guards and official charcoal makers away. The country folk wanted to continue their traditional wood harvesting, charcoal making and other foraging which produced marginal income.

Previously unaware of this curious episode in French rural history, I hunkered down on my return to Washington at a desk in the Library of Congress to read about this "women's war" in Peter Sahlins book *Forest Rites, War of the Demoiselles in 19th Century France*. In addition to acting up to cause trouble for the authorities, the cross-dressing revolutionaries were thought to be emblems of the strong women of the Pyrénées, who were at that time losing their traditional status as heads of the household and defenders of village rights.

The male peasants did not attempt to take on the identity of women, as might male transvestites. Rather, they adopted the abbreviated, caricatured signs of women without abandoning their masculine identity. By darkening the face with red or black, wearing a white shirt outside the clothes instead of leaving it tucked in, tightening the waist with a colored band, the men's clothing gave the impression of a skirt. On their heads they wore a handkerchief or a woman's headdress. Sahlins writes that these armed peasant men took matters into their own hands, chasing the royal charcoal-makers from the forests.

The Couserans, to the west, had experienced extensive revolts by farm workers against the nobility and government officials during the late 16th century, and like the Comté Foix (Foix county), peasants continued their rebellions during the 17th and 18th centuries, so there was a tradition of revolt when the monarchy occasionally attempted to restrict local people's traditional rights to use the forest. The 19th century "war" was a continuation of local practice.

At Illartein and at Bordes, peasant rioters presented themselves as Demoiselles to the village innkeepers, warning them not to give lodging to the official forest guards. Throughout the course of the revolts, workers deliberately used the rites of Carnival – the tradition of dressing up in costumes or cross-dressing, frolicking and drinking wildly in public. In July, 1829, men from Saint-Girons were arrested in Aspet. There I was, reading about Aspet under the dome of the Jefferson Building at the Library of Congress and I'd been in Aspet; knew the market and the wine bar.

The foresters had prowled around all day in elaborate disguise, running through the forests. They returned in the late afternoon to the village inn, where they spent a quantity of money on drink. According to the arrest record, they were led by Jean-Baptiste Lafforgue-Vidalou, who called himself "Captain" and was wearing a military uniform. "He commanded a troop of Demoiselles and seems to have a certain authority. He is, in fact, only a peasant who affects to speak French, he barely knows the language," states the record as transcribed in Salins' book.

Rioting spread during June and July of 1829 throughout the valleys of the Castillonnais, to the southwestern part of the Ariège. The revolt migrated farther south into the Pyrénées, up to Ustou, following the traditional route of summer transhumance (of cattle at that time) In the village of Fougaron on Sunday, 26 July, thirty-nine Demoiselles entered a cabaret and ordered wine. Fancifully dressed and led by three costumed men calling themselves "The Captain," "The Executioner," and "The Priest," these disguised men later went into the forest, where they destroyed five shelters erected by royal charcoal-makers.

The War of the Demoiselles wasn't the first time women's disguises served the revolutionary spirit. Sahlins writes about documents archived by the French government that describe Pyrénées region rebel peasants who appeared disguised as women. The purpose was to hide identity but also to jibe the authorities. Men dressed as women entered into the traditional women's role of acting in public for the public good. And the raucous cross-dressing men intended an affront to the status quo.

"The image of powerful and disorderly women might have been especially appealing to male peasants in revolt. For in the peasant culture of the Ariège, as throughout the central and western Pyrénées, women had traditionally been authorized to act in certain public contexts." Sahlins writes that the rural communities which in time were consolidated as the Ariège department had "valued the integrity of the household (casa) over the specific sex of the household head (cap de casa). The result was that households were not infrequently headed by women, who held that right not simply as widows but as legitimate heirs with public responsibilities and privileges as local citizens or neighbors. Such rights were recognized in the customary law codes of certain Pyrénées regions, such as Bareges, Labourde, Soule, and the Basque country, written down in the 16th and 17th centuries." Though little is really known about women heads of households in the Pyrénées during the Old Regime, "women were juridically empowered in the public domain of village life to a much greater extent than in other peasant societies of Europe."

In the Central Pyrénées, women were considered as capable as men in maintaining traditions and defending the integrity of the household. In addition to the rural unrest in reaction to restrictions imposed by the royal forest managers, the local women were affected by royal decrees concerning male primacy in property rights. The Napoleonic Civil Code of 1804 subjected women to patrilineal authority, undermining women's traditional status. Thus, a woman who would have inherited the family property because she was first born, lost her claim under the new decrees, and would be passed over in favor of the first male. He, in turn, marrying a woman from another family, further diluted the bloodline of the house as the symbol of Basque unity and family strength.

This education about the Guerre de Demoiselles occurred many months later. Right now, I was trudging across the same turf in the Ariége that those rebels defended against the encroaching bureaucracy from Paris. Using a local guidebook to rural lodgings, I'd found a farmhouse that was open to guests and phoned ahead. I was worried about relying on chance in this sparsely populated rural area.

Mr. Marcel Buffalon, the dairy farmer who owned the rental property in Gerus where I booked a night's stay, told me there's no relationship between the name of the town 'chein-dessus' and oak trees. My ears were deceiving me. According to the Larousse dictionary, oak is spelled chêne, not chein, and there is no entry for a French word chein. The words sound similar and in a region where so many dialects and languages overlay, I was still tempted by the idea that chein referred to oak. "I burn oak, the best wood,"Mr. Buffalon said, trying to resolve the conversation.

Over coffee served by his wife, who later whispered that her husband was going through a difficult time, Mr. Buffalon launched into an involved story about the old lady who many years ago lived in the small house up the mountain, in a hamlet a few miles from their farm. When Mr. Buffalon was a boy, he waved *bonjour* to the woman as he walked to school. Years later, when the old lady died, she deeded the house to the Buffalon family. That little house was the chalet they rented to tourists like me.

A man about my age barged into the room, bearing bags of food. Mr. Buffalon introduced his son, Jean-Bernard, whose day job is designing and building roads for the regional government. Later, when the old man was out of earshot, Jean-Bernard confided that his father was diagnosed with Alzheimer's disease, so I shouldn't believe every story the old man told me. However, the story about the elderly lady giving his father the mountain house was true.

While Mrs. Buffalon tidied up the coffee cups, the men invited me into the dairy barn to watch evening milking. A teenage grandson, Julien, and his father Serge, helped the patriarch handle chores on the farm. The road engineer son, Jean-Bernard, visited on weekends. During a lively supper they quizzed me about my journey and I asked the family about local lore. Jean-Bernard drove me out to the mountain house where I would stay. A one night rental was somewhat unusual because vacation chalet rentals are typically rented by the week, so I repeated my thanks to Jean-Bernard for opening the place up for my short stay. Alone again, I gathered fallen apples from the tree in a side yard to cook a compote for dessert. I was happy to have a little stove, a fireplace and the opportunity to cook – to do useful homey tasks. These trees have produced fruit for decades; I wanted to honor the fruit and the land. Most of all, I was mindful of honoring the woman whose house this had been. I had a feeling that she was frugal and kind.

Just passing through, a leaf on the fly, falling from branch to earth. There is nothing left behind but goodwill. On the way towards the Mediterranean I was collecting parcels of memories in the places where I stopped and with the people I met. My feet hardened, grew accustomed to the daily pounding. My pack was lighter because I knew what to leave at home. After a week of walking this second phase of the cross-France trek, I was beginning to find my rhythm.

This is my recipe for compote which can be used for any kind of tree-grown fruit.

Apple Compote

Peel and core 4 to 6 apples. Cut into rough chunks about 1 to 2 inches square. Put the fruit in a plain syrup made of 1/2 cup sugar and 1 1/2 cups water. Increase the quantity of syrup if more apples are used. Cook over medium heat and mash the fruit slightly as it cooks. Add more water if too thick. Flavor with vanilla, lemon, cinnamon or nutmeg to taste. Serves 4.

CHAPTER 6
Castles and Cathar Forts

Saint-Lizier to Mirepoix

Embraced by ramparts, high stone walls built into the largest buildings, the cathedral, the bishop's palace, and nobles' houses shape the core of Saint-Lizier. The small town on a hilltop is well secured from attack – medieval era land attack, that is. In the magnificence of the bishop's palace and the density of the fortified stone walls, you could say Saint-Lizier is a miniature version of Carcassonne, the fortress and capital of the medieval south about seven days' walk to the northeast. Carcassonne is a vast and storied city; Saint-Lizier more compact, but I could see vestiges of wealth and social status in the architecture.

Once upon a time, powerful bishops lived in Saint-Lizier as legal administrators of the entire Couserans region. This position of legal and religious authority was often contested by the neighboring region of Comminges, ruled by the Bishop at the Cathedral of St. Bertrand, which I'd explored the previous week. In those times, bishops lived in fortified palaces situated at the highest point, and Saint-Lizier followed the rule. The cathedral, enclosed and supported by ramparts too dense and high to be breached by hostile rabble or invaders, formed a defensive citadel joined with the Bishop's palace. During times of attack, or threat, people from the surrounding area sheltered in the cathedral or in courtyards between the buildings. Stables, huts for the servants, small gardens and other dependencies were tucked between the dominant buildings. Each grand building served as an effective fortification element for the other. The bishops and noble families, who were usually related because of the effort to consolidate power through marital brokering, accumulated great wealth by taxing agricultural crops, wool, wine, wheat and whatever else they fancied in exchange for protection from marauders. The protection racket engineered by the religious and civil leaders ensured security of their own assets, which included the agricultural producers. The threat to their assets was social and political revolt which was characterized by the authorities as religious heresy, thus justifying decades of violent persecution.

The contest for territorial and religious supremacy begat violence. The region was torn apart by the Albigensian Crusade, which operated under authorization of Popes Lucius III and Innocent III. In 1184 Pope Lucius III mandated that the Cathars be persuaded by trial to give up their beliefs that differed from the Roman Church's precepts. Pope Innocent III authorized an army to achieve the goal by force. This crusade was really a civil war, led by northern French armies who famously murdered whole towns, like Béziers, calling upon God to sort out the faithful among the dead, and Montsegur where the remaining Cathar refugees were burned on a pyre at the base of the mountain. The incentive for the northern mercenaries authorized by the Church hierarchy, was plunder. Soldiers kept whatever they looted. Local chiefs and their henchmen settled festering political and personal debts with the sword under the guise of the papal crusades.

Couserans, a feudal territory extending from the Mediterranean inland to Toulouse, was one of several fiefdoms controlled by noble families. In Roman times, the region's people were called Consorani, and that evolved into Couserans, the geographical name. Alliances were forged and contested with neighboring fiefdoms, but the Couserans (the Ariège is also part of this region) lay far from the power centers in Provence and Burgundy. The mountainous Southwest and the independent Basques were generally left alone.

Hostilities entrenched during the Albigensian religious war to stamp out the Cathars during the 12th and 13th centuries and the later persecution of Protestants during the Wars of Religion, 1562 to 1598. Political supremacy favored the Catholic Church and its richest allies. I'm not alone in wondering how so-called Christian entities could have fostered such violence and destruction, burning villages, uprooting vineyards and slaughtering livestock, laying waste to the region that rejected the corruption of the church and refused to pay taxes to the Burgundian dukes hundreds of miles away. The unsettled rebels of the south continued revolts and acts of civil disobedience such as the Guerres de Demoiselles, and participated in the national revolutions of 1789 and 1848 the nobles who controlled land use and agricultural commerce.

This region borders Spain, with Aragon and Catalonia to the south. Land was periodically annexed by marriage with neighboring counts, or lost during conflicts. Saint-Lizier's pinnacle of power was from the 11th to 18th centuries. When

Napoleon reorganized the political administration of France, creating a secular federal state in 1801, with power centralized in Paris, the bishops were displaced and Saint-Lizier became the administrative center for the district.

Gathering clouds burst just as I crossed the narrow bridge over the Salat River and slogged into Saint-Lizier. The tourist hotels along the road in the lower part of town were closed, of course. This was the off-season. The driving rainstorm soaked through the usually reliable Gore-Tex jacket and there I was without a room for the night, out in the cold and rain. During the afternoon, I'd passed small groups of hunters who were having a grand time passing the liquid courage and telling tales. Now I wished that I had stopped and chatted, queried them about nearby lodgings.

I plodded through streams of water, soaking my boots. The pack was already wet and dragged on my shoulders. My glasses fogged; I couldn't see signs. Up and up I trudged, on steep narrow one-way alleys to the oldest part of town where the cathedral and bishop's palace overlooked the surrounding valleys. This wasn't the first time I'd entered towns without a reservation for a room, but not on Sunday and not with a rainstorm hampering my sight. Was everybody behind shuttered windows and locked gates?

A woman in a car noticed me, rolled down the steamy window and asked if she could help. "Try La Liceroise, on the street at the top. Françoise rents a room." Soon, I was clanging an antique knocker on the tall wooden door of a five-story mansion on Rue des Nobles. There was no date carved on the lintel, but the other stone buildings on the street looked many centuries old. Minutes passed while I waited at the door. This was the right place; a signboard with the pension name hung above the door. Just when I was considering whether I should clank the metal knocker again, a woman peered out, smiling in welcome. "Bonjour, my name is Françoise," she said, patting strands of long grey-blond hair into a loose bun atop her head. Her ankle length dress reminded me of the earth mother style from the 1970s. "I have a room to rent on the top floor. You'll have a view of the bishop's garden," she promised. Even without the view, I wanted to stay. A cot in the cellar would have been fine.

But I'd learned to always take a gander at rooms, especially in this type of arrangement when the room for rent is inside the family quarters. The room under the eaves was too many staircases for Françoise to climb, she said, so she gave me the key and told me to find my way upstairs, and be sure to hang my wet clothes in the drying room in an air shaft off the stairwell.

Up in the little room, a charming retreat with its own tiled bathroom, piles of pillows and quilts, and a reading lamp by the bed, I took in the promised view of the ramparts, the medieval bishops' mansion and the walled garden. What luck, I'd landed in an historic mansion, complete with vast staircases, stone walls and, in the main reception rooms, twenty-foot ceilings. I made a mental note to ask about ghosts, but forgot to pursue the idea while I was there. In any event, the owner of La Liceroise, Madame Françoise Biesiada, drew on a fund of stories about the living.

The twin towns of Saint-Lizier and Saint-Girons are populated by an old nest of radical activists, Françoise told me one morning at breakfast. Most of the former radicals were now contented local bourgeoisie, Françoise asserted, but back in the 1970s, the police actively searched for hemp farms. "Now, people around here are more interested in growing organic vegetables than pot," she laughed. When the clouds broke and the rain stopped, I walked around the twin towns and noticed packs of bench-sitters in central Saint-Girons loitering near the river. The etiolated idlers were similar to the group with mangy dogs hanging around the post office in Oloron-Sainte-Marie waiting for handouts. These folks weren't political activists; they were barely awake. And most appeared to be way too young to have been questioning authority during the 1970s. The anti-authoritarians and activists of the past had become progressive bourgeoise homeowners long before the new millenium.

The farmer's market in Saint-Girons runs Saturday mornings all year round. According to Françoise, it was the place to purchase fresh fruit and "*bio*" (organic) local produce, honey, cheese, and nuts. Two Mondays a month there's a larger market at Saint-Girons, where vendors park their vans and sell all kinds of products – clothes, artisan creations, kitchenware, used books, bric-a-brac, shoes, pirated CDs and videos. My visit coincided with a Monday market, so I toured the stalls, but didn't find anything other than lunch supplies, bakery treats and snacks. I couldn't carry music media or crafts.

Françoise regaled me with stories about local politics, feuds over land use and the old days when the Masatoise, the anti-drug police, patrolled the region. She said Saint-Lizier was once known for its pot farms, but the mountains seemed chilly compared to Hawaii, California or Mexico where marijuana flourishes. Police don't have much interest in small time pot growers now, she said. Illegal immigrants, smuggling and the threat of terrorism preoccupy local law enforcement.

Françoise recounted the minutia of her efforts to care for Boris, her 18-year old son afflicted with a degenerative disease. I heard how she badgered the social workers and doctors, threatening court action if providers didn't install an elevator so she could move Boris around the house, or pay for the visiting physical therapist to help him exercise. Boris reclined in an elaborate red wheelchair and communicated with brief hand squeezes. Bold colorful artwork, created when Boris could still hold crayons, hung on the kitchen walls. Françoise's dogged pursuit of benefits for her son from the already generous French health care system was admirable, but her long talks drained me. My understanding of medical insurance is rudimentary in any language; parsing rapid-fire commentary in French about arcane regulations sent my mind reeling.

Boris' father is a telephone company executive with a job in another city, so he's frequently absent. One night we all ate together, family style. They were kind to me, inviting me for an aperitif as if I were a family friend, rather than a paying guest. I chatted with Élodie, their high-school aged daughter who wanted to be a park ranger. We talked about internships in the U.S. National Parks or volunteer work on the trails.

I couldn't decide if they invited me to join their table because I could speak a little French or if my cross-country trek sparked curiosity. Maybe I offered diversion for a family under stress. I've discovered there's a knack to projecting command of a language. Concentrate on listening, then insert a comment, joke or rebuttal at the right moment to advance the conversation.

Saint-Lizier is home to an unusual artist, Genevieve Seille, whom I met along with Gerard, her British musician-composer companion. Seille is an Outsider artist, a definition that signifies creative work in non-traditional forms and images. She showed me intricate whimsical boxes and cases she'd constructed. On the bare floor she spread out paper dyed with tea to tint it brown. She demonstrated how she paints and draws detailed representations of tattoo designs similar to Maori body art in New Zealand. The designs also resemble the painted tapa cloths painted by Aboriginal artists of Australia. While we sipped peppermint tea, I scrutinized the rooms. These two creative artists lived simply with very few objects in their house. A few rocks were arranged on a windowsill, an allegiance to nature. Her pens, paper and brushes were laid out and ready for work. I've noticed this in other artists' houses – the art materials and tools are ready; no clutter is left around. The house functions as a studio, with few possessions to distract them from creative action.

Françoise told me that Saint-Lizier's cathedral is an historic landmark that can't be missed. She also introduced me to the director of the local tourism office, Daniele Pélata, who led me around the historic center. The landmark site is actually two cathedrals. The eleventh century basilica was built of salvaged pieces from Gallo-Roman ruins, Daniele told me. Stone capitals atop pillars in the Romanesque cloister were carved in a style similar to the Daurade church in Toulouse. The tower is constructed of the same rosy red brick as Saint Sernin, the Romanesque Basilica in Toulouse which is a major stop for pilgrims heading towards Spain. Once again, I was reminded that the churches and cathedrals in provincial centers imitated the structures in the nearby cities – Carcassone and Toulouse.

The frescoes at St. Lizier date from the 15th century, yet I was startled by the resemblance to much earlier Byzantine figure painting and mosaics I'd seen in Ravenna, Italy. Maybe itinerant artists back then shared the same flat style. While we strolled around the cathedral cloister, drills whined and hammers rang as workmen labored on the tile roofs and refinished stone walls.

Specialists were engaged to refinish the frescoes in the upper church, Daniele said, but work hadn't yet started. Interest in the pilgrimage route through the Piedmont increased tourist visits and attracted funding for building restoration.

I strolled through the basilica and cloister defined with columns capped with carvings. The outer edge of the roof is decorated with small carved animals – a turtle, a lion and other beasts. A column near the main altar ends with a sculpted human foot at the base; long ago, the whole column was shaped as a human figure.

Saint-Lizier's hidden gem is the 18th century pharmacy. In 1756, the Bishops of Saint-Lizier inaugurated a hospital for the poor called the Hôtel-Dieu (House of God). The pharmacy inside was founded in 1764, and was established to serve those who lived in the region. It's somewhat unusual for a building associated with the church to have survived the various revolutions without a scratch, and this pharmacy is intact. The political center of the 1789 revolution occurred far away and communications in the mountainous south were slow and unreliable.

The guide wielded a key larger than my hand to unlock the dispensary. Once upon a time, women who were chatelaines of manor houses wore many heavy keys hanging from a ring attached to their belts. So much of the past continues in daily use in this part of France that I was frequently struck by the quality of construction and manufacture, the enduring habits continuing over the centuries.

The pharmacy walls were lined with shelves filled with glass jars and blue and white faience jars made in Martes de Toulasan, a regional ceramics and stone carving center dating back to the Roman occupation when Caesar invaded and divided Gaul (France) into three parts, as my high school Latin textbook stated. Some jars were marked "H" for huile (oil) or "S", for holding sirop (syrup). Labels such as Huile de Chien (Oil of Dog) shared shelf space with jars labeled "Elixir de Longue Vie" and "Huile de Camomille." I didn't learn what the Oil of Dog concoction was used for – homeopathic rabies treatment perhaps? I did acquire a recipe for Chamomile Oil.

Oil of Chamomile

Place 1/2 cup dry crushed Chamomile buds into a small sterilized glass jar or bottle. Cover the Chamomile with extra-virgin olive oil. Put a tight lid on the jar or bottle and place in direct sunlight for 2 weeks. After that, store the chamomile oil in the refrigerator and use whenever needed to treat muscle pain. Warm a small amount of the oil prior to use and massage thoroughly into the skin.

Dried Chamomile buds are sold at health food markets in the herb or tea section. In areas where the plant grows wild, harvest the flowers just at flowering. Spread on trays and dry in the sun or a room without moist air. Shake or stir the flowers occasionally while they dry to prevent mold.

Black marble tabletops were quarried in the Couserans and the table was described as a "grand antique," but I'm not sure if the guide meant the marble itself or the wooden cabinet. The washbasin was also carved from black marble and housed in a cabinet tucked in the corner of the room with a hanger for a towel. Above the basin was a pewter vessel with a spigot for the water and a custom built holder fitted in the wall for drying bottles or beakers turned upside down to drip into the basin. A reservoir below caught the waste water. This compact unit was built before running water was available, yet it offered an efficient, sanitary washing system. Centuries past, an assistant fetched water from the well and sloshed the waste out into the courtyard.

A large black marble mortar and wooden pestle used for mixing batches of remedies was stashed under a shelf with a curious device called a *sphère armillaire* to show celestial positions. Perhaps this was a diagnostic tool to determine planetary influences on a patient? Or which planetary alignments determined the time to mix, let's say, Oil of Dog with Henbane and Mullet?

Because it was an Episcopal collegiate, a cathedral where bishops ruled in residence, Saint-Lizier owned an important position on the pilgrimage route to Santiago de Compostela. Though the religious authority has waned, tourism has stepped into the breach. Daniele Pélata, from the tourism office, told me "our *halte* (rest stop) on the Chemin St. Jacques route is a three star pilgrimage lodging." She meant that typical pilgrim hostels don't offer hot water, privacy and a garden for reflection all for a modest fee less than $20 per night. The gîte shares space with an old folk's residence, the current function of the 18th century hospital.

In former times, and even now at some points on the route to Compostela, rest stops for pilgrims were at churches or monasteries. At Saint-Lizier's gîte, there are three beds, a kitchen, a common room and a shower, all quite clean and brightly lit. An Association of St. Jacques based in Saint-Lizier assists pilgrims on the road if they need help. Two heavily laden hikers in their mid 20s with packs teetering over their heads rested in the small garden. As Daniele led me out the door, we nodded at the pilgrims, said our *"Bonjours"*. I chatted with them briefly, asking how far they'd walked. They were on the way to connect with the Spanish camino.

Daniele showed me the logbook that pilgrims sign and told me about one German visitor who didn't know how to write – hard to believe since Germany has one of the highest literacy rates in the world, but there are always exceptions. She said the pilgrim route attracts travelers with a variety of backgrounds and life experiences. True enough; I'd already encountered an array of personalities on the path. I suppose I qualified as slightly unusual myself.

The scallop shell is one of the symbols associated with the Chemin St. Jacques. Pilgrims used to wear a scallop shell dangling around their necks. You'll see the shells carved in walls or used as design elements in churches and on road markers, shrines and statues all along the routes. I've heard that in Salamanca, Spain a building is covered with scallop designs – La Casa de Conchas. In all the literature and images depicting pilgrims on the way to Compostela, the scallop is a fundamental symbol, representing the abundant scallop harvests on the Basque seacoast. But hunting for the scallop shell insignia isn't so easy: a doorway may have become a window for the basement or an archway once adorned with the shell could be partially bricked up.

Daniele mentioned there are many old signs and markers made as early as 1533 on rocks or buildings that indicate the original pilgrimage route through the region; some are scallop shells, some are small crosses or year markers. In Castillion, a nearby town, a chapel is decorated with ancient frescos depicting St. James, also called St. Jacques in France, the namesake of the pilgrim route. Some people link the old children's song Frère Jacques to the Chemin St. Jacques because of the lyrics about morning bells, a signal to get up and out on the pilgrim path.

From Saint-Lizier eastward, I followed the Chemin du Piémont Pyrénéen, one of several protected historic paths that comprise the Chemin St. Jacques in France and lead to the path in Spain that ends at Santiago de Compostela. A group of dedicated local *randonneurs* (hikers) researched the history of the pilgrimage path, marked the trail, and wrote a short guidebook. Daniele gave me a copy since I'd be walking in that direction. In return, I agreed to verify directions and listings as I progressed.

Church Ruin at Clouquet, east of Saint-Lizier

The geologic landmark near Saint-Lizier is the Grotte du Mas d'Azil, an extensive warren of caves made by water eroding the rock wall. Electricité de France (EDF) owns a power plant that capitalizes the waterpower coursing in a stream that flows from part of the cave network. Further along, I came to the town le Mas-d'Azil with a museum of geological specimens and prehistoric artifacts from the caves. At the museum reception desk, a young woman sat crocheting Victorian style lace squares for a bedspread in a rosette design like my Great Grand Aunt Morrie used to make.

My Aunt Marion Drury Watson's life spanned 1860 to 1956. A traveler, she'd lived in India with her British Army doctor father and many sisters, moved back to Armagh in Northern Ireland, lost her nephews in World War I, lived in London for a time, traveled in France as her postcard collection attests and immigrated to Western Canada after World War I, eventually living in New York City and Cape Cod with relatives and ending her long life in Maryland, where I witnessed her death when I was six. She was a spiritualist who fasted on alternate days and taught me to read verse aloud before I was old enough for kindergarten – Stevenson's poems for children and also Byron, Burns, Tennyson, Kipling and other heroic bards of the Empire. When I knew her, she used a cane and no longer was able to walk distances, but I imagined my journey would appeal to her sense of international adventure.

The museum was closed, the crocheting-lady told me. I could wait until it reopened after siesta later in the afternoon, but I was itching to move onwards. The museum guardian agreed to show me some Paleolithic artifacts from a cabinet near the ticket sales counter. She pulled out a weapon that Cro-Magnon hunters probably used 10,000 to 40,000 years before the common era. The tool making was fairly sophisticated – a small ball sat on the staff to be launched at a target. She went through the motions of how to launch the ball aimed at a live target. A decorative bird figure was carved into the launching projectile. Cro-Magnon fast food.

This region is also known for the realistic female figures found in the caves, burial grounds and other sites. The figures are part of the collection at the Musée des Antiquités Nationales at Saint-Germain-en-Laye outside of Paris, but infrequently displayed because of their fragility. The figures include carvings of heavy breasted pregnant women with explicit sexual parts and smaller female statuettes of serene regal demeanor representing a goddess of that time and culture.

On a rural stretch of the path, an area noted on the map as Tout Blanc, where the hillsides were covered with large white rocks, possibly *cliquart* (fine grain quartz sandstone). I spotted a red squirrel and a black one gathering acorns. Surely the big white stones scattered in the fields gave the area its name, which means "all white". Hundreds, maybe thousands, of footstool sized rocks were embedded in the ground about two or three feet apart, some covered with moss. To me it look like debris from a storm of meteorites or a volcanic spray. Rocks clustered beneath groves of trees with twisted trunks. The rocks resembled white grave markers, although they were embedded in the soil any which way. I had quite some time to study the rocks because I left my walking stick propped against a farm wall and had to walk back along the same ground more than a couple of kilometers to retrieve it.

The day offered the usual challenges. The trek out of Saint-Lizier was made longer by ambiguities in the path as well as my inattention to the small pathway markers. At several forks in the route, where a hiker had alternatives, there were no "X" signs to indicate a dead-end. The default practice on sign-posted trails is that an X marks the path option not to use if the choice is ambiguous. Power line easements and fences crossed designated paths with no indication of which alternative to follow. Time slipped away as I patrolled back and forth to check junctions. To study map and compass, I leaned the walking stick against a wall. Farther along, I stopped to photograph a woodpile, a theme I'd been photographing ever since I noticed that each woodpile was structured differently, depending on how logs were laid and stacked. Then I realized my stick was missing. Shrugging out of my rucksack, I hid it under branches at the side of the road, thinking okay now, if this is gone when I return, all I will have is the shorts and T-shirt on my body, the dog repeller, my money and the walking stick, assuming it was where I'd left it.

Was I forgetting things and losing the path because I was so involved with the scenery? My mental focus on the history of the region, which took over my consciousness as I passed crumbling stone walls, graveyards and old barns, was a springboard to times long past. I was distracted that day because I was living in my mind, walking through imagined scenes from many centuries ago.

A man squirting chemical weed killer from a small tank reservoir strapped to his back came towards me from the field. As we talked about country topics – the weather, the hay, livestock – he spit for punctuation, a little dribble smearing the corner of his mouth. When enough polite chat elapsed, I bid him, "*Bon après-midi*," grabbed my stick, and returned to my rucksack still safely hidden by the woodpile further down the trail.

The sun was over the yardarm, dipping behind the trees, when I took a picture of sheep munching grass at the side of the road. A skeletal dog with pinpoint black pupils set in blue Malamute eyes patrolled the flock and stared at me with what seemed to be malice. A shepherd huddled at the side of the road. His eyes wandered in their sockets and were as disturbing to me as the dog's. He posed a figure like a desert hermit, stepping down from the pages of the Good Book. I asked him about

Caoué, but he said he didn't know that place. Quite possibly I pronounced the town name incorrectly. The shepherd shrugged towards one direction, counter to the route I believed led to Caoué. Stubborn me, I ignored his advice. It turned out the shepherd was right because the path doubled back on itself. My stubbornness added a few kilometers to that day's walk. My imagination was listening to my fear and I wanted to be near a settlement before nightfall. The wild eyed shepherd tested my complacency. Had I known how to breach the fence around the tree plantation and cross the river using the direction indicated by the shepherd, or just quit the path and head west after descending the mountain, I'd have reached the gîte before nightfall, but it didn't turn out that way.

Up on the mountain, I'd seen a compound near a clearing filled with abandoned vans and rusting farm machinery. Painted on a large cement block that housed a water pump, grafiti spelled out *"liberte"* (freedom). A motley crew of young folks lounged on sagging porches of the several decrepit houses tucked under the trees. Was this one of the former hippie enclaves that Françoise mentioned? Did the cars rusting on cinderblocks indicate I'd stumbled into redneck France? It seemed like one of the cars was a cream colored vintage Volvo, like the one my friend David planned to restore, but the car was actually a Peugeot of the same era. A snakeskin lay on the path, just after the abandoned cars. Wasn't that a shamanic symbol for good fortune? I tucked the skin between notebook pages. First Nations people honor shed snake skins for their valuable magic of regeneration.

Chased by Sheep

But luck was not really smiling on me. I'd ignored the queer shepherd's directions and added extra miles in the wrong direction. At twilight, the marked path disappeared. I was on private property, on the lawn of a new "starter-castle" house with a swimming pool, separate garage or stable and expensively trimmed shrubs. The house sat right on the path line. I noticed in the shadowy gloom that the path markers pointed to the gravel driveway and a paved access road. Designated hiking paths don't use private driveways, but I followed the markers, which led back out to the paved road. This was puzzling.

Night fell without my reaching the gîte. Lightly beating time with my hands on my thighs to match my strides, I considered that maybe a kind stranger driving by would stop, provide directions, or give me a lift. But there wasn't any traffic.

It was dark now and lights flickered in the window of a house that had been converted into a print shop. The owner was just locking up, but he offered to call the gîte for me. "Aha," he said, smiling at me, "the gîte is directly opposite, as the crow flies, but about two or three kilometers away, on the other side of the river. You'll have to go all the way into town for the bridge to cross the river." He pointed out the cluster of lights and launched me towards the town of Maury. A half hour later, I reached the bridge and crossed the Arize River. On the other side, I found myself on a tractor lane walking through a field in the dark with only a faint light in the distance as a reference point, a light that would be the gîte, I hoped. Gravel crunched underfoot. It was the drive leading to the gîte, which in the gloom appeared to be an enormous barn with several smaller cottages nearby.

When I tapped on the door of the main house, Michèle Duran, the hostess, quickly fetched me a glass of orange juice to restore my strength. I must have looked all in –probably in the low blood sugar zone as well– after the long walk and fighting the frazzled feeling of rising panic. I had made too many mistakes that day, wasted time and lost the path, ending the day unsheltered at nightfall.

Walking after dark with a fuzzy idea of the destination was a situation I hoped to avoid, but I found myself pressured in similar situations other times during the walk, especially when I took time out from walking to paint a watercolor or converse with people I met along the way, which was the whole point of the journey. Though I wasn't in any real danger in this benign corner of France and there was no reason to worry, fatigue provoked irrational fear.

As the days unfolded, there just weren't lodgings spaced at convenient intervals for tardy walkers like me. The distance between lodgings was aimed at the hiker dedicated to speed. Did I have to walk faster and reach a pre-set destination by nightfall? Should I stop early in the day as soon as I found a suitable lodging near the path? Neither option was a happy solution for my leisurely self, so I learned to cope with walking through dusk and dark. Future mountain treks would be earlier in the summer season when daylight lasts until 9 p.m.

At the gîte, Michèle Duran said she had just about decided I wasn't going to appear because it was so late. They were preparing for bed when the printer down the road called to let them know I was on my way. She hastily put together dinner for me – vegetable soup, roast chicken, fresh green salad and flan for desert. As Madame Duran ferried the food from her own kitchen to the community room where I was eating, she explained that when the lodge was busy during the vacation season, this was the dining hall. I spooned up the soup and recounted the evening on the path that lacked sign postings. "The path markers disappeared at an elaborate new house on the other side of the river," I said, waving vaguely in the direction from which I'd come. She nodded and tightened her lips. "There have been contentions" – that's the word she used - "with the neighbor over there."

"I saw a sign "Tuiliers" in the driveway where the path stopped," I added. *"C'est ça"* (That's it), Michèle replied. "The proprietor moves the path markers. He doesn't approve of the Chemin St. Jacques."

Hikers have legal right to use paths protected by preservation societies, even when the route stretches across private property. In most cases, the paths predate private ownership. Indeed, the Routes of the Chemin de Saint-Jacques-de-Compostelle in France were placed on the UNESCO World Heritage list in

1998. Yet the neighbor was trying to discourage the few walkers who came through this region by moving the signs. Michèle promised to mention my observations to her husband, who was involved in maintaining the official markers along the path.

Eric and Michèle Duran, my hosts at the Vergers de Sésame Gîte, raise heirloom apples, provide camping spaces, run the dormitory gîte and rent private rooms to guests on farm-stay vacations. No one else was staying there, so I slept alone in a warm, carpeted dormitory.

Fog misted through the valley when I awoke. The tall windows gave a grand view of the orchard as I sipped coffee and wrote about the previous day and evening. After breakfast, I tracked back along the real path, to the point where I'd lost the trail the previous evening. In daylight, I could see that the path markers had been angled to steer hikers out the driveway rather than past the swimming pool and into the woods, the path that led directly to the gîte, a mere ten-minute walk.

Late the next afternoon, I trundled over pastures, heading for Pailhes, where the guidebook promised a small hotel. I found a hotel all right, with a *fermé* (closed) sign, even though the door was ajar. I walked in and cried out *"Allô?"* but no one responded. Had I been really bold, I suppose I could have snuck in and stayed there. I asked a mechanic repairing a flat tire in the garage next door and he told me that the hotel owner lived across the street. She had no interest in my plight. "Go on to Pamiers," she said, "it's not far." "But I'm walking," I said. "Then hitch-hike," she snapped, shutting the door in my face. "Damn you," I snarled at the closed door. A woman passing by on the sidewalk heard my curse and told me to visit Jean-Luc at the *épicerie* (a small quick-stop store) near the highway. "He can help; he knows everyone," she said.

Jean-Luc listened to my tale and started phoning local farms and mansions that take lodgers. All were full. I was once again caught in a trap of inconvenience, a trap of my own making because of my desire to be spontaneous and to rely on chance to stimulate experiences. Well, I was having my fill of experiences.

"*Mon Dieu*, what to do," Jean-Luc said, over and over, generously making my problem his own. Between hurried calls asking about lodging for me and serving customers, Jean-Luc Dumont told me his biography. I had mentioned I write, which sometimes prompts people to share their life history. He was of Norman and Russian extraction, a writer and a poet, a political activist and a family man. With the sparkling blue eyes and reddish blond hair of the Normans and the excited focus that I've seen some Russians display when they have a mission to accomplish, Jean-Luc was a bright whirlwind of energy. While he dialed nearby inns and guesthouses, customers trooped into the store for cigarettes, milk and snack food. Each one greeted Jean-Luc Dumont and then nodded politely to me because I was standing near the cash register engaged in conversation with the proprietor. It's considered polite in France to acknowledge people in your vicinity even if you don't know them.

One chubby man studied the candy-by-the-kilo display rack, filling a sack with sweets while sampling a few pieces. A little girl waited patiently at the counter. I continued telling my story of walking across France while Jean-Luc told his between ringing up packs of Gitanes and bottles of milk. Eventually Jean-Luc Dumont asked the girl what she wanted. Was she with the man selecting candy? No, she whispered, her mother was waiting in the car and she wanted a pack of chewing gum, green wrapper please. Dumont fussed over the girl as he rang up the gum, apologizing for not noticing her sooner, explaining that he'd thought she was with the man ogling the jars of wrapped candy.

In this microcosm, I reset my mood and released my sour reaction to the hotel owner. She was entitled to a day off. I would let the authors of the guidebook to the path know about the closure that was different than their text. I noticed how manners are part of the general social interchange. Though many Americans characterize the French as abrupt and impolite, perhaps they refer to tourist venues in busy, impersonal Paris, or perhaps such visitors know nothing of the French language and customs. I've always been impressed how people in France, parts of Italy and in Mexico as well greet grocers, clerks, customers and proprietors. It's a civility we could all use. When you enter a shop, a bakery or a market, you say hello to the person in charge. If you enter a café or restaurant – not a grand place, just ordinary bars and cafes - you nod hello to the cashier and anybody nearby. When you leave, you say farewell or good afternoon. That's the way rural America used to be too.

When I return to the U.S., I feel the absence of these small social gestures that improve the quality of daily life. If I forget that I am in the States and say hello to shopkeepers and other customers in a small store, they sometimes turn with hostile cold stares, as if polite greetings are bizarre, as if I'm loony. But maybe that is changing; there is a public civility movement rising.

Jean-Luc tapped in the numbers to phone another guest house. After a few words, he reported to me. "This place has a room," he said, covering the telephone with his hand, "but the private bath attached to the room isn't working. The plumbing is broken." I could have the room at a discount. "Sure! No problem," I answered quickly. "It's far away," Jean-Luc said, after relaying the information that I'd be there soon, "maybe another hour on foot."

It took more than an hour to walk the five kilometers to Artigut, where the country inn was located. I was walking west now, a detour from my planned route, with the sunset in my face and on weary feet. A dinner party was in progress when I arrived, but the Dutch proprietors invited me to squeeze in at table. The guests included friends who had come from England to help cut and stack firewood, a reunion of sorts that the group enjoyed together each autumn, and others who were guests at the inn. Soon I was engaged in spirited conversation with a British vicar and his wife Jane. The vicar fit the stereotypical image to a tee with a hearty laugh, thinning white hair, a robust appetite for victuals and a long memory. He'd lived briefly in Chevy Chase Village as a boy and attended St. Alban's School, an Episcopal academy in Washington. The vicar was quick to add, once he learned I lived in the Washington area, that he lived in Chevy Chase before it became a posh neighborhood.

There was another complication besides the broken plumbing. The hostess and owner of the country inn, Corey Bloch, had broken her arm on the night of September 11th. She'd been extremely anxious about the hijacked airplane attacks on New York and Washington and headed outdoors in the dark for a walk to ease her tension. As she walked on the country lanes, a car came up suddenly and Corey overreacted to the headlights. She leapt sideways into a ditch without looking and fell, breaking her right arm. For Corey, and many other Europeans I talked to during the weeks after the September 11, 2001 massacre, the events were just as psychologically threatening as to residents of North America. Hundreds of

Europeans and others from around the globe were killed in the destruction that day. People from ninety countries perished, not just Americans, a fact that is sometimes omitted in short-hand descriptions of the tragedy. Indeed, I came to believe Europeans were more deeply affected by the attacks, despite the fulsome political rhetoric back home. Europeans actually had suffered devastating wars in their homelands and knew about the suffering that follows the abandonment of diplomacy. We set aside talk of the attacks that night at dinner, trying to focus on life beyond political posturing. The guests helped serve the dinner and clear the table to spare Corey the difficulty.

In the morning, I was invited to accompany Peter and Mieke Appleton, friends of the owners of the inn, on an excursion to visit a nearby town by car. I left my gear at the inn and piled into their station wagon, which they'd driven south from Holland. They wanted to visit the town named Carla-Bayle, birthplace of the philosopher Pierre Bayle. I had to confess to the Appletons that I'd not studied the philosopher, and had never heard of him. Later I researched his history.

Pierre Bayle, born in 1647, was a Huguenot exiled as an adult to Rotterdam, the grand port now paired as a sister city to Carla-Bayle. A liberal secularist philosopher, he was persecuted for his writings and lectures, hence the exile in the Netherlands. I discovered that Bayle was an early supporter of women's rights. At that time – and even now in some countries – women were held responsible for what had been done to them by men – abductions, forced incest, or rape. In Holland, Pierre Bayle attacked this hypocrisy. He spoke and wrote against a judicial and social system that penalized and viciously punished single women who became pregnant by whatever circumstances. Ahead of his compatriots, Bayle defended abortion and infanticide as superior alternatives to the systemic degradation and enforced poverty of women who became pregnant without a legal spouse, a fairly frequent occurrence then, as now. Bayle also pointed out that the continuation of this double standard depended on the collusion of other women who testified against the unwed mothers.

Bayle also read travel literature, which doubtless helped shape his opinions. During the sixteenth and seventeenth centuries, travel literature became increasingly popular and influential in Europe, as more people traveled and brought back tales from far-off lands. It's important to bear in mind that some of the travelers' tales were fantastical, especially the reports of humans growing tails and streets paved with gold. The Far East, in particular China, came very much to the fore at the end of the 17th century and provided an important example of social tolerance, a stark contrast to the persecution and religious fanaticism in Europe. Travel accounts about such countries had an impact on Bayle during his exile in Rotterdam. Bayle had suffered persecution and waged a lifelong campaign against narrow thinking. He died in 1706.

For people living under the brutal extremism carried out by Christians of all types, examples of other ways of treating humans offered a beacon of rational light. As more people traveled and brought back tales of tolerant civilizations, philosophers such as Bayle incorporated a wider world-view into their writings, moving Europe toward more enlightened social organization not based on political power derived from religious affiliation.

What serendipity to happen upon this town that figured in the evolution of human rights. Centuries ago, economic prosperity in Carla-Bayle derived from the town's position as a trading center for indigo blue dye made from woad plants (Isatis tinctoria) grown in Europe, until cheaper indigo (Indigofera) was imported from the tropics. I already knew about the economic significance of indigo in the region because revenue from *pastel* (as indigo crops were called in France) cultivation had made Toulouse and the region extremely wealthy. I'd lived in Toulouse during the 1980s, visited a few of the 17th and 18th century mansions built by *pastel* merchants.

Peter Appleton drove. He was an accountant, and was quick to notice the big houses next to the town hall where agricultural sales and trading occurred in centuries past. A few hundred years back, accountants and clerks tallied up the value of indigo, wheat and other crops sold and shipped from this town. The spacious trade exchange buildings were decorated with relief designs depicting sheaves of wheat over the doorways. I could see evidence of the town's security and prosperity in the church dated 1687, a grand mansion dated 1602, and the town hall dated 1754. A large plaza in the center of town paved with marble inlays was built more recently, according to my companions, who consulted a Dutch guidebook.

The front door of a handsome house at the top of the hill was open. An attractive man and woman sat at a small table in front of the steps, drinking coffee. The blue shutters attracted my attention, as did the gauzy white curtains fluttering in the tall windows. I sauntered up and posed a question to the man with the gray ponytail drinking coffee. "Is this place your house?" Three large pieces of amber hung around his neck. He smiled and laughed, said yes. Then he invited the three of us to come upstairs. Mieke Appleton sucked in her breath with surprise that I'd so easily gotten all of us invited inside. Once again, I realized how it helps a traveler to know the language. I may be kidding myself that I also knew a bit about the culture, but my take on the situation was that a couple drinking coffee outdoors in front of their house signal that they are in public, open to casual greetings. If they'd been on the porch or at an open window, they would be in private space.

It turned out that ponytail man was a well-known artist, at least in these parts. As we chatted, I asked about the curious perforated metal cornice over the 3rd floor balcony. The punctured tin cornice and voile drapes shielded the balcony and gave it a New Orleans Belle Époque look. We trooped upstairs out onto the balcony and looked out over the town. Paintings by Mr. Re, the owner, hung in the stairwell and walls. His partner pointed to his signature as we climbed the stairs. The painter made colorful Gauguin-style figurative compositions.

While we were on the balcony, ponytail man – Mr. Re, I assumed – told us the story of his house. Previously, it was the business office, or registry office, for a rich family that owned some 90 agricultural properties during the 19th century. Farmers lined up to pay the percentage they owed the landowner after the harvest was sold. The artist said the farmers paid the landowner half their crop earnings. He found books listing the assets, numbers of sheep or hens, tools, plows, all written in miniscule script. The books were stored in the house when the artist bought the place a few decades ago. A matriarch inherited the assets of the wealthy family and after she died, the registry house was closed for 50 years. He told me that he bought it for next to nothing.

Could I find a fine old pile for a pittance and fix it up? Luck was part of the equation, like this artist had when he found his house, but I lacked the financial resources to try a real estate adventure. Across the way, slightly down the hill, we could see workers restoring a brick house with the roof sinking inwards. Mr. Re supplied the details: It was bought recently by an Englishman, presumably at a price that wasn't next to nothing.

We returned to Hans and Corey's country inn, a property which is a dependency of the nearby Chateau Thibaut. I gathered my gear and steadied myself for walking onwards. When I asked Corey about the pony-tailed artist, she told us the gossip about him. "The painter has a house in St. Tropez and a German girlfriend in Tahiti, plus a wife here in Carla-Bayle," Corey said. "Everybody talks about him." Presumably the young woman we saw with him was a client or agent, because her manner, clothing and jewelry just didn't signal rich artist's wife to me.

Corey escorted me up the lane to the edge of the forest and warned about isolated farms ahead, not out of any specific alarm, but just so that I would realize the path was remote. I wasn't worried; the day had hours of daylight to spend. Many of the shuttered farm houses were flanked with neatly arranged piles of firewood , so I indulged my current image theme – the woodpiles of the Pyrénées. Woodpiles are easy to photograph since they don't move and each woodpile is stacked in a different pattern.

Wind buffeted across the hills constantly, rustling the cornstalks and saving me from the heat. After the woods, I trudged through cornfields and fields of hops, a plant that looks like short corn about two feet tall, with a stalk of green grains at the top. Sunflowers remained in the soybean fields which were already harvested. I smelled cut grass as I strode across fields snapping with grasshoppers, moths and butterflies.

Scattered flocks of cyclists churned by on the road when I got there, mostly men over age 60 with lean and hard muscled legs. Where do they hang out when not cycling? How could I meet some of these attractive and hardy men? Friends chided me later for not making an effort in that direction. I contented myself with watching these fit fellow outdoors enthusiasts. They peddled up a hill in clumps, then a solo cyclist would come lagging behind, and another pack of cyclists would stream by. It was not the Tour de France because the Tour ended months ago, with Lance Armstrong earning yet another win. My detour to the inn the night before caused me to veer far off the marked Chemin du Piémont Pyrénéen, so I walked on pavement until I could reconnect with the trail.

Madière, a town west of Pamiers

After crossing the Ariège River, I was officially in Pamiers, a town that history records as significant during the Albigensian Crusade against the Cathars. I expected to encounter castles, watchtowers and museums. I talked to some kids on bikes waiting at a crosswalk and asked where to find the center of this very old town now fringed with bare yards, ugly apartment buildings and factories. Do you know of any hotels, I asked, forgetting that youngsters have no need for hotels.

Eventually I found my way into town, across the wasteland of suburban sprawl that filled the flat area near a huge metal factory named Fortech. "Big factory for a little town," said the hotel manager in the morning, articulating local pride. Before I settled in for the night, I searched for a news stand and bought extremely detailed topographic maps to cover the land features for the next few days of walking.

A castle loomed above the town and there were signs with the French government logo pointing up, indicating an historic site, but I couldn't marshal the energy to pursue the history that I came there to explore. Was I getting weary of the walk? Pamiers bothered me. The buildings were cement and cinderblock; the residents congregated in shopping plazas, not cafes or parks as in other French towns I'd passed through. At the pedestrian piazza in the middle of town, youngsters hung out in groups taunting each other and passers-by. I didn't imagine it: they were laughing at the funny woman wearing the battered straw hat with raven and goose feathers stuck in the brim. There's no doubt that the shorts, scuffed and dusty boots, walking stick and pack added up to a picture they didn't understand. Summer holidays were long over; what was the strange woman doing? Cars cruised the narrow streets and the youngsters called greetings to their friends. Objectively, I knew the scene was benign, but my sense of threat was high.

Guests saw me as I entered the hotel and murmured to each other about the Chemin-de-Saint-Jacques, as if I couldn't hear them. It seems I'm the pilgrim again. I slumped on the bed in a cross and tired heap. Unable to motivate myself to read or write, I punched numbers on the remote control blipping through television news and a French version of the travel channel. The American President Bush II, is in Chicago exhorting Americans to fly, take vacations, and go see Disneyland to get over the shock of the destruction of the World Trade Center in New York. A travel expert on French TV says how irrational it is for travelers to change plans or cancel tours to the Middle East. Libya, he said, is probably the safest place to be right now. I watch a program about long distance walkers in Africa and learn of a website that tracks explorers walking the Arctic Circle. Another travel channel showed the Train Jaune (Yellow Train) that chugs up the Pyrénées west of Perpignan from Villefranche-de-Conflent through the Cerdagne region to Bourg-Madame on the Spanish frontier. The two bridges and 19 tunnels for the high altitude train are a marvel of civil engineering. Maybe I would get there later in the journey. With the most cloud-free days in France, the Cerdagne seemed like it would be my kind of place.

Ludies

I peeked through the glass windows of the brick garage adjacent to the country inn. Mannequins draped in antique women's dresses, complete with lace jabots, parasols and high topped leather boots stood at silent attention in the display room. Was this a museum? A seamstresses' workshop? A costume warehouse for a community theatre?

An older couple strolled around the lawn of the late 19th-century country house which obviously had been refurbished recently, given the stacks of brick and lumber near the garage. They said the owner was gone and they were locked out. It was about 4 p.m. and I had no other choice of lodging for miles and miles. How odd – a locked mansion that was supposed to be an inn. They were eager to tell me their strange story. The previous night, they'd driven from Niemes with two friends from Cannes, they explained, finishing each other's sentences. They gestured to a luxury sedan where a German shepherd dog crouched in the rear seat. Their friend who drove the car complained of chest pains and had gone to the hospital the night before. Now, they were waiting to find out what was to be done. They had keys to their bedroom which was in a separate guesthouse, but the lounge and dining facilities of the inn were off-limits while the proprietors were away.

No surprise that the driver had chest pains the night before. Four large adults and a German shepherd crammed in a fastback sedan for 600 kilometers spelled stress. After hearing their story, I asked if I could take the dog for a walk, since he didn't look too happy locked in the car. "Oh, he likes it in there," insisted the woman. This rang false to me. Have you met a dog that prefers being locked in a car to running outdoors? I persuaded them to let the dog out under my supervision. Poor creature, treated like a lapdog with toenails so long he could barely walk. I attached his collar to a leash, and wrestled with a stick so he could chew, leap and vent his pent up aggression. He chewed the stick until his tongue bloodied. That dog was troubled.

Meanwhile the hostess returned with her friends. She was alarmed that the German shepherd was out of the car, though on a leash and under my control. He might attack the geese or the rabbits in the cages, or her small dog, she said. The mannequins wearing old dresses were her hobby, she told me. She'd amassed a museum collection of 19th-century bourgeois clothes and accessories. "I buy clothing at estate sales or when old houses are auctioned," she said. She fluttered her extended eyelashes. "It's easy to find out when the old houses come up for sale. The elderly ladies are dead; their heirs don't want these clothes." While a room was prepared for me, I toured the dress collection. It struck me that these dummies were wasp-waisted ghosts at a cheerless reception dressed in silks, voile and batiste. The clothing was pretty, but not really extraordinary in terms of design, fabric or trimming. Nice bourgeois dresses on silent middle class dress dummies.

Pierre, the host, told me they bought the place three years ago. The house had no roof on it when they acquired the property. "I did the work myself," he said, "except the electricity and plumbing. I brought in a mason to help, but really," he said, "no one knows old bricklaying anymore. Best to do it yourself."

The rooms where the other couples were sleeping were formerly a brick pigsty, now repurposed into guest suites. Pierre plastered the ceilings, tiled the floors, and directed workers to install baths and lights, he told me. They offered me a room in the main house which was decorated with tacked up draperies forming a headboard and bed curtains effect. The bed itself was a large folding cot under a mattress. A framed vanity mirror was vintage dime-store, not an antique. The place was as fake as a stage set. The dinner was disconcerting too. I was supping with a bunch of right wing Le Pen types who revere the military and attribute the nation's economic woes to immigrants from North Africa and other former French colonies. Jean-Marie Le

Pen, the political head of the Front National, a nationalist-fascist party in France, was gaining support from the middle class who believed that France's problems stemmed from the influx of Algerians and Muslims, not to mention blacks from the Caribbean and West Africa. They had a long list of demographic groups to blame for whatever they didn't like about the times they lived in. I braved a few retorts and settled for saying that they reminded me of some Americans I'd encountered.

I'll admit that the main course – sliced grilled magret de canard (duck breast) – and the plate of sliced garden tomatoes was worth the wait. I was extremely grateful that the tomatoes made it round to me several times. The man with chest pains remained in hospital, but the missus turned up at dinner dressed in a knit ensemble none too clean and reeking of perfume. Was she on the prowl with hubby under observation in the hospital? Maybe the dog sat on her lap during the long car trip. The other couple was more normally clad for French people on vacation, in polo shirts and pressed slacks. They all were headed to a military reunion of the regiment that the two men had served in, a weekend of old boy camaraderie, with wives on the side.

Grilled Magret de Canard

Now that magret de canard is more widely available in U.S. and Canadian supermarkets, it's easy to prepare this low fat, high protein meat. In France, magret refers to the breast of a Moulard duck which has been fattened with corn to be used for fois gras. Magret has a dense flavour and the pectoral muscle used for the breast cut is thicker than usual because of the bird's corn diet. Some chefs prepare magret with a pepper sauce or serve the meat with grilled figs or peaches.

Preheat oven to 450 degrees F. Score the skin side of the magret in a diagonal crisscross pattern. Brush both sides of the meat with olive oil. Season with sea salt and pepper. Heat an iron skillet over low heat. When the skillet is hot, place the breast skin side down. Brown the magret for 8 minutes. Turn the duck meat over. Place skillet with seared meat into preheated oven for 5 to 8 minutes, or until the center is rare. Remove from oven. Let the meat rest on a heated platter for 5-7 minutes. Slice the meat on a 45-degree angle into thin slices.

Mirepoix

When I arrived at the Hotel du Commerce in Mirepoix, I called Jean-Louis in Toulouse. We talked about the chemical factory explosion there the previous week. He told me the sidewalks were covered with glass from blown out downtown store and office windows. Jean-Louis had been staying at his girlfriend's house and had checked the security of his own apartment and then went to work at the main post office the day of the accident, the 21st of September.

Since he asked, I told Jean-Louis about my day's walk: about a mountain that gave me trouble, about logging roads that branched off in many directions, and about wrong headings caused by my map reading errors when I didn't check the compass or follow my nose, which would have been smarter. "Down is always down," he said. "Have a rest; take an extra day on your next segment."

In contrast to his good advice, up on the mountain near the monastery at Manses that afternoon, I'd stamped around stupidly, retracing my route in several places, thinking I could find a shortcut through the muddy logging roads. At one frustrating junction, I even tried to find my way across brush and cut up trees that lay on the ground as barriers. The limbs and branches were too dense to climb through, too tall to climb over efficiently. End-of-day fatigue confused me. I stopped and slurped down a half-liter of water mixed with a packet of Ener-C, a vitamin mix that boosted blood sugar. I had a little talk with myself: You need to get off the mountain and quit flailing. It's going to be dark soon. There are no villages for miles and no lights to help you find landmarks. Get off the mountain!

I wasn't afraid of encountering people in the dark. I knew I was alone out on the trails. But especially after the fall and the broken wrist earlier in the pilgrimage walk, I did worry about twisting an ankle or cracking my shin if I tripped on an obstruction in the dark. Sure, I had a flashlight, but the darkness of the rural Pyrénées night is profound, with no ambient light, no streetlights, no beckoning glow of a gas station or all night market down in the valley. After that period of chasing my tail on the Manses mountain path, I was hell-bent on getting to Mirepoix. Once again, I was blowing into town after dark without reservations. I hoped the town was big enough to have several hotels, maybe even a place with more than one star.

Down the last inclines from Manses to the hamlet of Mazonette, a perky blue car pulled out of a lane and stopped. A man about the stature of de Gaulle unfolded himself from the car. *"La randonneuse!"* he crowed, bowing over my hand. Had he heard about the American woman walking alone on the pilgrimage path? Maybe the tourist office staff in Saint-Lizier had spread the word. He told me he'd constructed and placed all the markers from Pamiers to Mirepoix. I said, "Thanks, it's a great trail, but up on yonder mountain, there is a little problem. A bulldozer has knocked down the signs and you can't find your way." I didn't actually say "yonder" but used a reflexive French equivalent, *"cette montagne la,"* with a backwards wave of my hand. He was gracious, responding to my complaint. "Well, you can see the church spire down here and just descend towards it," he answered, which is what I had done. We parted with more good wishes and he drove off with a horn toot, while the small woman in the front seat waved.

In Mirepoix, I easily found a room at the Hotel de Commerce. I was too tired to eat dinner and after chatting with Jean-Louis, fell into a blank stupor watching the news on television. My feet stung. There was no getting around it. I didn't recall feeling such pain during the walk the year before. I clicked past a movie that featured young dudes driving around in a van and girls smoking, a quaint version of teenage lifestyle, much milder than the violent dramas about youths that appear on American television. Was there a huge difference between recent graduates in France and in the U.S.? The post-graduate young adults I hired to be aides at the newspaper were involved in furthering their music or writing careers. They worked long hours at several jobs to support budding artistic work. Many young people I'd met in France were unemployed or underemployed and they anticipated bleak job prospects. Did the Americans know how valuable it was to have flexible employment situations even if the pay was low and educational options while they advanced their creative dreams? Did the French consider themselves fortunate to have free medical services and government financial support while they looked for a job? I didn't know the answers and the people I'd talked to in France or that I knew in the U.S. composed too small a sample for me to form a valid conclusion.

The BBC showed life in Pakistan and Afghanistan. The news announcers debated whether the U.S. will attack Kabul. Will there be war in Afghanistan or not? What is the next hotspot waiting to erupt in violence? The television reporter turned to Malaysia for man-in-the-street comments from Muslims. "America should take action peacefully, not take action emotionally," said one man. "The twin towers in Kuala Lumpur are still up."

CHAPTER 7

Out After Dark

Mirepoix to Camps-sur-l'Agly

"Get up early to catch the morning light," my father advised. The words crept into my dreams and I jolted awake. It was Sunday morning and Mirepoix offered uniquely preserved late Medieval buildings to photograph. Way down here in the southwest, the 20th century wars of mass destruction hadn't leveled the half-timber and exposed brick buildings. Mirepoix was destroyed during the Catholic campaign to oust the Cathars from the region. A new town was built over the ruins on a grid pattern with the central square bordered by solid houses. The upper stories of these stocky houses jutted out over sheltered walkways around the central square. The half-timbered building style uses massive hand-hewn logs to frame the walls, which are filled in with exposed brick or plaster. Mirepoix's central square dates to the 13th to 15th centuries and some structures are older than that.

With my Dad's advice in mind, I downed my coffee and baguette with unusual speed and headed out into the early morning mist. Soon the daylight would be strident, not soft, with crowds crawling through the heritage sites. Like a few other market towns in southwest France, Mirepoix retained the town square of centuries past. Mirepoix draws tourists from all over Europe – almost to the point of being a theme park concept of an antique market town, though it is indeed authentic. Subtract the tour bus idling near the largest restaurant, turn off the electricity and you're pretty close to the way things were in the 14th century. Take the cell phones out of the picture and change the merchandise back to raw materials and squint, and you have a timeless market scene. Farm vendors set up small tables to hawk dried flowers, honey and fall produce. Guys stood smoking in the background rocking on their heels as they talked about business, one with a racing sheet rolled under an arm

Mirepoix attracts a steady turnover of visitors on the tourist circuit in Southwest France. Authentic pre-Renaissance architecture brings some groups. But most visitors come here for the novelty of seeing a market town functioning as it did centuries ago. I prowled around the narrow streets in the crisp September air aiming my lens so that modern objects – cars, street lamps, signs and newspaper boxes – were out of the photo frame. Before the mist lifted, I'd snapped photos of the cathedral towers and the low wooden arcades where merchants from the prosperous Languedoc region of France once traded their goods. Today's shopkeepers were selling art, crafts and custom clothing; their buyers were middle class tourists from northern cities and day-trippers from nearby cities like Toulouse and Montpelier. The daily commerce of contemporary Mirepoix took place in the side streets beyond the historic town center that aimed to snare the tourist trade. I watched a crafts gallery owner arrange hand-woven shawls and baskets. She chatted with a friend and I shamelessly eavesdropped as they discussed the migrating sexual pairings of people they knew, evidently a source of endless interest.

After shooting the Gothic spires veiled in a picturesque froth of mist and studded with flocks of birds, I wanted to explore the interior of St. Maurice Cathedral before the tour buses unloaded. Two buses were already parked near the café where earlier I'd hunkered at a table near the window and sipped my coffee. Though the schedule of services and hours of opening tacked on the cathedral door stated 10 AM as the opening time, the doors were already open.

Mirepoix was a Bishop's seat and the cathedral is remarkable in that its nave, the largest in Europe, according to guidebooks, is wider than it is high. Market towns, with their reliable income and populace tied to the land, were logical places for the church to establish a strong presence. The large houses around the main square and the long colonnades with wood ceilings indicated prosperity.

St. Maurice was a knight, if the armor and mail draped on his statue were to be believed. I nodded hello to the somber statue. There was a notable Saint Maurice who figured in the military crusades to wrest Jerusalem from the Muslims. One website names Saint Maurice as the person who retrieved the lance that pierced the side of Jesus on the cross. Another describes Maurice as an Egyptian. Alone, I slowly paced the nave, stopping at chapels dedicated to various saints – Anne, the Virgin Mary, the Lady of Lourdes, Therese – all women. The chapel dedicated to St. Marguerite had been converted to a war memorial and names were listed under the gory image of Jesus' open chest and the exposed red and bleeding heart. No wonder the rock and roll high priestess Patti Smith and social prophets Bob Dylan and Leonard Cohen reference this same image of suffering in their poetry and song lyrics. Raw sacrificial energy doesn't come any riper than the bleeding heart of Jesus. The names of people sacrificed in the world wars and the bleeding heart affected my feelings. The war memorials reminded me how vulnerable all of us are to the whims of political leaders. Whether the leader is self-appointed, elected or anointed by a religious authority, the people sent to fight aren't consulted. While national leaders may claim wars are prosecuted with due process, history shows wars are always entered too hastily and without sufficient attention to the cooling effect of diplomatic intervention. I prayed for those who suffer war, that primitive, unintelligent action, unconscionable to people of evolved conscience.

A small sign on a wall described a labyrinth in the Chapel of St. Agatha under the cathedral. This discovery excited me, even though I could not enter the crypt to get to the tile labyrinth because restoration work and excavation were underway. Mosaic and tile labyrinths were embedded in the floors of some cathedrals built during the Middle Ages in France – Amiens, Reins, Chartres and others. The measured circular patterns in a labyrinth lead to a central turning point. Labyrinths dating to pre-Christian times appear in many locations – Rome's colonies in North Africa, in Italy, Crete, Indonesia, and India. In Medieval churches, it's thought that labyrinths were used for walking meditation and as a symbol of the journey of human life. Buddhist walking meditation expresses the same concept, but without a specific form or pattern for walking.

Labyrinth walking is in revival now, largely through the initial efforts of Lauren Artress of Grace Cathedral in San Francisco. Labyrinths provide an unfolding pattern that leads into the center of a circle, which symbolizes the destination and the beginning of the path back to the perimeter as a form of spiritual focus and unity. I had written about the spiritual revival of labyrinth walking for the Washington Post years ago and had meditated on several labyrinths. Modern labyrinths are constructed outdoors for use at any time, and some churches unfold large painted canvas labyrinths for indoor meditation and healing walks.

According to the description taped on the wall of St. Maurice Cathedral, this labyrinth was very small. How disappointing that the St. Agatha chapel was closed while excavation and analysis proceeded! I speculated that the small 60 centimeter (about 2 ½ feet) diameter pattern may have been used as a model or a decoration, or to suggest meditation. By comparison, the labyrinth set in the floor of the cathedral at Chartres, which dates to the year 1200, is over 12 meters (42 feet) in diameter, a vastly different scale to this labyrinth pattern in the Mirepoix Cathedral. Labyrinths should be large enough for adults to walk through 11 circuits of the path. No one could walk on a pattern less than a meter wide. Perhaps when labyrinths were no longer popular or fell out of official favor, this small labyrinth was hidden as a reminder.

Ha! My conspiracy hunter alter-ego clicked on high alert: Could modern day church officials know that labyrinths attract visitors seeking spiritual exercises, but they're hesitant to allow access or show the examples of the walking meditation used in the past by devout Catholics because it deviated from standard practice? Further, a conspiracy theorist might speculate, the undulating imagery of the labyrinth path could be compared to a stylized interpretation of the loops and curves of mandalas and are feminine in orientation. Leonardo da Vinci's notebook of anatomy drawings show studies of female forms and an abstract design of swirling loops on the same page.

The labyrinth at Chartres, the masterwork of cathedral architecture, dates to 1205. Some references state the cathedral was constructed atop a Druidic worship center and who knows what water-earth-wind-fire centered spiritual system pre-dates the named religions. Dr. Lauren Artress, the motivator of renewed interest in labyrinth walking, writes of having to push stacks of benches from the main floor of the cathedral at Chartres in order to uncover and walk that labyrinth in the early 1990s. That was my experience too when I visited Chartres in 1966 and again in 1989. Chairs attached to kneelers were still crowded over the Chartres labyrinth during my visits in 1999 and 2000. Perhaps by now the labyrinth is uncovered for meditation.

I studied the photo and description of the labyrinth in St. Agatha's chapel. This labyrinth measured three tiles by three tiles, for a total of nine tiles. No information was offered about the size of the tiles, but research on the internet turned up a website that refers to the "maze at Mirepoix." Mazes confuse with dead ends and tricks whereas a labyrinth is one undulating path to the center and back to the circumference. The Mirepoix labyrinth dates to 1537 and it is designed to scale so that it can be adapted into a standard size labyrinth for walking. Considering the religious wars in southwest France during the 16th century, when groups hid their spiritual practices, I speculated that the mini-labyrinth may have been a model designed to preserve the concept in miniature in a private underground chapel. Was this labyrinth used by someone who could no longer walk in meditation and instead traced the path with a finger? Was this labyrinth the last example of what was once a mystic tradition in the Catholic Church?

Paintings of female saints cover the walls of St. Maurice. Blue backgrounds with red trim are accented with gold fleur d'lis, the symbol of the Virgin and Joan of Arc. Gold stars draw the eye upward and suggest the celestial domain of the venerated saints. The decorative motifs and painted ornamentation was probably 19th century vintage and referenced classical symbols of the universal feminine. Yet men hauled the stones and carved the columns.

Devotion to female icons transcends the history of the region. From the Venus of Brassempouy carved some 25,000 years ago to the venerated Black Madonna figures secreted in village chapels to the 18th and 19th century apparitions of holy maidens in grottos, the connection to the supernatural female element endures. Even the Cathars sustained the devotional practice. Meticulous documentation by 14th c. Inquisition lawyers of the beliefs and practices of Cathar villagers examined in historian Emmanuel Le Roy Larurie's book *Montaillou* indicates the local people prayed to the Virgin Mary as a redeemer in her own right. not just in her orthodox role of intercessor.

Mirepoix was a Cathar stronghold until Simon de Montfort, the unrelenting leader of the papal crusade, destroyed the old city in 1209 after finishing off Puivert, a rebuilt castle I would see in a few days. The construction of the grand cathedral of St. Maurice, begun in 1343, reasserted the strength of traditional Catholicism in the region. The ornate tower appeared to float in the frothy mist that was burning off with the rising sun.

Pigeons flapped close and settled on eaves and nearby trees, ruffling their feathers. Grizzled men cadged cigarettes from friends and nursed their first glasses of red wine for the day.

The wooden pillars that supported the old covered colonnades that border the central square of Mirepoix reminded me of the trimmed and trained plane trees along the roads. The bulky pillars supported shops and houses and a deep covered walkway around the square. I sketched the massive columns and mused about the process of building the town core so many centuries ago. The constructors took their model from a thick tree trunk. Were the farmer's crops so rich they could finance the town center built to last centuries and beyond? Or was Mirepoix's market square built to reinforce the political and cultural dominance of the ruling religious class?

Forests and trees remained on my mind as I pushed on through Cathar Country, as the tourist signs proclaim, an area that extends from Albi through Carcassonne and Toulouse south into the highest mountains in the eastern Pyrénées. Forests were being replanted in these parts, but the trees were young and of a uniform size that indicated this was a tree plantation, not a real forest.

The open spaces also attracted my notice. The pastures and prairies, planted with clover or rye or resting fallow, provided intervals between built-up towns. How in this modern and sophisticated country, can fields and meadows be little different than six or eight hundred years ago? It is because France values its small farm holdings and supports them. Federal subsidies for agricultural industries like sugar, cotton and beef in the U.S. go to small farms in France. These fields weren't industrialized farmland, but small holdings, developed in proportion to human need and community size. The roads and paths followed the edges of the fields and hugged the clines of natural topography. Trees were planted at roadsides for shade. The fields weren't nudged by bulldozers pushing the soil into a form to accommodate roads, as is the case in automobile-centric North America. Much of the Southwest France is rural, though during the years I've been visiting and living in the region, Toulouse and its suburbs have expanded. The quiet rural scene is changing somewhat; there are highways and roundabouts in France too, cutting through the old pastures and diminishing the perimeters of the ancient towns.

The *Grandes Randonnées* (long distance paths) GR-7 and GR-36 lance through the Southwest, tracing the routes used by the so-called heretics in their flight from the Pope's mercenaries in the 12th and 13th centuries. I anticipated revisiting some of the mountain-top castles that I'd climbed up to during earlier trips.

Excursions focused on the history of the Cathars have brought prosperity for the tourism industry in these parts. When I first visited Southwest France in 1982, travel brochures focused on the history of indigo commerce more than the saga of the Cathar sect. By 2002, the roadsides were studded with brown and white signs pointing the way to the next Cathar historic site. I was dismayed, but not surprised, to find brochures for theme parks depicting the violence and brutality of the crusader era, a natural fit for the blood lust pop culture of our times. The Cathars did not die in peace. Those who remained after the Inquisition, torture and imprisonment were burned alive en masse. Fire and mayhem ushered their demise and lit the way to their version of paradise. We've heard all the official excuses for murder that governments and religions dish out. Modern day terrorists follow a long tradition of imposing fundamentalist obsession through random bloody violence. History also shows countless instances of institutionalized brutality and murder of civilians that was sanctioned by organized religions, government officials and their myrmidons.

During the easy pleasant walk from Mirepoix to Chalabre, on the GR-7, I nodded greetings and exchanged information with other hikers out on Sunday excursions. The trail south from Mirepoix began on an old railroad track about a quarter mile from the cathedral. A woman gathering walnuts told me the converted railway path was intermittently sign-posted. She was right - occasionally the trail marks vanished, but the landscape was open. A wrong turn wouldn't lead to being lost in dense woods. I noticed that the GR-7 overlapped the pilgrim path to Spain.

Just north of Lagarde, the path skirted the high stone walls of a ruined chateau. "Château féodal ruines" (feudal chateau ruins) was marked in miniscule print on the map. I longed to find a foothold to scramble up the walls and see what was inside. A boy was playing in a yard adjacent to the chateau wall that was topped with barbed wire and untended climbing roses in bloom.

The ruin at Lagarde was spooky, evoking a mystery movie atmosphere, even under the brilliant blue sky. The walls were intact, about six meters high with thorny vines and climbing roses covering the stones. Small trees grew out of crevices in the walls and bigger trees grew inside, overhanging the ramparts and stone walls. Trailing roses formed a thicket to prevent anyone except determined youngsters from sneaking inside the castle. A dog barked menacingly as I hastened away. I looked back at the castle, which had been neglected for decades, perhaps centuries. What dismal secrets did Lagarde hide?

Later on, I learned more about Chateau Lagarde. It was constructed in the 14th century by heirs of Guy de Lévis, a lieutenant installed as ruler of Mirepoix and its environs by the vicious Simon de Montfort who burned through the Southwest during persecution of the practicing Cathars. In the cycle of returns, it was fitting that this castle was in ruins.

The sun radiated on the gravel courtyard at the abbey and chateau in Camon on the Hers River. Built in 778 and reconstructed after floods in 1316, the abbey saw new life as a hotel restaurant in the 21st century with a pretty interior court and vines clinging to the walls. I needed a break, so I settled myself at a table in the patio cafe, placing my rucksack on a nearby chair. Piles of empty dishes bore witness to a big lunch consumed by a British group at the next table. Always willing to eavesdrop on English speakers, I heard that they were staying at a chateau in Quillan. One woman caught my attention and said she'd seen me walking by a bridge the previous day when they'd been touring in a van. Yesterday had presented many bridges, but I agreed that perhaps the bridge she was thinking of was near Vals where I had stopped to take a photo of the date and manufacturer's mark on the iron bridge, because such a solid old structure caught my attention. The narrow iron bridges are being replaced with cement bridges when roads are widened. I vaguely recalled waiting at the bridge for a mini-van to pass so I could take the picture.

Conversation turned to manor houses snapped up by wealthy Northern Europeans who renovate and move in, later selling at enormous profit to other Europeans or Americans. They made no apologies for their own purchase of a chateau, and suggested that without the spur of interest in restoration and investment brought by newcomers such as themselves, the abandoned great houses would crumble to ruins. I'd certainly seen boarded up stone barracks with brush covering the exterior fences. And I'd talked with workers who labored in the grit of derelict mansions. Newcomers who undertake such a project need a substantial reserve of money, dedication and hands-on construction skills to complete the restoration. Those who don't do the work themselves need even greater assets. I wished them well, hoped they continued to plaster and mortar their cash into the local economy.

Who hasn't had fantasies about living in a rural outpost in France? That day I walked past a train station for sale, a former railway crossing guard's house. The guards operated the barriers that prevented cars – and animal-drawn vehicles in the past – from crossing the tracks when a train approached. As automatic systems replaced the human guardians, and as train routes consolidated, some of the houses were abandoned or sold. The train guard's house with the *En vente* (For Sale) sign lacked a compelling view and the oddly shaped yard abutting the track was insufficient for a vegetable garden, but the idea of living in the rail guard's house, especially one near a hiking trail, set my mind adrift as I moseyed along the abandoned tracks which were now overgrown with grass and marked as a hiking path. Earlier I'd had scrambled off the trail to uncover brush growing over a small pile of trash including old bottles and rusted cans. Among the trash covered by dirt and vines along the abandoned railroad tracks I'd scuffed up a small glass vial marked *"L'eau d'vie"* and "2.5 cl." Perhaps this bottle once held "medication" since *L'eau d'vie* is blistering grain alcohol. I saved the bottle to add to my collection of travel treasures that includes animal skulls and bones, fossils, feathers, blue Sastun marbles, pottery shards, sand, shells and stones.

There were other train manager houses and guard stations along my path. Some were abandoned and overgrown with grass, but many were occupied. One former train station was converted to a chicken house. Hens pecked and scratched the ground where taxis and porters with bags once stood. A local train that connected market towns and commercial centers to rural areas was a key economic link before widespread car ownership.

At Vals, close to where the English woman had seen me at the bridge, there's a church built inside a grotto. I crept up the narrow stone stairs that twisted along several alcove chapels built into the cave which is topped by a 14th century tower and fortification. I counted twenty-three steps carved out of rock that connect the series of chapels deep within the cave. A 12th century chapel sits at the top of the stairs closest to the tower which caps the rock formation on the outside. Historians believe the innermost chapel is pre-Romanesque, which would mean it was a pre-Christian sacred site within the rock formation.

I took photos of frescoes on one level of the interior, but the images were so faint and the light so dim they barely registered on the film, despite flash. This place looked more authentic than the austere figures outlined in frescoes in the church at St. Lizier, which suggested to me a redo by a recent well-meaning amateur's hand.

The rocks around the church dwarfed a Volkswagen beetle car. I looked briefly in the cemetery behind the Vals chapel, but it was uninspiring to me. Steps away from the church, I stumbled upon an archeological ruin of a Roman era stone platform and walls, according to the explanatory plaque mounted by the local cultural administration. Back in the commercial sector of Vals, a handful of row houses and a car repair shop, I heard the buzz and whacks of saws and hammers, fairly common sounds in villages in these parts where residents and newcomers refurbish old buildings. As I walked through the town, a boxer dog sallied up, wagging its tail and hips, approaching me with great friendliness, possibly catching the scent of the German shepherd I'd led on a run earlier. On one old door, a sign advertised regional economic financial assistance to restore old buildings. Do the English and other Northern European ex-pats who are restoring historic old mansions and castles qualify for this economic assistance? That remains to be discovered.

East of Vals, acting on the guidebook description that promised the church at Teilhet has historic interest and was well preserved, I climbed the steps to the church door. It was locked tight, with not even a crack to peek through. This had also happened at Le Carlaret, north of Ludiès when I rattled the church doors, but they were bolted.

A woman was working in the garden of her rather fine country house in Teilhet. I marveled that she was weeding a garden while dressed in a blue and white striped business shirt with a ribbed white tee shirt underneath – elegant attire. Another example of the effortless chic that French women achieve even for their gardening work clothes. I would wear baggy shorts and a loose old tee-shirt for my gardening outfit. A vine covered garage, neatly painted sheds, trimmed shrubs and edged flower beds all signaled house pride. The man of the house appeared briefly on some errand in the garage. Our conversation turned, as it did during those weeks after the calamities in the United States and Toulouse, to violence and war. The woman's long serious face was saturated in doubt and disappointment. The terrorism attacks in the United States and the unexplained explosion in Toulouse were causing many people great fear in this region, she told me.

In the forest north of Chalabre, the town that was my goal for the night, I encountered several young men grinding their way on knobby tire motorbikes down the path. They waved and grinned at me as they whizzed past. I came across them again about an hour later. They were parked at a fork in the path, so we exchanged greetings. I met the same group again near Lac Montbel. One guy had fallen and wrenched his shoulder. They wore snug spandex outfits and the bikes were just out of the showroom, brand new. The injured chap was gathering himself together for the long walk out to medical assistance. With a shoulder injury, he couldn't control his own bike and didn't think he could manage to ride behind one of his mates. It was not for me to mention that it probably wasn't legal for motorized bikes to chew up the GR paths intended for hikers, mountain bike riders and equestrians. The knobby tires cut deep trenches that fill with water after it rains. The muddy ruts erode, leaving slick exposed hillsides, dangerous and unpleasant for cyclists and walkers like me.

A different type of cyclist met me as I approached the town when I paused at a bridge near a sign announcing this was Chalabre. The woman stopped her bicycle to direct me to a hotel – the only hotel. Her weathered face, dress and sweater spoke country thrift. She was peddling a beat-up bike and the carrier box was crammed with lettuce and other vegetables. We talked about kitchen gardens – I missed mine – and she said the vegetables grew in her part of a communal garden on the outskirts of town.

Rural France, far from busy cosmopolitan centers, lives by traditional ways. Shutters are locked at sunset; everybody is up before dawn. Families grow and harvest vegetables, and sell the surplus at market. The bakeries and creameries offer their products on a delivery wagon that serves the villages and hamlets. Old folks stay in the family house with younger generations and are buried nearby. While there are cars, big screen televisions, computers, internet, iPods and mobile phones, the time-honored pace of rural life endures. That's one objective for my walk – to observe slowly the daily rhythms of agriculture and food production, the lifestyle known for centuries, now at risk.

There were folks along the way who cast a curious eye at me, perhaps suspiciously, wondering about the hiker's staff and backpack. They quickly turned their heads when they saw I'd caught them staring at me. We travelers can be nearly invisible in a city, but the stranger in a small place is often thought foreign, an intruder. Octavio Paz's autobiographical account of his philosophical evolution, reports that he felt "the foreigner is always under suspicion." I had perceived hostile scrutiny during my trek, but I'd also discovered that the foreigner can be welcomed as a friend. In many cultures, a stranger is sacred, endowed with magical or religious powers.

Older couples ate in silence and a few families gathered in the hotel restaurant for Sunday dinner. The working men prepared for Monday morning by chanting the 21st century equivalent of plainsong by praising contemporary gods of soccer while anointing themselves and the tables with mugs of draft Kronenbourg. Despite the German sounding name, this is a popular French pale lager, from a company founded in 1664. Men in jeans and sports jerseys crowded around the tables in the bar and a few enthusiastic women also cheered the Marseilles soccer team on television. They chanted in slow syllables, "Al-lez, al-lez, Mar-sei-ialles – Al-lez – al-lez!" (ah-LAY, ah-LAY, Mar-SAY-YAY!) over and over again. A waiter explained the chant because I couldn't quite understand the words in the local accent. "Go, go, Marseille, go, GO."

Many of the merrymakers were under age 30; clearly not all of younger generation was leaving the region for better jobs in big cities. The population of St. Girons, where I'd stayed some days ago, was now 7,000, less than half the population in 1850. The relative poverty of the Ariège region demonstrated how French government revenue migrates to large cities, even with farm subsidies and unemployment insurance for rural provinces. Some of the local infrastructure dates to the '80s, the 1880s, that is. I was so impressed by one cast iron bridge over a fast-flowing canal that I stopped to take photos. The iron bridge bore a panel with a maker's name and date more than a century ago. Bridges were well-made, meant to last. Construction now can be irregular and slapdash. Masonry skills have deteriorated if you compare brickwork and stone construction on older chateaus and walls to contemporary cinderblock construction.

Farmers were barely getting by on their tax subsidies. Livestock were left to pasture in random places, locations chosen for proximity to water. Or families without land would house their animals destined for market or table on fallow land belonging to neighbors or the community. I saw pigs rutting in the dirt atop a mountain, in a little compound on a rocky field. They looked at me as I went past, but didn't move or get up to follow my movement as sheep would. I saw horses tethered to graze far from human habitation and other livestock left to their own devices in remote pastures. Sheep farmers depended on the annual transhumance, moving sheep to fresh pastures away from the farm, to give the land closer to home a chance to re-sprout.

The Chateau de Mauléon, overlooking Chalabre, is closed for renovation, to be opened in a year or so. Hotel staff had volunteered to help clean the chateau that day. "We'll have *son et lumier* shows like other chateaus," the desk clerk told me. Chalabre wanted a share of the tourist revenue generated by sound and light shows at the royal castles in the Loire Valley. During the entertainments, recorded hunting horns and battle sounds play while lights illuminate parts of the castle and a narrator describes historic events.

That night I dined on terrine poivre verte, lamb chops with grilled vegetables and fried potatoes, and sipped a 1999 Minervoix Chateau St. Louis. Between courses, I scribbled in my notebook about my purpose during this journey. My editor friend Lisa told me before I left Washington that the older solo woman reader would appreciate a book that defines and opens a way for women of a certain age to engage with the world. Perhaps my book could be model for older women on how to step forth alone into the world. I started writing about what the walk meant to me and why others might read it. So you're 49 or 64 and not getting around as much anymore. Now is the time to grow your own woman. Fran, another friend, also an editor, had years ago urged me to write a book about my approach to living an artful life. Any way you look at it, now is the time to do the things you always wanted to do. Too many adults, especially women, are scared of living fully. I wanted to communicate that you don't need anyone to validate your life experience.

In the end you're going to be alone – just because you are female and last longer. So you might as well start now to have the fabulous life you were planning to have. Do it – whether it is learning masonry and building a summer house or setting up an art studio or learning to swim in the ocean or playing golf or writing a family history. Some people sublimate their desires on community activities, saying yes to anyone who asks for help – better to be the generous older woman named anonymous who provides scholarships for needy girls.

Were you planning to become a veterinarian, a clothing designer, farmer or a parachutist? Get moving; your bones will hold out if you do move enough, but if all you do is think and talk about it, your bones are already too fragile for real life. Worrying about what others think destroys women's ego and paralyzes their ambition. Forget about what others think or say. Act according to your self-determination.

Meanwhile, there's the drama of rural France. The European Dynamic – English, German and Dutch folks arriving to buy up local property and coexisting, but perhaps annoying the local French folks. "The U.S.A is our best friend," I hear, but later, when the U.S. President launched a preemptive war against Iraq, that sentiment expired. When the generation that experienced the U.S. effort and support during World War II passes on, will that connection be forgotten? Too many Americans have a weak grasp of history and have forgotten – or never knew about – France's essential role in the success of our revolutionary nation.

The hotel manager, a young woman who told me that she had started the job in July and would have the next day off after four months of seven-day-a-week labor, explained the popularity of the singer Serge Lama whose songs were playing in the bar. He lives in the Southwest of France and his lyrics resonate with young and old. She asked me to let myself out in the morning and just leave the key on the desk. "Close the door firmly behind you," she said. I appreciated the trust.

Puivert Castle

Puivert Castle, a squared fortress with a distinctive crenelated tower, served as a landmark for the next day's destination. Visible from a long way off, this castle was one of the defensive strongholds during the Albigensian crusade and figured in the history of the of troubadours. In popular history and novels, itinerant troubadours are sometimes confused with Cathars because both groups hailed from Langue d'Oc. The poet musicians who celebrated chivalry and a romantic way of life achieved prominence just as the Cathars were being smudged out.

Ezra Pound, the iconoclastic Idaho native who alienated himself from the United States by making radio broadcasts supporting Mussolini, was enthralled by the troubadours. The poet believed he had a constitutional right to freedom of speech, but he was tried for treason. Declared "of unsound mind" in 1946 he was imprisoned in St. Elizabeth's Hospital for the Insane in Washington, D.C. until 1958. That's a long time for a creative artist to be locked up. He returned to Italy – not hard to understand why – and died there in 1972.

Ezra Pound's wartime actions are controversial, but there's no doubt of his literary genius, energetic ego and independent views. Long before his misguided expression of sympathy for fascists, he followed the footsteps of troubadours during the summer of 1912, walking several hundred miles through this region. He covered the seventy-odd kilometers between Foix and Axat on foot in two days leaving the main road to clamber up to the hilltop ruins of the Cathar stronghold of Roquefixade. In 1919, he returned to the area with his wife Dorothy Shakespear and they climbed another Cathar refuge, Montsegur.

Pound saw the region through the romantic lens of the troubadours and his notebook reveals wordplay and self-mockery. "To goon on pilgrimages" is a respectable & ancient habit, it implies a shrine, etc., but to go for mere mts. is decadent, I presume, & modern…Of course the quest of adventure is another matter, that also is respectably medieval, but I can not be said to be seeking adventure – a greatly overestimated commodity – for the pleasant ones one can never mention & the kind that make good telling are usually very fatiguing & uncomfortable while they last..." He even compares his foot journey to Julius Caesar's travel in the region.

My route skirted several Cathar castles, the last refuges of the sect. History calls the rampage, massacres and pillages by the northern troops a crusade against heretics, but in reality it was a political and religious consolidation by the north against the prosperous and politically independent south. One might describe the decades of church-sponsored aggression as a sad example of human greed fueled by religious self-righteousness.

At various inaccessible mountains between Toulouse, Montpelier, the Pyrénées and the Mediterranean, the Cathars retreated to fortified castles atop rocky peaks. Some of the castles were pre-existing fortresses where members of the religious sect holed up until the last of them were put to the fire in March, 1244. Castles occupied by the victorious mercenaries from the north were subsequently rebuilt and used to defend the frontiers, which makes it difficult to visualize what the castle fortresses looked like during the romantic troubadour era or the earlier Cathar period.

At table with the other guests at the Puivert gîte, I learned that many of them use the gîte as a base of operations and go out on bicycle, afoot or on horseback for the day. All of us are active people who enjoy physical challenges. We traded stories about the outdoors and environmental destruction – stories of 4x4 trucks cutting through forests or encountering screaming motocross bikes on the forest trails. These experienced travelers agreed the state of forest paths was worse in France than in the U.S. "The French aren't disciplined," said the nurse, an amiable chap, but finicky. He rode the Cannondale 840 parked on the terrace and traveled with an older fellow on a Specialized Rock-hopper. They were gear-heads, talking about equipment when general conversation lagged. He shared a cure for dry hands – smear on Vaseline, then put on rubber gloves and sleep that way. That might give you soft hands in the morning, but ick! Who would sleep with rubber gloves on?

A Canadian couple arrived late at the Puivert gîte with the license 997 APT, a rental car from Toulouse. I've seen APT licenses twice now, which has significance for me because those are the initials of my Canadian friend and travel companion during the mid-1970s. This couple hailed from Laval, near Montreal. They dressed alike in polo tops and shorts and fussed with their plastic bags of food, refusing the cooked dinner offered by the gîte. In the morning, they planned to drive to Bordeaux on the Atlantic. "Two days to cover the Pyrénées," they crowed. I sealed my lips: it had taken me weeks to walk the same distance and they were allowing two days. Michel, who helped manage the Puivert gîte, makes marionettes, charming figures with elaborate costumes. He creates and sells hand puppets too. I promised to send a postcard to his kids and gave them a few postage stamps and an American coin commemorating New York state.

Before the crusade against the Cathars, Puivert was a fiefdom known for sponsorship of the arts and poetry. The castle at Puivert served as a meeting place for troubadours in the Roussillon region and a hospitable refuge for poets and troubadour musicians traveling east to Provence. Hence Ezra Pound's interest. However, the castle that stands in the 21st century is not the same structure as the Medieval fortress. With the array of websites and books about the history of the Cathars, it's difficult to sift fact and legend. Various sources on Cathar lore describe a lady named Alpaïs, the sister of the lord of Montsegur and wife of Bernard de Congost, who received the

Cathar Consolatum, a ceremony similar to the Catholic blessing and anointment with salve, before her death in 1208. Despite the prohibitions against the Cathars, the family continued its affinity with the sect. In 1232, Bernard de Congost also received the Consolatum at Montsegur. His son Gaillard participated in the massacre of the Pope's crusaders at Avignonnet, an event that triggered even more aggressive destruction by the invading army. Saissa, the daughter of Alpais and Bernard de Congost, stood firm in her Cathar faith and sang hymns with the few remaining Cathars as they were burned alive at the foot of Montsegur in 1244.

The religious persecution screened the reality: political greed. Simon de Montfort, the general who burned cities, massacred townspeople and eventually wiped out the Cathars, turned over the conquered land and castles to his myrmidons, subverting the established noble families of the French Midi. The Puivert castle and land went to Pons de Bruyères, one of the northern crusaders, and the property passed to his son Jean. In 1310, the grandson of Pons, Thomas de Bruyères, married Isabelle de Melun and enlarged and repaired the chateau.

I stared at the chateau and painted it in the setting sun. I hoped families in the region retained some historical knowledge of the atrocities committed against the Cathars. When I mentioned my interest in them, people would nod in recognition, but in conversation, it was rare to find anyone with deeper knowledge than the facts offered on a wayside historical marker. A typical response would be: Cathars owned the castles and the army burned them out. That is true, but misses the point that the army was there on a trumped-up mission to subjugate a civilized, peaceful and prosperous population who disagreed with the corrupt religious hierarchy.

Are the stories of 700 years ago taught in French schools today? I doubted that many understood the political greed and religious oppression of that era, nor did I have evidence that anyone is interested in the complex dualist philosophy of the austere Cathar beliefs. The Cathars embraced vegetarianism, celibacy and simple living while rejecting the ultimate authority of Rome, but I thought their self-mortification was bizarre. There's a legend, or perhaps a local truth, about La Dame Blanche, said to be an Aragonese princess who liked to sit on the border of a lake on a rock shaped like an armchair meditating on the beauties of the countryside. A flood rose and took away her perch, and she persuaded Jean de Bruyères to divert the water and lower the lake, which created a river through the lower part of the Puivert village. Truth? Fiction? A stream did run through the lower part of the village, just behind the gîte.

In the Bois de l'Espezel, I met a man and a woman on horseback. They were from Munich and had moved to the region, they told me in English. Perfect land for keeping horses and riding. Soon after, a dog joined me. The young black Labrador with gangly legs and a dash of a collie ancestor in his face, trotted along behind me for several miles starting at Nebias. He had a longer and narrower snout than a pure bred Labrador, which I knew well from looking after my friend Jill's Labrador retriever, Watson. My new companion stuck with me all the way up and over a small chain of hills, on red dirt tracks. The dog found a ditch with trench water and slurped it down, frolicking in the water.

When we approached a farm at Brenac, several dogs yapped to keep my canine companion at bay while a quartet of puppies circled around. A ruddy-cheeked farmer, head topped with a well-greased beret, ambled out. Another man appeared, introduced by the beret-wearer as his son. Both men were quite thin, long legged and lanky. As an American, I'm not used to seeing trim older adults in good health. This farmer reminded me of Mr. Buffalon, the aged dairy farmer at Gerous, who even at age 70 worked every day. I didn't learn the names of these farmers, but we discussed the weather, the dog that was following me, the crops and the fruit harvest.

Soulage castle is gone now; the village sits atop the stone ruins. Soulage was an ancient fiefdom of the family de Peyrepertuse, a castle that defended the surrounding territory, protecting smaller landowners in exchange for taxes or a portion of the harvest. According to the footpath guidebook, in 1217, troops defending their territory and Cathar religion struck out under the leadership of Guillaume of Peyrepertuse to meet Simon de Montfort on the battlefield. But the sleepy village offered no traces of these events long past.

The light burned down and reflected on the red dirt, the trademark of this region called Roussillon, deriving from *roussir*, which means to turn red or to scorch. I shielded my eyes with sunglasses and a brimmed hat. Heat and bright sunlight shined harshly on the red dust of the hills which caked on my boots.

Ezra Pound wrote of the light at Quillan, "Whether it is a haze of heat or whether it is only the effect of sunlight & of great distance, I do not know but there come with these mts, as the sun lowers, a color at once metallic & oriental, as of a substance both dim & burnished."

Quillan shimmered below and I saw a town laid out on a grid, crowded with buildings and lines of traffic. Streaming out of the factories were cars and vans filled with workers headed home after the workday. Entering and exiting Quillian, I noticed a Formica factory, the largest building on the landscape. I passed a hitchhiker with a sign spelling out "Lemoux." I yelled across the roadway, *"Bonne chance!"* (Good Luck!) At that exact moment, a car pulled up. He waved and yelled back, *"Je doix une salud."* (I owe you one.) We were travelers crossing paths sharing and shifting the beacon of luck and serendipity. Later, I passed a guy in cycling Spandex savoring a beer as he peddled. We smiled and waved at each other, knowing we'd both spent the day outdoors working hard. I felt terrific, as usual, except for aching feet. Later, I medicated myself with aspirin and codeine-laced anti-inflammatory pills.

I hoofed through the town quickly, using sidewalks until I could find a turnoff that followed the Aude River. At a tennis club out in the country, I asked for water and directions to the gîte at Granes, where I planned to stay the night. It had taken me the best part of the day to walk the distance to Quillan some 14 kilometers as the crow flies and probably more like 20 when you factor in the topography and the snaking paths. And I wasn't finished yet.

Late in the day, I arrived at St. Feriol, a village near Quillan. Needing help to navigate the path through vineyards to the Granes gîte and horse ranch ahead, I asked directions of a woman sitting near the gate to a large well-kept lawn. With her sat an elderly man and two adolescents who obviously had developmental disorders. The woman led me across the vineyards and then spontaneously with tears in her eyes told me about her grandchildren, the twin youngsters I'd seen. "One reads, the other can do nothing," she said. "My husband can't help because he's sick too. My son and his wife leave them with me all day. I'm seventy-four," she said. "What will be become of them when I die?" To distract her, I offered to take her picture, which pleased her mightily. She smiled, started arranging her clothes and patted her hair. I made good on my promise, sending her copies of the photos after I returned home.

Signpost in Corbières Region

Camps-sur-l'Agly to Chateau de Peyrepertuse

Rain punched out of the sky as I started marching up the D14, a twisty back road headed up the mountains east of Bugarach. It was too late in the day to chart a path through fields and forests, so I stuck to the macadam. The sun had already set and I figured nightfall was an hour off, but rain hastened the dark. Late that afternoon, at the large gîte at the base of Pech de Bugarach where I'd planned to stay the night, I'd entered logistical free-fall. A group of students and adults were slapping cards on a picnic table in front of the gîte. A pile of backpacks leaned against the wall. "We're full," said the manager – "a school group."

Scurrying around the town, I had searched for a room. A tour leader at another inn with no vacancies lectured me. "You should call ahead." She was about my age and professionally groomed. Stung, I shot back, *"Il n'y a pas de téléphone en montagne."* (There are no telephones in the mountains.) This got a laugh from the students in her group and provoked her. "You shouldn't go adventuring; it's foolish," she said. Up riled my Irish dander. "This isn't an adventure!" I spit out, using the word in the French context – "adventure" meaning a wild-goose-chase. She pinched her nose and mocked. "This sure is an adventure." She nodded to my sweat soaked shirt and rank odor. The students laughed again, this time at me. At the time I couldn't see the humor in this impromptu street theater.

No phones in the mountains, but there was a phone booth in town. I called La Bastide, the gîte at Camps-sur-l'Agly listed in the pilgrimage pamphlet as several miles further. "There's room in the dormitory," the woman told me, "but come as soon as possible. Dinner is in a couple of hours." I struggled to contain tears of gratitude for the promised bed, about five miles ahead.

At le Linas, a six-house hamlet, the sky was dark with low streaks of light just over the horizon. Rain spattered on the brim of my cap. Over the phone, the woman had given directions: "Turn right at a little road after you pass the sign for le Linas." Could this rutted track leading into a field be the road she described? I took it, hoping. Then stopped and wasted precious seconds to pull on rain pants and a raincoat. The fields were soggy and I didn't know where I was going, but at least I would be dry.

Fifteen minutes later, I had no idea whether I was on the correct "little road". It wasn't really a road, but a cart track that led into woods and a series of unfenced pastures. At the top of the hill, I could see lights below in the valley, a mile or two further. What streams, muddy fields or swamps lay between my position and those lights? My flashlight batteries were just about dead; I had forgotten to replace them. In fact, I'd passed no village with a store that sold batteries, so it couldn't have been helped. *Mei-you fa-tze* as the Chinese say, "Nothing can be done." In my imaginative narrative, I was a Cathar heretic on the run, albeit one clothed in Gore-Tex and stout boots. As I trudged through the fields, clumps of tall grass sluiced the pants. Mud sucked at my boots. I hitched my pack closer and tightened my jacket hood.

Then I saw the boars.

Less than thirty feet away, two boars tussled each other in the murky dark. Even in the windy and rain-streaked gloom, I could see them. Chilled and alarmed, I felt hackles rise on the back of my neck. Boars are small, but they charge at great speed and their tusks are as long as my arm. These two boars maneuvered their tusks, bouncing off each other. Were they fighting? Were they playing? Would my presence enrage them? It was swordplay that I witnessed, not aggression. These animals were cavorting in the field, in their element. I skirted them, marveling at what I'd seen in the drizzle and the last gray-blue light of evening.

The cart track split. Which way, I dithered, consulting the topographic map with the feeble beam of the dying torchlight. No Energizer bunny here. Rain turned the paper map into pulpy mouse bedding. I was hoping for clues: which direction to La Bastide, but there just wasn't enough information on the map and in the dark I couldn't see any physical landmarks ahead. Sure, a compass heading might have reassured me, but without light, I couldn't read the arrow or the map inclines. In any case, the map was a torn mess. Worst-case scenarios flashed through my imaginary adventure film. I wasn't afraid because it was dark, I was worried what I'd do if I didn't find the farm. Maybe I could huddle under the trees. Already shivering in the rain jacket, I had no desire to spend a wet night outdoors. Memo to self: bring one of those insulated survival tarps that fold to pocket size.

There had to be farms nearby because I'd seen electric lines off to the south and west. Resolving to follow the deepest ruts, I tramped onward for another three-quarters of an hour, passing over a modest hill crest. The track across the fields gave way to blacktop, for which I was grateful, because surely a car must pass sooner or later. I figured I'd been walking on a tractor road instead of the "little road" from le Linas. I must have finally stumbled across the road described by the manager at La Bastide. The rain had slackened a bit. Prospects were improving. Ahead was a house with a single light in the window and a car parked outside. Two dogs raged inside the house as I approached, but no one responded to my knock. I continued walking on the narrow blacktop road, which was the width of a suburban bike path in Maryland.

Car headlights crossed the road in front of me. The vehicle slowed as I approached. I was in full rain gear – dark purple coat and black pants – but I'd tied a white shirt to my pack as a safety measure once I'd found the paved road. The driver was the owner of the La Bastide, trying to find me when I didn't arrive at the expected time.

Gratefully, I settled into the dorm at La Bastide in Camps-sur-l'Agly. Twelve Norwegian hikers had booked most of the sleeping space and they were downstairs about to tuck into supper. They'd soused through several bottles of red wine while they waited for me. European gîte etiquette indicated holding the meal until the last expected guest arrived, which was why the manager wanted me to arrive promptly. I smelled the aroma of garlic and a juicy stew. The guide for the Norwegian group, an Englishman from Newcastle named Julian who lives in France with his French wife, invited me to join their table. Introductions followed, all around the room. There was Inge, who headed up the national tax office in Oslo. Next to me on the wooden bench sat Sven, an attorney, and at his side, his wife Vanessa – call me "Nessa" she said – a medical researcher. Per, Inge's husband, wrote a flight manual for Boeing in the late 1960s. Another one in the party, Warte, had spent time in Lynchburg, Va. and Schenectady, N.Y. with her husband, who now works in Moscow doing something in oil. They were a lively group of high-level professionals on holiday.

During the course of the evening's revelries, I learned the history of their group. They'd been setting off together on various trips or self-improvement projects for ten years, said Inge. "We were all at a party, just sitting around. We were in our 50s and thought we should do something special. One of our daughters was learning to dance, so we thought we'd all learn to dance, and that started it. Ever since, we've been doing things together, learning or traveling. Now we travel to hike and we still dance." The others laughed and contributed their own stories about their years of group travel, ski outings, dances and dinner parties.

The Norwegians also sang, breaking into drinking chants and bawdy ballads during dinner. Afterwards, the best singers entertained all of us with charming songs in English, French, Norwegian, Swedish and bits of other languages. One song chorus featured knocks on the table, which Julian thumped with his fist or improvised with cutlery on the many bottles of no-label red wine. The day's disappointments retreated with the excellent meal skillfully cooked by the German mother-in-law of the owner who found me on the road. First course was a big green salad with a spinach tart, followed by Beef Bourguignon. We were also served rice, and after the main course, cheese and a custard-filled rolled cake.

Bœuf à la Bourguignonne - Beef Stew with Red Wine, Onions and Mushrooms

Correctly spelled Bœuf à la Bourguignonne, the dish has been shortened on menus and in cookbooks to "Bourguignon."

- 2 lbs. beef, top round
- 4 oz. salt pork or streaky bacon
- one large onion, sliced
- 1/2 tsp. each, various herbs – thyme, parsley, tarragon
- 1 cup red wine
- 2 tbsp. olive oil
- 1 tbsp. flour
- meat drippings
- 1 cup meat stock
- several cloves of garlic, peeled and slightly crushed with the side of a knife blade
- 1 bouquet garni made of thyme, parsley, bay leaves - to make a bouquet garni, place the herbs in a small piece of cheesecloth and tie securely
- 8 oz. small mushrooms, a dozen of more small whole onions or shallots, for garnish

Cut the meat into slices about 2 1/2 inches square and 1/4 inch thick. Place in a glass or earthenware dish. Season with salt and pepper, cover with sliced onion, herbs, olive oil and red wine. Marinate from 3 to 6 hours.

Place a tablespoon of beef dripping into a heavy stew pan. Cook the bacon which has been cut into 1/2 inch thick matchstick length strips. Add the whole peeled small onions or shallots and let them brown, turning them frequently over low heat. Remove the bacon when the fat becomes transparent and remove the onions when they are light brown. Set the onions and bacon aside. Place the drained marinated meat into the fat and brown quickly on each side. Sprinkle the meat with the flour, shaking the pan to distribute the flour into the fat. Pour over the strained marinade. Let it bubble over the heat for less than a minute. Add the stock. Put in the garlic and the bouquet garni. Cover the pan with a close fitting lid and let it simmer for about two hours. Add the bacon and onions and the whole mushrooms which have been washed and cooked in butter or olive oil for several minutes to remove moisture. Cook the stew another half hour. Remove the bouquet garni and garlic cloves before serving.

Serves 4 to 6 people. The first two hours' cooking can be done in advance, the stew cooled and fat removed. When ready to finish the cooking, reheat the meat gently with the bacon, mushrooms and onions added. A less expensive dish can be made using chuck roast instead of topside round and an extra 45 minutes cooking added. If no small onions are available, cook chopped onions with the stew but remove before making the table presentation for serving.

Bottle after bottle of red wine appeared on the table from the cellar below, fetched by Richard, the gîte owner, a genial character with mutton chop sideburns and unruly hair that added to the diameter of his significant head. When I mentioned that I'd seen the boars tussling in the rain, Richard nodded sagely. "Even hunters don't see boars playing like that. You have good luck."

Sven, the Norwegian lawyer, engaged me in a long conversation about the purpose of my walk and the book. I explained, "The focus is on encouraging people to explore their purpose in life. If a person wants to do something, they should set out and do it. My view is that if a person is happy in their life, whatever the pattern, so be it, but if a person hesitates to live their full life, perhaps there should be a push from an outside source." He nodded and agreed. I told him that I had the idea that my walking project might be a model for those stuck in their ways. It could show how a project can be carried out, one step after another, more or less easily, if you let the road bear you onwards, even with difficulty. My attention is focused in the present during the walk, because inattention leads to errors such as losing the trail, or falling. My walk was a metaphor for embracing and managing change in life.

I hadn't thought much about purpose to this point in the walk, but his question focused me in a way that I hadn't yet articulated. Who needs to read this book of yours, asked Sven. "People, especially women, who are afraid of the woods, of solitude, of dealing with unexpected problems," I answered, improvising. And I also thought about how walking contains a pacific quality that beats with each step, each breath, to create a further experience, an onward purpose.

When I reached the tiny village of Duilhac-sous-Peyrepertuse, I looked up, craning my neck. Far above, the Peyrepertuse castle blended into the rocky surrounds. Two kilometers of ramparts surround the castle. At a distance the constructed fortifications fade into the background of rocky cliffs. Even in daylight, it's hard to distinguish where the castle starts and the limestone rocks end. In the late afternoon light reflecting on the stone, pink, gray and cream colors were integrated with the mountain face. I stopped and pulled out my painting kit and water to capture the castle above.

From my perch, I could see Duilhac below and the bell tower where the gîte was located. As I painted, a group of rock climbers finished up a day's effort. Out of the corner of my eye, I watched them collect their gear and load the cars.

The day had gone easily at first, but then there was a serious climb on a torturous rocky path. My feet hurt from twisting to get a grip on the loose rocks. In the Gorges de Galamus, a deep canyon with a 6-foot wide road cut into the canyon wall, I proceeded cautiously. Cyclists rolled past on the narrow pavement, their legs pumping slowly in the heat. A few cars crept by, easing around the narrow turns. A few areas were wider, allowing drivers to squeeze past.

Up ahead was the sign that announced the last department in the eastern Pyrénées. I was nearing the end of the journey and decided to think things over at a hermit's cave that's become a tourist attraction. Caves and grottos in the Gorge de Galamus were once inhabited by monks, or other refugees from society. This hermitage, dedicated to St. Antoine, overlooked rushing water that showered off the opposite wall of the canyon. Cement stairs led down to a shallow cave that didn't set a mood of tranquility with the roaring River l'Agly below. It seemed inappropriate for a spiritual hermitage to have a surly gatekeeper charging admission. I scrambled onwards to the historic Cathar fortress.

The Chateau de Peyrepertous loomed above, worthy of the colors I brushed on the wet paper. I captured the pink and grey rocks and the castle crenellations. Suddenly, gunshots cut the mountain air. I looked behind me, below, back to the area where the rock climbers had been. No hunters were in sight and in any case, it wasn't Sunday, the day when hunters usually go out. The shots continued at defined intervals, every few minutes. Could there be a target range nearby? I finished the painting in a hurry and hauled out the orange fleece vest to tie on my rucksack so I would be visible in the landscape of gray, rust and brown.

Later, I learned the gunshots were air explosions, not real guns, and the noise serves to scare the *sangliers* (boars) from the vineyards. I heard this from a nice man cleaning an old Yamaha 1967 bike on a narrow street near the gîte in Duilhac-sous-Peyrepertuse. I was ambling back with groceries and wine clutched in my arms when I came across him. We talked about old motorcycles – which brands we'd owned over the years. He pointed out the stripped-down features on the bike – no plastic fender, no covers or tricked up gimmicks, and flat black paint on the gas tank and motor cover. At the end of our conversation, François – ponytailed and cool – and probably around my age, introduced himself.

He asked to see the label of the wine I'd bought – La Reserve du Reverend, a 1999 Corbières. He crowed, "I picked the grapes that year!" A small engraving of the Chateau de Peyrepertuse decorated the label of the wine produced by Peter A. Sichel (pronounced "seashell," explained François) in Cucugnan, a town nearby. François said that the Sichels were Dutch and well placed in Bordeaux. The locally bottled wine made from grapes picked by the man I was talking to and grown in the fields I'd passed through presented a satisfying cycle to me.

The energy of the land has showed itself to me in many ways: in the two boars playing in the gloom yesterday evening before the rain thundered down, in the orange seed pods bursting from dried iris or lilies finished for the season but offering fertility for next spring, and in the streams I'd seen where handmade stone dams route water that a long time past drove gristmills.

The austere landscape of the Corbières, a barren rocky region, is difficult to cultivate except for grapes. In the past, the wine was for domestic consumption; the yield was insufficient to sell or trade. The limestone gorges and gaps in the hillsides absorb rain without any benefit to the soil. But agricultural techniques have improved in the past 100 years. Corbières now exports wine and large-scale California vintners have established vineyards in the region to expand market operations.

Peter McPhee writes in *Revolution and Environment in Southern France, Peasants, Lords, and Murder in the Corbières 1780-1830* about the region and how he examined departmental records of vineyards in the eastern Corbières.

The landscape of the modern Corbières was shaped by the struggle over who owned and used the *garrigues*, the local name for limestone hillsides covered with brush and brambles too dry for cultivation. People were polarized about how the land should be used, whether for forests and woodcutting or sheep pasturage and wool production. Sheep tore out the bushes that held the earth and the exposed earth eroded under rain, wind, and storms. The barren landscape may be starkly impressive, but it is an injured land, just now recovering from centuries of sharp hooves and plant tugging teeth.

The expansion of the vineyards in the region came after the French Revolution, when local forge and tannery industries declined. In 1828, the Corbières region was mainly inhabited by nomadic shepherds who produced high quality wool, prized by the cloth industry "because it was as good for warp as it was for weft, an advantage no other wool had." Merchants came to buy the wool from afar but now there were fewer producers than there had been before the Revolution. The pastures had been subject to clearances and erosion, and the silted riverbeds caused vineyards to be the best hope for the future. The nomadic herders became agricultural people. With the sheep gone, the land healed, allowing the slow recovery of the environment. This is a rare example when the transition to a monoculture – grape cultivation – actually had a positive effect on a sensitive environmental region.

Today, the landscape of the Corbières is rough and silent except for the hunters shooting boar in the mountains on Sundays and the pop, pop, pop of the automatic noisemakers used to repel the boars from the vineyards in the valleys. The *chasseurs* are a link with the past, a longtime custom that puts food on the table and keeps the boar population in check. The prevalence of boar (some locals call them "field pigs") is seen by environmentalists as *"la calamité du sanglier"* (the calamity of the boars). I heard several sides of the hunter debate during my travels. Should they continue hunting for sport? Should it be abolished? The hunters didn't need to forage for dinner meat anymore, but if the boar were allowed to increase, they'd ruin the fragile environment, negating all the gains achieved by removing the sheep and turning the land to vineyards. Hunting was part of the local tradition. Hunters also ensured that the people's right to public land continued.

The sheep have all but disappeared in this area, even though there is now abundant fodder and the reduced demand for cheap table wine, which the Corbières has typically produced, has led villages and vintners to transform the economic equation by producing less quantity but higher quality wine.

That night in the dining room of the gîte I sipped the wine and jotted down quick calculations in my journal. My ticket home was dated the 18th of October, which meant I had 13 days remaining. As I mused about future plans, townspeople assembled in the mayor's office and council chamber on the floor below.

CHAPTER 8
Death in Duilhac

Duilhac-sous-Peyrepertuse to Quéribus

The town council was meeting in the gîte because a town employee died that day, the gîte manager told me. Nicole, the deceased, had been the tourism office representative at the chateau. I had visited the Chateau de Peyrepertuse in September, 1997. Could she be the same cheerful woman who helped me with information about the castle and the region for a travel article I was writing? Later, I checked my notebook from the 1997 trip to the region, and confirmed that I had interviewed the same woman. She died of lung cancer at age 48 after six month's illness. Solange, the gîte manager, confided this in a hushed, steady voice. "The whole village is upset," she said. "We're devastated. She was the spirit of the chateau and worked so hard."

While the town councilors met downstairs and decided what homage to offer Nicole's family to acknowledge her service to the town, I met the other guests at the gîte. A German couple crossing Europe on a tandem bicycle had claimed the private bedroom. Not realizing the room was already occupied, I stuck my nose in the door, to be scolded that the room was taken. On the other side of the building, in the eight-bed dorm room, a young couple – Laurent and Morgane – have spread their clothes and gear over several bunks. I threw my pack on a top bunk near a window away from their nests. We shared wine and talked. They, too, are long distance walkers. Laurent lived in the USA for awhile as a student; now he's an agricultural economist. I felt like I was the grand old gal of travel and they were youngsters just starting out.

We laughed about my initial worry that the gun "pops" of the machines in the fields were live fire. Morgane, who had been a day laborer in the vineyards, said the first cut is for the *sangliers*. I guess she meant that the vintner gives the imperfect or not quite ripe first fruit to the boars. Perhaps as an offering, perhaps because the first cutting isn't the best.

Jean-Pierre, Solange's husband who also helps manage the gîte, is a perky fellow, sexy and laughing. His sturdy torso is barely covered with an Everlast weightlifters' shirt with the sleeves cut out. When we shake hands, I feel that his palms are muscular, indicating a man who makes things. He wheedles his wife's permission to escort me back to the gîte after I'd gone to their house to get bed sheets. He sneaks a couple of shoulder squeezes as he hands me the keys and sheets. He puffs a small cigar as we walk from their house up to the town hall gîte. We talk about my walking route and what I will write about. "Probably I shouldn't tell too much about the Corbières in my book," I said, half joking. "You might not want caravans and tourist buses coming through." "They're already here," said Jean-Pierre. "Those English are stiff," he said. "They won't drink a *pastis* with the men in the village."

That day in the woods, I had noticed paw prints – about the size of a baby's fist – of a small animal with five toes and asked Jean-Pierre about it. Probably a skunk he said. The marks were on the path through the forest along the L'Agly River that also courses through the Gorges de Galamus.

During my conversations with François, the motorcycle man, he told me that all the vineyards are being bought up by Americans and Dutch. They take out the old vine stock and replant the rootstock farther apart so the vines can be cut by machine, he told me, putting locals out of work. He demonstrated how the special grape cutting scissors are held by the workers. The under blade is flattened and not sharp, so it won't cut your fingers and the top blade is very sharp so it can whack off the grapes easily. "You stand with feet apart and knees slightly bent," he said, "so it's easier on lower back". I noticed he wore a spandex kidney support belt, like United Parcel Service drivers.

During my meanderings through Duilhac, a 1961 Citröen *deux chevaux*, which is a utilitarian two cylinder (*deux chevaux* means two horses but the car has more than two horsepower, but not by much), passed by and the driver stopped to give a man a lift. I noticed the vehicle because in 1985, my companion Serge and I had driven around a fair portion of the Mediterranean Sea, across Portugal, Spain and France, down Italy and across Sicily and North Africa in a 1961 Citröen *deux cheveau* which we'd paid a mechanic to modify with a more recent used engine. It's an inexpensive sturdy, slow vehicle with a distinctive curved back that resembles a beetle.

Morgane and Laurent go to the dorm room to pack and I stay in the common room to give them privacy. As I plunge deeper into the wine bottle, my musings turn to the future. Why not stay in Duilhac an extra day or longer to explore this remote region, learn more about winemaking from the motorcycle man who harvests grapes, join the harvesters in the fields, tramp around the castles of the Cathars? This region figured during World War II as well, when clandestine fighters risked their lives to escort Jews fleeing Occupied France, or downed Allied pilots across the mountains to Spain.

I considered the events of the past few days. The scary night when I walked across the fields to La Bastide and the subsequent encounter with the prospector in his orange Renault van that other guests at the gîte in Granes had talked about. The prospector with his metal detector cultivated the image of a rustic character dressed in a black felt sombrero and denim overalls. This man obviously was well schooled in local lore and history, since he told me that library research leads him to the right places to prospect for coins, hardware, tools and other artifacts. His finely tuned ear and metal detector can even turn up pieces of gold, he said. Marie Vionne at the gîte in Granes told me that while this man, who has a reputation as a local eccentric, may dress and act like a movie character that Dennis Hopper might play, he does find significant items of historic interest. Metal detectors are illegal here, she said, but it's unknown whether police enforce the rules.

I also thought about my know-it-all attitude and stubbornness, particularly about maps. This walk is giving me insight to my weaknesses. I decide that the route is going to go a certain way based on map reading and ignore the visible reality or what local folks say. This is a lesson. What is visible offers important information, perhaps more so than my interpretation of the symbolic evidence on the map. The question for me was how to integrate this self-awareness into life. I will be applying a different perspective after the walk ends at the Mediterranean Sea. Only a few days remained of my solo trek. I hoped my future path would lead to an international work assignment, and there were other careers I had plans to explore. Rather than relying on one option, perhaps I should take a compass reading for future paths.

Cats screeched outside. About a half-hour ago, a town councilor waved up at me from the courtyard below. He saw me writing at the table and I went down to speak to him. The councilor introduced me to several council members – a couple of young men and several women, including the proprietor of the pizzeria where I'd purchased the bottle of wine. I asked the pizzeria-café owner about coffee. "Not too early," she said. I knew she was thinking about tomorrow's funeral services. "How about 9:30?" I asked hopefully. *"Pas de problème"*(That's not a problem), she responded.

My own voyage is reaching a turning point. Part of me wants to stay in the Pyrénées because I enjoy the serendipity and excitement of the unknown offered by the road. Part of me, my feet especially, screams with fatigue. Each step on this journey moved me into fresh terrain, mapped by others, but not known to me. This is the magnetic essence of long distance foot trekking, the unknown.

The church bell tolls for dead Nicole. I see cars parked along the street near the cemetery set into the hillside above the town. Cypresses screen the gravestones and reach up towards the old stone chateau-fortress on the top of the mountain where she had worked. Her extended family runs the Vieux Moulin hotel, so it was closed last night to honor her memory. I suppose the Norwegian hikers from Camps-sur-l'Agly who told me they had reservations there were accommodated elsewhere.

The faces of villagers show sad concern. People cluster, the women in dark pants suits, navy, gray and black; the men with wet comb marks in their hair, uneasy in sports jackets and their good trousers. During the service, the men huddle together outside the church, talking and smoking. Inside, women and family members pray, shuffling to their feet when the priest enters. Bells creak and roll – no jubilance in the ringing.

Weather repeats the somber mood. The mist casts a heavy gray layer, covering all the mountain ridge tops, seeping into the town. The air cannon to frighten the boars booms and pops. Tractors toting cut grapes plow upwards with their purple cargo. The harvest cannot stop. Below the village, workers walk back and forth in the vineyards, cutting. A lone cyclist mounts the hill to the chateau.

Later in the day, I walk slowly to the cemetery. Bundles of flowers, red, pink and white roses, asters, birds of paradise, and cyclamen are placed just inside the iron gate to the cemetery. Flower arrangements wrapped in plastic bore cards: "To our colleague, from the Mayor and Municipal Council." "To our cousin." "To my spouse." "To our daughter and sister."

This morning, the bakery truck passed at 11:30, tooting its horn for customers. Outside one house across from the cemetery, a small table stands draped in black with a small handwritten sign: "The family is not receiving." Whether the notice refers to that house, or perhaps was attached to a guest book during the burial service, I don't know. The entire village was galvanized by the death and funeral. People are indoors, except for the grape pickers, working steadily below in the valley. I honor her memory by painting watercolors of Duilhac-sous-Peyrepertuse and its vineyards. Back in the village, I hear people consoling each other with phrases you'd expect to hear in a close-knit community. "It's sad." "That's life, but so short." "She will be missed." "She had a grown son." "Her work at the Chateau was her life."

François, the motorcycle man, told me that Nicole's son was in the army and he was told that his grandmother had died. When he got to town, he learned the deceased was his own mother. "I saw the veins jump on his head," François said. "He had close cut hair, you know, for the army. And his hands were fists, like this." François told me about the scene, his eyes red rimmed and burning. "I'd never seen the veins pulse in a man's head before, like something you read in a novel."

In the evening at the Vieux Moulin which was open again, François leaned into a conversation with a woman at the bar. After the waiter took my order, I glanced over and saw that the woman had moved away and François was now alone. I went up to him and asked about the funeral and invited him to join me if he hadn't yet eaten. He smiled with a rhetorical "why not." Olivier, the council member who I'd met at the gîte, was a co-owner of the restaurant and he came to the table. The men discussed the funeral and how the rest of the family was handling Nicole's death. After dinner, François said I was welcome to join a group of his friends at the photographer Alex Mayan's house so I tagged along.

The photographer lives and works in Perpignan, but also maintains a house in the village. Alex and his wife Bea greeted me with the ritual four kisses on alternating cheeks. Folks skated chairs back to make space around a large table. We traded travel stories and mountain lore, and compared camping experiences.

My notebook lists phrases from that long night, which turned into a wake for Nicole. Among the group were folks related to Nicole or co-workers at the Chateau de Peyrepertuse. We talked about Les Saints Innocents, a group who did good works during the nationalist fascist regime of Spain's Generalissimo Francisco Franco. Christian or Alex mentioned the name of a writer or film director, Mario Camus. Much later, I did an online search and unearthed a film titled *Les Saints Innocents* directed by Mario Camus. That must have been the film we were discussing; my command of French falters after midnight. At one point François rushed out to feed his cat, Scarface, pronounced "skarfas," and returned with the cat draped over his shoulders like a scarf inside the jacket collar.

Next morning I will be leaving. The group is kind to me, filling in the gap that the funeral leaves by embracing me – the stranger – and sending me onward. We kiss and hug, trading email addresses. I considered staying on for a day or two, but it was the right moment to leave. Time to head south, cross the Quéribus ridge and hoof through the vineyards to Estagel, where I know there is a small hotel. It was still grape harvesting season, so I would see activity in the vineyards I passed through.

During these days and nights of casual discussions with the locals, I learned that many hectares of vines are being ripped out and replaced with new varieties bred for the modern palate. Vines are now braced on wires strung between posts instead of allowed to grow naturally, spread out along the ground or on low lines, like the vines in fields I'd walked through in the Minervois and Roussillon regions. On machine harvested vines, the leaves turn brown after the fruit is cut, whereas a hand cut vineyard will show various colors: purple, violet, red, orange, green and yellow leaves – colors the Fauvists painted.

As I moved slowly away from Duilhac-sous-Peyrepertuse, morning fog enveloped the low-lying fields, but the sky was clear, sweeping away the gloomy impression of yesterday's dull sunken sky. The morning mist made for easy walking. I sniffed the odors in the mountains – lavender, thyme, pine trees and, down near the houses, sweet scented purple flowering vines.

During the day I realized: this is it – the end of my walk, of all this open-ended freedom. Farewell mountains. Bye-bye country villages. Yes, I could return, but the freshness and surprise wouldn't be the same. Adventure to pursue in the future will probably take me on other routes through the Pyrénées. I thought about the warm farewells the group of new friends bade me in the wee hours of the night. We kissed the usual four times on the cheeks, which is traditional in the Southwest. François, with the cat curled around his neck, said in a mix of French and English, "*Je suis content to gain your connaissance.*" (I'm happy to have met you.)

As I plodded out of Duilhac in the morning mist, Alex pulled up behind me in a red station wagon, on the road that crosses the vineyards, and we surveyed the landscape together. He gestured to a burned stretch of land to the south. "That was done by angry hunters," he said, "against my friend. She owns the land, had horses pastured there. The barn burned and probably she has no insurance coverage." I guessed that the hunters believed they had the right to the land before this current owner acquired the property.

Cucugnan, the next village, owes its popularity with tourists to literary significance. Alphonse Daudet, sometimes called the Dickens of France, told rustic stories of Provence, using Cucugnan as a setting for the *Curé of Cucugnan*. Calcaire, the limestone mountains in the region, figure in the stories, along with windmills, taciturn villagers and clever padres. I paced through Cucugnan, not pausing for its tourist attractions, but it turned out that I would return within an hour. Duilhac exhibits an authentic quality; tourists flock to the castle and ignore the village so the community retains its feeling. On the other hand, just a few kilometers away, the village of Cucugnan is its own tourist magnet and may have lost its essence. Maybe my distinctions are hastily stitched, but this was my true impression at the time.

Is it that I expected the walk and the open road to yield great human connections and so, in the ending days, I was particularly attentive, hoping to notice the essential qualities of the communities, to meet new friends and understand how they lived? From the minute I saw François tinkering with his bike, I was drawn in. And from that first conversation when he spoke English, thinking I was not able to understand French, we moved to speedy French and a sympathetic late night round table conversation with his friends. It was 3 or 4 a.m. by the time we left Alex and Bea's place. Maybe it was the novelty of having a visitor from elsewhere; maybe it was the village's loss of Nicole that made the evening so poignant.

I appreciated that they welcomed me into their circle, to be part of the evening. Did they recognize the mythic role of the traveling stranger who appears by chance during a time of crisis for the village? I arrived just after she died. I left the morning after her funeral. I'd met her before; spent time with her relatives and colleagues at an improvised wake. Not to assume any extra importance for myself, but to look at the role with a sense of timeless folk legend, that is what prompted my thinking.

And what was this figure I spied across the vineyards? A hunched figure was wrapped in a poncho, stick tapping the ground while a massive pack hulked on the person's back. I had been gazing ahead, thinking about the past evening and the people picking grapes in the distance. And here was a strange figure on the path. A local woman? A lost *Anglaise* (English woman)? The woman walking alone – was this a vision of a pilgrim across the vineyard?

We approached each other. It was like meeting myself.

This figure was another long-distance-hiking woman. About my age, Louise hailed from Quebec, and was walking the footsteps of the Cathars, lugging a huge pack which created a hunched profile. No softie like me, she camped where she pleased alone, and bathed in rivers. "Compostela," Louise scoffed, "anyone can walk, but the Cathar footpath is physical." She's right: the route to Compostela de Santiago in Spain is a long path, but not as mountainous. We trade stories and she shows me her gear: a tent, a sleeping bag, a foam pad, plastic ground cover and all kinds of camping tools stashed in a heavy resin waterproofed pack. She also sports a smaller pack worn backwards over her chest, for water and food she can reach without stopping. Louise told me that she stays in gîtes once a week to bathe properly. Otherwise, she washes in any creek she finds in the forest.

In my view, Louise risked severe body stress carrying all that equipment in a huge backpack. I estimated her body weight to be merely 110 pounds. She must be very strong! Her long tee shirt soaked with sweat, clung to her thighs and chest. Exercise tights covered her legs, gaiters encircled her ankles and she wore light-weight hiking boots. She'd coated her rucksack with resin for waterproofing, a good idea in theory, but worn against a thin cotton shirt, the plastic coating might cause irritation. She waited tables to earn money for travel and planned to return to hike a rough trail in Spain the following summer. I was in awe of her effort and dedication.

Canadian hiker Louise Legault in Cucugnan.

Though I itched to continue east, we walked back to Cucugnan together and stopped at a cafe. Out on the terrace, we sipped cappuccino and exchanged addresses and photos. She was passionate about Pyrénées history and willing to skip the comfort zone to experience authentic immersion in the region. My comfort requirements after a day of sustained physical effort were significantly different than hers.

I could smell the sea through the hillsides covered with clumps of wild lavender, thyme and low piney bushes. Hunters on the south face of Quéribus nodded hello as I tromped past. When I asked about their take, they gestured to the dead boars in the back of a white van. Yanking out my red scarf and orange fleece vest to increase visibility, I heard one of the hunters sound the horn, meaning the hunt was over for the day. Through acres of vineyards, I descended towards the Mediterranean Sea.

Estagel to the Mediterranean Sea

Had I been taller, I think I could have seen the Mediterranean from the slopes of Quéribus, the last significant elevation before the flatland leading to the water. Among the scents of wild sage, lavender and maturing grapes, I could just sniff the faint saltiness of the water about 25 miles east. I mapped my own path on dirt farm lanes that parallel the River l'Agly, which was a dry rocky gully in many places. The wide blue snake on the map was mostly wishful thinking inland near Estagel.

The sun glared on the white salt fields and pale gullies. Without the forests to provide shadow, the vast plain in front of me blazed with early morning light. I aimed to reach the Mediterranean Sea by nightfall on October 7th.

Joseph Conrad's thoughts on Mediterranean light better convey my own that day after a funeral and at the end of my journey. "The sea, perhaps because of its saltiness, roughens the outside but keeps sweet the kernel of his servants' soul. The old sea; the sea of many years ago, whose servants were devoted slaves and went from youth to age or to a sudden grave without needing to open the book of life because they could look at eternity reflected on the element that gave the life and dealt the death." Even though I wasn't going to sea, I felt the pull of the water, the promise of completing the journey. The emptiness of the open sea was a continuation of the wide stretches of land that I walked across.

In Estagel, where I spent the night at the base of the mountain ridge, I made an effort to call friends in Milan, Switzerland and Kosovo to let them know the long hike was nearly over. A young woman chain-smoked in the phone booth and gabbed nonstop. Waiting for her to finish the call, I studied the main square of this town about five miles southwest of a military training facility – the Champ de Manoeuvres de Rivesaltes. On one street, there's Morgan Coiffure, another Morgan in the coincidental chain of names. Was the original Morgan that spawned the evidently popular name come European entertainer, or the historic British motor car, or perhaps, Morgan le Fay, the Arthurian sorceress. A lineup of bars and video arcades competes for Saturday night trade, perhaps catering to military men on weekend leave.

I return to the phone booth and stare steadily at the woman. The light in the booth illuminates mouse brown hair and shadowed eyes. She's in her twenties, worried about money or something emotionally vital, judging by the distracted shuttling of her eyes as she chatters into the receiver. She hangs up, dials another number, lights another cigarette. I pace the area and ten minutes pass. Through several calls, she's ignored me. Standard French behavior for such a situation is to move in close, about arms length from the booth, and glare. I gritted my teeth because I would have to be rude to her to catch her attention. This is the way: hold your ground, be pushy if you need to be, but stay cool. Rapping on the glass or yelling – that's too much emotion. Now she responds when she sees me staring through the glass near her shoulder. I don't back off or look away. She opens the door and pokes her head out, puffing smoke. "Oh, sorry, I'm just finishing," she says. "I can't reach my friends." As if she hadn't noticed me there for the past quarter hour.

The booth stinks of Gitanes and she rattles her keys as she flounces off. I slide in a phone card and dial. No answer in Milan. No answer in Switzerland or Paris. No answer in Kosovo and no answering machine. Just like the nervous Gitanes smoker, I can't reach my friends either. I leave messages where I can, saying that I'll be visiting soon, don't know when, after the walk is over.

Men in the bar stare out at the street. They are silent and bored, not looking at anything in particular, just the passing scene. The Saturday evening is young; they're not drunk yet. Chairs and tables in front of two bars, side by side, migrate into the sidewalk where the whole town, or at least the male part, was hanging out. The sports bar – television blaring soccer or car racing in the background – actually looks quite nice under the trees in the warm night. Three women sit outside at this bar, but I decide not to have a drink. I feel out of place in my walking shorts and boots at night in October, even if the air is bath water warm. Estagel is almost a suburb of Perpignan, one of the great cities of the Mediterranean. I'm not in the mountains now.

I stroll around town, working up an appetite. Today's walk wasn't very long, with the time out for coffee and talk with Louise, the hiker from Quebec. Youths lean on the doorway of another café-bar farther from the main square. The boys aren't menacing, just waiting for something to do or for friends to arrive, huddled against each other smoking and chatting, some listening to music on headphones. Snap! It hits me: Is this my last night on the road?

Head nodding with fatigue, I tucked into a heavy meal to fuel my body with calories for the next day. Dinner started with fish soup, followed by coq au vin, (capon stewed in wine) noodles, Crème Catalan (custard), water and red wine. I couldn't finish the main dish and it was too soggy with the sauce to take along in my backpack. And the salad, – well, with a certain kind of intentionally wilted French salad, you never know if the elegant brown tidbits are slices of the internal organs of animals or rare mushrooms. I bit and the morsel felt like seaweed, tasted fungal, but other slivers exposed by my fork through the fronds of wilted lettuce looked like scientific illustrations of stomach lining, but, in fact, I was eating morels. Taste was more significant than observation.

Crème Catalan

This delectable recipe for Crema Cremada or Catalan crème brûlée is adapted from *Honey from a Weed*, Patience Gray's collection of recipes from the western Mediterranean.

- 4 egg yolks
- 4 tbsp. granulated sugar
- 2 tbsp. flour
- 4 cups whole milk or 2 cups half and half with 2 cups regular milk
- half a stick of cinnamon
- dash of grated nutmeg
- 1 fresh lemon rind, grated
- 1/4 cup superfine granulated sugar for caramelized topping
- 4 ceramic ramekins or a 8" shallow glass ovenproof dish

Beat the egg yolks in a bowl with the granulated sugar. In a shallow bowl, mix the flour with a little milk to make a paste. Pour remaining milk into a saucepan, add the cinnamon stick, nutmeg and grated lemon rind. Bring to a boil, then remove the pan from heat and let the perfumed milk cool. Strain the perfumed milk onto the paste mixture in a non-reactive sauce pan (stainless steel, glass or enamel) and heat gently, stirring constantly. The mixture should thicken and when it comes to a boil, pour the *crème* (custard) into a shallow oven proof dish or into small ceramic serving dishes. Cool to room temperature, then refrigerate for 4 to 6 hours. Immediately before serving, sprinkle the top of the custard with superfine sugar and gently burn the surface with a chef's blowtorch or place the ramekins under the broiler for a few seconds until the top of the custard is browned and sealed with the caramelized sugar.

The morning was cool and I stepped briskly through vineyards. Two runners came up behind me, then turned around, trotting back uphill. A family drove out on the dirt track into the vineyards, stopped the car at the side of the fields and piled out for a stroll. At Mas de Jau, a large vintner, the vines in the fields were supported on wire, indicating that this vineyard was harvested by machine. Some of the fields were labeled with signs stating: "experimental." Industrialized agriculture is replacing the small patches of individual growers who once sold their grapes to a collective.

In Rivesaltes, I stopped for refreshments. Polished smooth red paving blocks covered the surface of the central plaza. The buildings around the square muffled sound and provided a room-like feeling to this intimate public square, similar to the small neighborhood plazas I'd encountered in other Catalan cities – Perpignan and Barcelona. Cafe Babou in the corner looked the place to be on a Sunday afternoon. Men grouped around all the tables. Where were the women? Cooking Sunday supper for the family, probably.

Walking east out of town, I passed a woman seated on a wrought iron bench. She looked at me with a hopeful look, as if she wanted me to stop and talk. I sat down on the bench and asked for directions in order to engage her in conversation. Then we chatted about the weather, the region and other basic topics. It's not the content that counts, but the fact that the traveler stopped and shared a moment with the one who may not be able to travel anywhere, who lives in a culture where women, especially as they age, live on the fringes of public life. I excused myself after about ten minutes, saying the pull of the coast was drawing me onward.

Less than five kilometers farther on, I lost my way. I was striding along the south bank of L'Agly River, heading towards a major highway labeled on the map as the Autopista Catalane, which arrowed south into Spain. Surely I could find an underpass. But my overland trajectory bumped me into the elevated highway: no passageway to cross and no underpass. Consulting the map, I realized that I'd misread where the highway featured exit ramps and underpasses. It would take time to make a long detour to find a passage under the autopista and the quickest route was through grove of trees that defined a gypsy camp. Caravans and RVs were parked bumper to bumper on a paved expanse the size of a shopping mall parking lot. The Roma people or gypsies in France and other European countries live freely on the fringes of towns. They congregate in orderly camps, do business in the town in their traditional nomadic occupations – running carnivals, repairing cars and welding, trading, and recycling metal. Gypsies and locals don't bother each other, although the dominant economic class may gripe about the encampments.

As I strode through the densely packed lot, past large RVs or expensive powerful sedans hitched to white camping trailers, I saw domestic stability. Women scrubbed clothes in plastic barrels or hung laundry on makeshift string lines. Men worked on engines or rolled cigarettes to smoke under the trees. Little kids stared at me and fled. The bolder ones smiled and sashayed up for a closer look as I tramped through. At one camping van, I poked my head inside and said hello to teenaged girls doing each other's hair and older women who were sorting kitchen supplies. They smiled and giggled. I toyed with the idea of taking photos of them, but I didn't, feeling too shy to urge the women to pose. Was it embarrassment at intruding, fear of their reaction, or a desire to appear nonchalant, rather than a photo-snapping tourist? The moment of camaraderie passed and I headed out of the encampment. Within minutes I was scooting through a cement tunnel under the roaring traffic, holding my nose against patches of piss, and analyzing the graffiti for political meaning. From the trash – soda and beer bottles, crushed cigarette packs – I could see the pedestrian underpass served as an adolescent hangout.

On the other side of the highway, a levee divided farm fields of vegetables, mostly artichokes. Hunters knocked off shots and I could see them walking with rifles. The guns sounded a rhythm: pop-pa, pa-pa, pa-pop. This wasn't a machine generated sound designed to deter boars from vineyards. In cultivated fields, the hunters pursue rabbit or quail, and boars range freely in the region. Rifle blasts this close made me jumpy. A family strolling along the levee and a man on bicycle peddled unconcerned. A guy exercised his dog by driving a car on the raised riverbank slowly behind the dog, with the leash hooked around his hand on the steering wheel. An astonishing display of sloth, but maybe the dog liked the faster pace set by a car. Up ahead, I spotted a woman walking a little terrier while shooting the breeze with hunters a few feet below the levee in the artichoke fields. If the locals are unconcerned, that's probably a signal that the hunters aren't going to wildly misfire in the direction of the levee. I gulped water and checked my watch. Could I dip my toes in the sea before nightfall?

Through the last few miles near the beach, I passed vacation campgrounds but only one was open. Even though the night was coming fast and I still hadn't reached the water and scooped sand from the beach, I paused to ask about lodging. "No hotels are open now," said the campground owner, "and we have no vacancies here. The season is over." I tried to negotiate access to a caravan, explaining that money wasn't a problem. He shrugged in that bored indifferent way that tells the weary traveler she's out of luck.

Bone tired, hungry and worried about reaching the sea before absolute darkness, I didn't consider turning back, to stay another night inland and find the beach in the morning. The momentum of the long day and prior weeks pushed me onwards. I had to finish the walk and finish it now!

Working on Alternate Plan B, I scouted places where I might curl up and sleep in the rough without a tent, huddled in the low pine woods near the Mediterranean. But sleeping outdoors with no food and no covering seemed a sorry end to the cross-country walk. I believed that luck must favor me after I finished the walk.

Just as the sun set, I glimpsed the Mediterranean at Torreilles-Plage. I was excited. All done, at last. With days of momentum behind me, I raced down to the sea and snapped a photo of my feet in the surf. Up on the edge of the beach, a man was tinkering in the back of his truck, baiting long fishing poles. He was setting up for night fishing. I put my boots back on and plowed up the sandy slope to ask if he knew of any nearby hotels that might be open. He turned to me and burst out, "America, boom-boom." At first it seemed he was telling me there'd been another attack, like the destruction of the World Trade Towers the month before. We hunched over the back of the truck and listened to the shortwave radio. He chewed on a cigar and continued baiting fishing lines. As I listened to the news broadcast in French, I realized that it was about the bombing of Kabul, in Afghanistan, by American forces. The bombing had started more or less when I dipped my feet into the Mediterranean Sea. We continued to listen in horror to the radio describing the first rain of bombs on Kabul. "But why Afghanistan?" we asked each other. The Afghani people didn't destroy the World Trade Center, it was Islamic extremists and they are everywhere. I realized that the distressing events of 9-11, which had occurred at the same time I was entering French territory through the Channel Tunnel, were transmuting into the beginning of war on the evening of October 7th, 2001, even as I sloshed my feet in the Mediterranean Sea. What horrible symmetry! I had walked well, and hard, but war greeted me at the end. This was a rough, bitter finale to my weeks of spirited effort and walking meditation focused on peace.

I left my boots by the truck and dug my heels into the sand on the way back to the surf. The sand grated my feet and the cold water swirling around my ankles eased tired muscles. I scooped a tablespoon of sand into an empty container, repeating the gesture I'd made at the Atlantic Ocean. The wet sand was to remind me of what I'd done. A year later, after the walk was settled in my mind, I found the containers of wet sand and tipped the contents into a cactus plant, part of a budding passion to use things up, to put things in useful places. The sand fit the cactus and fulfilled its purpose. Stored in an old film container, it was just a reminder, a souvenir.

Like the war that started that night, the end of the walk dragged on and on. By 7 p.m., I dipped my feet in the Mediterranean after a blistering march of more than 34 kilometers, then I had to walk through three more villages to find a hotel room for the night, finishing the day with my longest stretch of more than 40 kilometers. There were closed campgrounds and boarded-up ice cream shops. I searched on foot through towns to the north, asking for a room at a fancy inn and a business hotel, with no luck. Two of the three hotels in St.-Laurent-de-la-Salanque were locked. The third one was above a bar filled with guys burning off testosterone.

The television newscast referred to the U.S. attacks on Afghanistan as *"la Riposte américaine."* In the rowdy bar, I could barely hear the reporter and my thoughts were conflicted, full of sorrow at the news of war. I couldn't help wondering at the spikes of violence, the events that bracketed my walk. World Trade Center attacks on the day I arrived in France weeks before; bombs falling on Kabul the evening I finished the walk. George W. Bush on the big screen explained that God blessed his crusade while techno-blast rhythms rumbled from the jukebox. I chewed the dry pizza I'd bought from a take-out truck a few kilometers back, and sloshed back a couple of Kronenbourg drafts from the bar. The walk was over.

The guest room was tucked into an attic with skylights that I couldn't open, but this place was graced with up-to-date plumbing in the largest bathroom since the chateau in Basque country, hundreds of miles behind me. I heard doors open and close during the night, and yes, I chained the door and hiked a chair under the knob. What a way to celebrate the last night of my walk, sleeping above the biggest bar in town. A machine groaned and rumbled intermittently during the night.

The bar was transformed in the morning – floors clean, chairs lined up at each table. Instead of young rowdies, the clientele pushed baby carriages and carried shopping totes. Old men at corner tables hoisted glasses of *vin rouge* to start the day. Chic women sipped coffee and tucked tendrils of hair behind their ears. The barman was the same shaved-head fellow who closed the place down last night. I handed over the key and thanked him for a good night's rest, despite the rumbling sound. "Oh, that's the refrigerator for the bar," he told me and wished me good day.

The *Riposte américaine* replayed on television. Images of U.S. President George Bush were incongruous in the sports bar. Marching Pakistanis took to the streets of Karachi, while American planes bombed Kabul and Herat. How long would the U.S. be mired in this unruly harsh landscape and tribal history that had defeated the controlling efforts of the British Empire in the 19th century and the Supreme Soviets in the 20th? I ordered another coffee and stared at the people who ignored the first bombs of the televised war and continued their purposeful day. I felt like it was the first day of the rest of my life.

NOTES

Inspiration

Hugo, Victor. *The Alps and Pyrénées*. Trans. John Manson. London: Bliss, Sands & Co., 1898.

Maillart, Ella K. "My Philosophy of Travel." *Traveller's Quest.* Ed. M.A. Michael. London: William Hodge Publishers, 1950.

Mercier, Louis-Sébastien. "Going on Foot." *The Picture of Paris Before and After the Revolution, 1740-1814.* London: George Routledge and Sons Ltd., 1929.

Pirsig, Robert Maynard. *Zen and the Art of Motorcycle Maintenance: An Inquiry Into Values.* New York: Bantam Books, 1974.

Stark, Freya Madeleine. *Baghdad Sketches.* London: John Murray, 1937.

Thoreau, Henry David. "Walking." *The Atlantic Monthly* 9.56 (1862): 657-674.

Introduction

The history of human walking is covered in lucid and entertaining detail in Rebecca Solnit. *Wanderlust A History of Walking* (New York:Viking, 2000). See Chapters 4, 5, and 14 on pilgrimages, labyrinths and attitudes towards women walking alone.

"How little the French people really know of the Pyrénées": Henry Blackburn, *Artistic Travel in Normandy, Brittany, the*

Pyrénées, Spain and Algeria (London: Sampon Low, Marston & Co. Ltd., 1892), 149.

"Walking with intent": For background on prayer walking, see Linus Mundy, *The Complete Guide to Prayer-Walking* (New York: Crossroad Publishing, 1996) and Cheryl Canfield, *Peace Pilgrim's Wisdom: A Very Simple Guide* (San Diego: Blue Dove Press, 1996).

"Church does intervene in the pilgrimage": Nancy Louise Frey, *Pilgrim Stories On And Off the Road to Santiago* (Berkeley: Univ. of Calif Press, 1998), 127. For details about pilgrimage certification and requirements for an "authentic" pilgrimage, see Chapter 4, especially pp. 126-129, and pp. 158-162.

"the kind of journeying that marks": Phil Cousineau, *The Art of Pilgrimage: The Seeker's Guide to Making Travel Sacred* (Berkeley: Conari Press, 1998), xxiii-xxiv.

Chapter 1

For general background on Basque political and cultural history, see Mark Kurlansky, *The Basque History of the World* (New York: Walker & Company, 1999).

"During the Nazi occupation": Sources for background on WWII refugees and Resistance fighters include John Dunbar, Peter Eisner, Agnès Humbert and Mark Kurlansky.

"there is nothing in France more beautiful": Henry Patrick M. Russell, *Biarritz and Basque Countries* (London: Edward Stanford, 1873), 71.

"I found a Roman-era cart road": Douglas Streatfield-James, *Trekking in the Pyrénées* (Surrey: Trailblazer Publications, 1998), 75.

"Seen through the eye of the geographer": Claud Schuster, *Men, Women and Mountains, Days in the Alps and Pyrénées* (London: Ivor Nicholson, 1931), 26.

"The country is charming": Russell, 130.

"During the summer of 1843": Victor Hugo's sketching trip ended when he learned that on September 4, 1843, his daughter Léopoldine had drowned with her new husband in a boating accident on the Seine near Villequier, a tragedy that shaped the author's future work and political life. See, Victor Hugo, *The Alps and Pyrénées* Trans. John Manson (London, Bliss, Sands & Co., 1898).

"Sare was a pleasant place with a comfortable hotel": Russell, 123

"the Opoka Inn and describes the church": Russell, 126

"Faisan au Riz Basquais Pheasant with Spiced Rice": Elizabeth David, *French Provincial Cooking* (New York:Penguin Books, 1981), 486-487.

Chapter 2

"The family house passes": Sandra Ott, *The Circle of Mountains. A Basque Shepherding Community* (Oxford: Clarendon Press, 1981), 202.

"highest concentration of type O blood in the world": Kurlansky, 19-21.

"This Basque unity is": Hugo, 178.

"narrowest and most vertigo-inspiring on the GR-10": Streatfeild-James, 78.

"Menhirs, also called standing stones": Sources on regional topography and archeology include: Jacques Blot; Glyn Daniel; John Sturrock; Ruth Wallis, Otis Sawtell and Ida Treat; Mary Watts.

"a stone *olha*, a summer hut that shepherds use": Adam Nicholson, *Long Walks in France* (New York: Harmony Books, 1983), 212.

"Syllables, each with specific meaning, are tacked together": Jean-Baptiste Orpustan, *Les Noms de Maisons Medievales en Labourd, Basse-Navarre, et Soule* (St.-Étienne-de-Baïgorry: Editions Izpegi, 2000), 153-157.

"Transhumance, or seasonal migration of herds, had been practiced": Marc Bloch, *French Rural History* Trans. Janet Sondheimer (Berkeley: Univ. Cal. Press, 1966), 204.

Chapter 3

"Shirley MacLaine's book": The actress-writer's account of her pilgrimage journey to Santiago de Compostela, may have boosted the popularity of spiritual tourism. Shirley MacLaine, *The Camino, A Journey of the Spirit.* (New York:Simon & Schuster, 2000).

"The Protestant forces of Jeanne d'Albret, invaded": Ott, 5.

"an heir or heiress who was 'of the house' (etxenko)": Ott, 202.

"R. Tait McKenzie, sculpted the Scottish-American War Memorial": Theresa R. Synder, *Guide to the R. Tait (Robert Tait) McKenzie, 1867-1938 Papers, 1880-1940.* (Philadelphia: University Archives and Records Center University of Pennsylvania, 1991).

"World War I had a huge impact on agriculture": Annie Moulin. *Peasantry and Society in France Since 1789* Trans. M.C. and M. F. Cleary (Cambridge: Cambridge Univ. Press, 1991), 136-137.

"The Second World War is remembered as a 'black period'": Ott, 10.

"crowned by a Byzantine style cupola": Marie-Astrid Sady and Michael Sady, "Faith and Stone: The Romanesque Era in the Western French Pyrenees" *Focus* 41.Spring (1991), 2.

"Hunting is one of the traditional uses ": Groupe d'histoire des forêts Française, *Histoire des Forêts Française* (Paris: Centre Nationale de la Recherche Scientifique: Institut d'Histoire Moderne et Contemporaine, 1982), 169.

"vast transfers of forested land from clergy and noble families": Henri Gaussen, "Les forêts de la vallée d'Aspe" *Revue Geographique des Pyrénées et du Sud-Ouest* 3 (1932), 146.

"every community had its permanent arable land": Bloch, 28.

"'Gave' is the local name": Hugo, 334.

"left bank of the river above Lestelle, a pilgrim resort": Thomas Cook. *Cook's Handbook for the Health Resorts of the South of France, Riviera and the Pyrénées* (London: Thomas Cook Ltd., 1905), 214.

"black stone madonna put in care of Premonstratensians {in} 1345": Ean Begg, *The Cult of the Black Virgin* (New York: Penguin, 1996), 222.

"Bernadette's vision also changed from a small fairy spirit": Ruth Harris, *Lourdes, Body and Spirit in the Secular Age* (New York:Viking, 1990), 72

"The Bétharram sanctuary had been destroyed": Russell, 112 citing Denys Shyne Lawlor, *Pilgrimages in the Pyrénées and in the Landes* (London:Longmans Green, 1870).

"Lourdes could be a breeding ground": Harris, 237.

"The Church was wrong to canonize so few women": E. M. Cioran, *Tears and Saints* (Chicago: Univ. Chicago Press, 1999), 49

"the most romantic of stories": Harris, 19.

"In some of the barrow graves seated skeletons": Glyn Daniel. *The Prehistoric Chamber Tombs of France* (London: Thames & Hudson, 1960), 139.

Chapter 4

"Anne Lister, a self-assured 19th century": Sources consulted on Anne Lister and climbing in the Pyrénées Mountains include Frank Cunningham, Jill Liddington, Anne Lister, Antonin Nicol, Kev Reynolds, Claud Schuster, and Cicely Williams.

"tapes and loops adjusted to tie up her skirts": Cicely Williams, *Women on the Rope. The Feminine Share in Mountain Adventure* (London: George Allen & Unwin Ld., 1973), 27-31.

"The Lac d'Estom is, I think, one of the most solitary": T. Clifton Paris, *Letters from the Pyrénées* (London: John Murray, 1843), 138.

"While the Romans took the waters at Bagnères-de-Bigorre": Denys Shyne Lawlor, *Pilgrimages in the Pyrénées and in the Landes* (London: Longmans Green, 1870), 248.

"downed British flyer trying to escape occupied France": John Dunbar, *Escape Through the Pyrénées* (New York: Norton, 1955), 69.

Chapter 5

"a son of Herod the Great": Laura Riding Jackson, *Lives of Wives* (Los Angeles: Sun & Moon Press, 1995), 323.

"A cult of St. Bertrand emerged": Sady, 5.

"I had been nervous about flying": Fear about flying commercial airlines in mid-2001 increased after reading Marc Reuel Gerecht, "The Counterterrorist Myth." *The Atlantic Monthly* July/August, 2001.

"You don't need a weather man": Bob Dylan, "Subterranean Homesick Blues," *Bringing It All Back Home* (New York: Columbia Records, 1965).

"In France the old men": Henry Miller, *Air Conditioned Nightmare* (New York:New Directions, 1970), 116.

"The male peasants did not attempt to take on the identity of women": Peter Sahlins, *Forest Rites, War of the Demoiselles in 19th Century France* (Cambridge: Harvard Univ. Press, 1994), 28-30.

"when the monarchy occasionally attempted to restrict": Sahlins, *Forest Rites*, 19-20.

"The foresters had prowled around all day in elaborate disguise": Sahlins, *Forest Rites*, 80.

"powerful and disorderly women might have been especially appealing": Sahlins, *Forest Rites*, 26-31.

"valued the integrity of the household": Sahlins, *Forest Rites*, 27.

"women were juridically empowered in the public domain": Sahlins, *Forest Rites*, 27.

"women were considered as capable as men in maintaining traditions:" Sahlins, *Forest Rites*, 27 quoting Henri Cavaillès, *La vie pastorale et Agricole dans les Pyrénées des Gaves, de l'Adour, et des Nestes* (Paris: A. Colin, 1931), 77-78.

Chapter 6

"In Roman times, the region's people": John Sturrock, *The French Pyrénées* (London: Faber & Faber, 1988), 134.

"realistic female figures found in the caves": Jean-Pierre Duhard, "Réalisme de l'image de la femme dans l'art Paléolithique" *Eskonews*, 2004: 10-29/11-5.

"Pierre Bayle attacked this hypocrisy": David Wootton. "Never Knowingly Naked" *London Review of Books*, 2004: April 15, 26.

Chapter 7

"labyrinths were embedded": Sources consulted for background on labyrinths include Lauren Artress, *Walking a Sacred Path: Rediscovering the Labyrinth as a Spiritual Tool* (New York: Riverhead Books, 1995) and these websites: The Labyrinth Society, Maze List, Places of Pilgrimage and Adrian Fisher's World Maze Database.

"Labyrinths dating to pre-Christian times": The Labyrinth Society. Resources. Retrieved from http://www.labyrinth.org

"labyrinth measured three tiles by three tiles": Places of Pilgrimage. *Mirepoix Labyrinth.* Retrieved from http://www. placesofpilgrimage.pilgrimsall.org/Earth/Labyrinth%20 Mirepoix.html

"The Mirepoix labyrinth dates to 1537": Maze List. *Cathédrale, Mirepoix.* Retrieved from http://www.mudge.screaming. net/Mirepoix.htm

"Even the Cathars sustained the devotional practice": Emmanuel Le Roy Ladurie, *Montaillou: The Promised Land of Error.* Trans. Barbara Bray. (New York: Vintage Books, 1979), 306-307.

"a church built inside a grotto": Sturrock, 153.

"the foreigner is always under suspicion": Octavio Paz, *Itinerary.* (New York: Harcourt, 1994), 11.

"a stranger is sacred, endowed with magical": Arnold Van Gennep, *Rites of Passage.* Trans. M. B. Vizedom and G.L. Caffee (London:Routledge & Kegan Paul, 1960), 26.

"The population of St. Girons": Douglas Botting, *Wild France* (San Francisco: Sierra Club Books, 1994), 131.

"Excursions focused on the history of the Cathars": For background on the history and philosophy of the Cathar sect, see Barthes, Brenon, Coincy-Saint Palais, Hamilton, Herbert, Ladurie and Oldenbourg.

"He covered the seventy-odd kilometers": Richard Sieburth
and Ezra Pound, *Walking Tour in Southern France:Ezra Pound
Among the Troubadours* (New Directions, 1992), 47.

"Whether it is a haze of heat": Sieburth, 51.

"To goon on pilgrimages": Sieburth, 48.

Chapter 8

"The landscape of the modern Corbières": Peter McPhee,
*Revolution and Environment in Southern France, Peasants, Lords,
and Murder in the Corbières 1780-1830* (Oxford: Oxford
Univ. Press, 1999), 203.

"good for warp as it was for weft": McPhee, *Revolution*, 204,
quoting the mayor of Lagrasse in 1828.

"This is a rare example when": McPhee, *Revolution*, 243.

"The sea, perhaps because of its saltiness": Joseph Conrad,
An Outcast of the Islands (Lunenburg: The Stinehour Press,
1975), 8-9.

"Crema Cremada, Catalan Crème brûlée": Patience Gray, *Honey
from a Weed* (San Francisco: North Point Press, 1990), 295.

"la Riposte Americaine": riposte refers to a quick thrust used in
fencing or a retort in a fast paced conversation. In this case,
the riposte describes the hasty - and ill-considered - launch
of American bombing raids on Afghanistan in response to
the attacks of September 11, 2001.

BIBLIOGRAPHY

Adrian Fisher's World Maze Database. *France - Medieval Christian Pavement Labyrinths*. Retrieved from http://www.maze-world.com/FranceMedChrMazes.htm.

Artress, Lauren. *Walking a Sacred Path: Rediscovering the Labyrinth as a Spiritual Tool*. New York: Riverhead Books, 1995.

Bardwell, Sandra, Miles Roddis, Gareth McCormack, Jean-Bernard Carillet, Laurence Billet, and Tony Wheeler. *Walking in France*. New York: Lonely Planet, 2000.

Barthes, Mireille, Dominique Baudreu, Anne Brenon, and Jean Duvernoy. *Le Sentier Cathar: De la Méditerranée aux Pyrénées*. Bordeaux: Rando Éditions, 2005.

Begg, Ean. *The Cult of the Black Virgin*. New York: Penguin, 1996.

Belloc, Hilaire. *Pyrénées*. London: Methuen & Co., 1909.

Blackburn, Henry. *Artistic Travel in Normandy, Brittany, the Pyrénées, Spain and Algeria*. London: Sampon Low, Marston & Co. Ltd., 1892.

Blot, Jacques. *Archéologie et Montagne Basque*. Donostia: Elkar, 1993.

Blot, Jacques. *Le blog de Dr Jacques Blot*. Retrieved from http://jacquesblot.over-blog.com/.

Beer, Jane M., Peter McPhee, and Charles Sowerwine. *Bibliography of the History of Women in France*. Melbourne: Australian Historical Association, 1990.

Bloch, Marc. *French Rural History*. Trans. Janet Sondheimer. Berkeley: Univ. Cal. Press, 1966.

Botting, Douglas. *Wild France*. San Francisco: Sierra Club Books, 1994.

Brenon, Anne. *Les Femmes Cathares*. Paris: Librarie Académique Perrin, 1992.

Bunbury, Selina. *Rides in the Pyrénées*. London: T. Cautley Newby, 1844.

Canfield, Cheryl. *Peace Pilgrim's Wisdom*. San Diego: Blue Dove Press, 1996.

Cavaillès, Henri. *La Vie Pastorale et Agricole dans les Pyrénées des Gaves, de l'Adour, et des Nestes*. Paris: A. Colin, 1931.

Cioran, E. M. *Tears and Saints*. Chicago: Univ. Chicago Press, 1995.

Cierbide, Ricardo. *Le Censier Gothique de Soule*. Saint-Étienne-de-Baïgorry: Editions Izpegi, 1994.

Coincy-Saint Palais, Simone. *Esclarmonde de Foix: Princesse Cathare*. Toulouse: Privat Editeur, 1956.

Conrad, Joseph. *An Outcast of the Islands*. Lunenburg: The Stinehour Press, 1975.

Cook, Thomas. *Cook's Handbook for the Health Resorts of the South of France, Riviera and the Pyrénées*. London: Thomas Cook Ltd., 1905.

Costello, Louisa Stuart. *Béarn and the Pyrénées: A Legendary Tour to the Country of Henri Quatre*. London: Richard Bentley, 1844.

Cunningham, Frank. *James David Forbes, Pioneer Glaciologist*. Edinburgh: Scottish Academic Press, 1990.

Daniel, Glyn Edmund. *The Prehistoric Chamber Tombs of France*. London: Thames & Hudson, 1960.

Didon, Catherine, and Philippe Moitron. *Châteaux de Midi-Pyrénées*. Prehecq: Editions Patrimoines et Médias, 1997.

Dunbar, John. *Escape Through the Pyrénées*. New York: Norton, 1955.

Duhard, Jean-Pierre. "Réalisme de l'Image de la Femme dans l'Art Paléolithique." *Eskonews*. 29 Oct. 2004. Retrieved from http://www.euskonews.com//0274zbk/gaia27404fr.html.

Eisner, Peter. *The Freedom Line*. New York: Morrow, 2004.

Fenton, Mark. *The Complete Guide to Walking*. Guilford: The Lyons Press, 2001.

Freund, René. *On Foot to the End of the World*. Trans. Janina Joffe. London: Haus Publishing, 1990.

Frey, Nancy Louise. *Pilgrim Stories. On and Off the Rod to Santiago*. Berkeley:Univ. of Calif. Press, 1998.

Gadant, Monique. Ed. *Women of the Mediterranean*. London: Zed Books, 1986.

Gaussen, Henri. "Les Forêts de la Vallée d'Aspe." *Revue Geographique des Pyrénées et du Sud-Ouest* 1932: 3.

Gerecht, Reuel Marc. "The Counterterrorist Myth," *The Atlantic Monthly* 2001:July/August. Retrieved from http://www.theatlantic.com/doc/200107/gerecht

Gray, Patience. *Honey from a Weed*. San Francisco: North Point Press, 1990.

Grierson, P. J. Hamilton. *The Silent Trade*. Edinburgh: Wm. Green & Sons, 1903.

Groupe d'histoire des forêts Française. *Histoire des Forêts Française*. Centre Nationale de la Recherche Scientifique Institut d'Histoire Moderne et Contemporaine, 1982.

Guillaume de Puylaurens, *Chronique 1145-1275. Chronica magistri Guillelmi de Podio Laurentii* (1203-1275). Ed. and Trans. Jean Duvernoy. Reprinted: Toulouse: Le Pérégrinateur, 1996.

Hamilton, Bernard. *Crusaders, Cathars and the Holy Places*. Aldershot: Variorum, 1999.

Hamilton, Bernard. "The Cathar Churches and the Seven Churches of Asia." *Byzantium and the West, c. 850-c. 1200*: proceedings of the XVIII Spring Symposium of Byzantine studies, Oxford, 30th March-1st April 1984. Ed. J.D. Howard-Johnston. Amsterdam: Hakkert, 1988, 269-95.

Harris, Ruth. *Lourdes, Body and Spirit in the Secular Age*. New York: Viking, 1999.

Harrison, Kathryn. *The Road to Santiago*. Washington, DC: National Geographic Directions, 2003.

Herbert, Zbigniew. *Barbarian in the Garden*. New York: Harcourt Brace Jovanovich, 1986.

Hitt, Jack. *Off the Road -A Modern Day Walk Down the Pilgrim's Route Into Spain*. New York: Simon & Schuster, 1994.

Hugo, Victor. *The Alps and Pyrénées*. Trans. John Manson. London: Bliss, Sands & Co., 1898.

Jackson, Laura Riding. *Lives of Wives*. Los Angeles: Sun & Moon Press, 1995.

Jacobs, Michael. *Northern Spain-The Road to Santiago de Compostela*. San Francisco: Chronicle Books, 1991.

Kalaora, Bernard. *Le Musée Vert ou le Tourisme en Forêt*. Paris: Éditions Anthropos, 1981.

Konnert, Mark W., Peter Barrs, and Carine Barrs. *The Christian Travelers Guide to France*. Grand Rapids: Zondervan Publishing, 2001.

Kurlansky, Mark. *The Basque History of the World*. New York: Walker & Co., 1999.

Labyrinth Society. Retrieved from http://www.labyrinthsociety.org

Laborde-Balen, Louis, and Jean-Pierre Siréjol. *Le Chemin d'Arles ver Saint-Jacques-de-Compostelle*. Bordeaux: Rando Éditions, 2006.

Ladurie, Emmanuel Le Roy. *Montaillou: The Promised Land of Error.* Trans. Barbara Bray. New York: Vintage Books, 1979.

Lawlor, Denys Shyne. *Pilgrimages in the Pyrénées and in the Landes*. London: Longmans Green, 1870.

Le Breton, David. *Eloge de la Marche*. Paris: Éditions Métailié, 2000.

Layton, T. A. *The Way of St. James*. London: Allen & Unwin, 1976.

Liddington, Jill. *Female Fortune, Land, Gender and Authority: The Anne Lister Diaries and Other Writings, 1833-36*. London: Rivers Oram Press, 1998.

Lietaud, Henry. *Oloron Ste. Marie ce Pays Qui Est le Nôtre*. Gelos: Le Luth, 1970.

Lister, Anne. *I Know My Own Heart: The Diaries of Anne Lister: 1790-1840*. Ed. Helena Whitbread. London: Virago, 1988.

MacLaine, Shirley. *The Camino, A Journey of the Spirit*. New York: Simon & Schuster, 2000.

Mahoney, Rosemary. *The Singular Pilgrim, Travels on Sacred Ground*. New York: Houghton Mifflin, 2003.

Maxwell, Constantia. *The English Traveler in France 1698-1815*. London: Routledge & Sons, 1932.

Maze List. *Cathédrale, Mirepoix*. Retrieved from http://www. mudge.screaming.net/Mirepoix.htm

McPhee, Peter. *A Social History of France 1789-1914*. London: Routledge, 1992.

McPhee, Peter. *Revolution and Environment in Southern France: Peasants, Lords, and Murder in the Corbières 1780-1830.* Oxford: Oxford Univ. Press, 1999.

Miller, Henry. *The Air Conditioned Nightmare.* New York: New Directions, 1970.

Morland, Miles. *A Walk Across France.* New York: Ballantine Books, 1994.

Moulin, Annie. *Peasantry and Society in France Since 1789.* Trans. M.C. and M. F. Cleary. Cambridge: Cambridge Univ. Press, 1991.

Mundy, Linus. *The Complete Guide to Prayer-Walking.* New York: Crossroad Publishing, 1996.

Munro, Eleanor. *On Glory Roads, A Pilgrim's Book About Pilgrimage.* New York: Thames & Hudson, 1987.

Nicol, Antonin. *Les Grands Guides des Pyrénées 1787-1918.* Oloron: Editions Monhelios, 2002.

Nicholson, Adam. *Long Walks in France.* New York: Harmony Books, 1983.

Oldenbourg, Zoé. *Massacre at Montségur. A History of the Albigensian Crusade.* Trans. Peter Green. New York;Pantheon Books, 1962.

Orpustan, Jean-Baptiste. *Les Noms de Maisons Medievales en Labourd, Basse-Navarre, et Soule.* Saint-Étienne-de-Baïgorry: Editions Izpegi, 2000.

Ott, Sandra. *The Circle of Mountains. A Basque Shepherding Community.* Oxford: Clarendon Press, 1981.

Paris, T. Clifton. *Letters from the Pyrénées.* London: John Murray, 1843.

Paz, Ocatvio. *Itinerary.* New York: Harcourt, 1994.

Places of Pilgrimage. Retrieved from http://www.placesofpilgrimage. pilgrimsall.org/Earth/Labyrinth%20Mirepoix.html

Reynolds, Kev. *Walks and Climbs in the Pyrénées*. Cumbria: Cicerone Press, 1993.

Rowe, Vivian. *Basque Country*. London: Putnam, 1955.

Rudolph, Conrad. *Pilgrimage to the End of the World*. Chicago: Univ. of Chicago Press, 2004.

Russell, Count Henry Patrick M. *Biarritz & Basque Countries*. London: Edward Stanford, 1873.

Sady, Marie-Astrid, and Michael Sady. "Faith and Stone: The Romanesque Era in the Western French Pyrenees." *Focus* 41. Spring (1991): 1-5.

Sahlins, Peter. *Boundaries: The Making of France and Spain in the Pyrénées*, Berkeley: Univ. Cal. Press, 1989.

Sahlins, Peter. *Forest Rites, War of the Demoiselles in 19th Century France*. Cambridge: Harvard Univ. Press, 1994.

Schneider, Robert A. *The Ceremonial City, Toulouse Observed 1738-1780*. Princeton: Princeton Univ. Press, 1995.

Schrader, Franz. *Pyrénées Courses et Ascensions*. Paris: Privat-Didier Editions, 1936.

Schuster, Claud. *Men, Women and Mountains*. London: Ivor Nicholson, 1931.

Sheldrake, Philip. *Spirituality and History. Questions of Interpretation and Method*. London: SPCK, 1991.

Sieburth, Richard and Ezra Pound. *Walking Tour in Southern France:Ezra Pound Among the Troubadours*. New York: New Directions, 1992.

Synder, Theresa R. *Guide to the R. Tait (Robert Tait) McKenzie, 1867-1938 Papers, 1880-1940*. Philadelphia: University Archives and Records Center University of Pennsylvania, 1991. Retrieved from http://www.archives.upenn.edu/faids/upt/upt50/mckenziert.html

Solnit, Rebecca. *Wanderlust A History of Walking*. New York: Viking, 2000.

Streatfeild-James, Douglas. *Trekking in the Pyrenees*. Surrey: Trailblazer Publications, 1998.

Sturrock, John. *The French Pyrénées*. London: Faber & Faber, 1988.

Van Gennep, Arnold. *The Rites of Passage*. Trans. M. B. Vizedom and G. L. Caffee. London: Routledge & Kegan Paul, 1960.

Vital-Mareille, Joseph. *Les Trésors d'Art de L'Aquitaine*. Bordeaux: Raymond Picquot Éditeur, 1945.

Wallis, Ruth, Otis Sawtell, and Ida Treat. *Primitive Hearths in the Pyrénées*. New York: D. Appleton & Co., 1927.

Watts, Mary Theilgaard. *Reading the Landscape of Europe*. New York: Harper & Row, 1971.

Wigram, Edgar T. A. *Northern Spain Painted and Described*. London: Adams & Charles Block, 1906.

Williams, Cicely. *Women on the Rope. The Feminine Share in Mountain Adventure*. London: George Allen & Unwin Ld., 1973.

Wootton, David. "Never Knowingly Naked" Rev. of Common Bodies: Women, Touch and Power in 17th Century England. *London Review of Books* 15 Apr. 2004: 26-27. Retrieved from http://www.lrb.co.uk/v26/n08/david-wootton/never-knowingly-naked.

Young, Arthur. *Travels in France During Years 1787, 1788, 1789*. Intro. J.Kalow. New York: Doubleday, 1969.

5687537R0

Made in the USA
Charleston, SC
21 July 2010